After the Tears

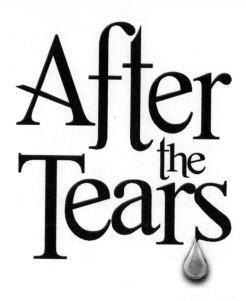

After the Tears

Helping Adult Children of Alcoholics Heal Their Childhood Trauma

Jane Middelton-Moz & Lorie Dwinell

Health Communications, Inc.
Deerfield Beach, Florida

www.hcibooks.com

Library of Congress Cataloging-in-Publication Data

Middelton-Moz, Jane, 1947-
    After the tears : helping adult children of alcoholics heal their childhood
trauma / Jane Middelton-Moz and Lorie Dwinell.
        p. cm.
    Includes bibliographical references and index.
    ISBN-13: 978-0-7573-1513-8
    ISBN-10: 0-7573-1513-5
        1. Adult children of alcoholics—Psychology.   2. Alcoholics—Family relationships.
    I. Dwinell, Lorie, 1939-   II. Title.
    HV5132.M53 2010
    362.292'3—dc22

                                                                        2010023155

Publisher: Health Communications, Inc.
            3201 S.W. 15th Street
            Deerfield Beach, FL 33442–8190

Poem on page 62 reprinted with permission.

Interior illustrations by Carol Hobart. © 1986
Back cover photo of Jane Middelton-Moz by Beltrami Studios
Back cover photo of Lorie Dwinell by Bill Dwinell
Cover design by Justin Rotkowitz
Interior design by Lawna Patterson Oldfield
Interior formatting by Dawn Von Strolley Grove

To the Adult Children of Alcoholics
who have taught us so much about the
strength of the human spirit
and to those ACOAs who have turned their pain
into the gift of helping others to heal.

from Jane:

My loving husband, John R. Fletcher,

the wind beneath my wings,

My brother, Alex E. Ward, who was always there for me, and

The memory of my parents, Jane and Bill,

who never had the opportunity to recover from alcoholism

or heal their painful wounds of the past. I thank them for the

gifts they gave me and for doing the best they could.

from Lorie:

The memory of my two brothers, David and Bill Dwinell,

and to my mother Betty Lou Archer.

Mom, I so desperately wish there had been avenues

for healing childhood wounds when you were the age many

of the readers of this book will be. In the face of

tragic losses and abuse, you tried so hard to heal and

not be broken by your history. God knows you tried

and tried again and I admire you for that.

In Memory

Janet Geringer Woititz,
a giant in the ACOA field, whose books on
children of alcoholics and alcoholic families have
touched and are continuing to touch
the hearts of millions.

Della Hill, Judalon Jeffries, Vera Manuel,
and Dr. Rudolph Moz, who dedicated their careers
to working with ACOAs, alcoholic families, and
families affected by generational trauma.

Daughters of the Bottle

until i was twenty-two
i didn't think anyone else
had a drunk for a mother
then i met lori, joanie, and susan
i recognized them immediately
by their stay-away smiles
they were leaders in their work
competent imposters like me
who would say they were sorry
if somebody bumped into them on a crowded street
i call on them once in a while
they always come
children of alcoholics always do

—Jane Middelton (Moz), from *Juggler in a Mirror*, 1980

Contents

Acknowledgments

WE WOULD LIKE TO THANK all who have influenced and touched our lives through our careers as therapists, authors, public speakers, community interventionists, and teachers. Thank you for entrusting yourselves to our care and for teaching us so much about courage, strength, and resiliency.

We owe an intellectual and emotional debt to the following giants in our field: Bob Ackerman, Claudia Black, Joan Borysenko, Stephanie Brown, John Bradshaw, Patsy Carter, Stephanie Covington, Tian Dayton, Christina Grof, Harriet Lerner, Jerry Moe, Pat O'Gorman, Phil Oliver-Diaz, James Pennebaker, Daniel Siegel, Peter Steinglass, Sharon Wegscheider-Cruse, Charles Whitfield, and Mary Lee Zawadski. The depth of intellect and passion for understanding the human condition you have brought to the important work we are all committed to is enormous.

A special thank-you to our editor, Candace Johnson, for her constant support, compassion, expert help, talent, and knowledge.

We would also like to thank Peter Vegso, Gary Seidler, Kim Weiss, Suzanne Smith, Lorrie Keip, Craig Jarvie, Terry Burke, Doreen Hess,

Tanya Woodworth, Larissa Henoch, and the editorial and art departments, as well as the entire staff at Health Communications, Inc., for their continued support throughout the years.

We would like to thank Karen Bingham, Jeanie Ferguson, Lucille Harms, Ann Harrmann, Lenny Hayes, Tiffiny Hubbard, Marilyn Janzen, Ruth Mueller, Yvonne Rigsby-Jones, Sarah Aloupa, Kim Sebastian, Carol Hobart, and Phil Wells for their part in helping to make this book a success.

Jane would like to acknowledge the wisdom, love, heart gifts, and endless support of her loving family: my children, Shawn, Jason, Damien, Lisa, Forrest and Sarah Middelton, Annie Van Avery, Melinda and Michael Knight, Suzy Goodleaf and Diane Labelle, and Michael and Laura Fletcher, for sharing your uniquely wonderful selves and being the cherished gifts you are; my precious grandchildren, Logan, Canaan, Anastasia, and Mira Middelton, Christopher and Ryan Flannery, Sarah Potter, Lily and Emma Knight, and Sage and Jamie Goodleaf-Labelle, for their continual gifts of laughter, wisdom, and love; my mother-in-law, Rose Fletcher, and my sisters-in-law, Jeanie Ferguson and Kathy Medici, for your kindness, laughter, and loving welcoming. All of you make me a very wealthy woman.

Jane would like to give her heartfelt thanks to her office manager and friend, Diane Laut. Diane, I don't know what I would have done without you for the last twenty-three years. There are no words for the support, talent, and heart gifts you have given me.

Jane would also like to say a heartfelt thank-you for the love, friendship, and continual support of Rod Jeffries, Harold and Joy Belmont, Elaine Lussier, John and Sharon Krueger, Wanda Gabriel, Jimmy and Robin Nicholas, Terry Harrmann, Rebecca Martell, Annie and Don Popert, Jeannie May, Gina Delmastro and Alex Smith, Bob and Sharon Horr, King and Gayle Lyons, Shirley Walker,

Jean Jacque Guyot, and Bill Laut. Your conversations, support, and prayers as I worked on *After the Tears* have been more meaningful than you can possibly know.

Jane would like to express her gratitude to her coauthor, Lorie Dwinell. You have offered so much to our field from the earliest days. You truly are a "pioneer." I am grateful for our journey together developing the thoughts, insights, and compassion that went into the writing of *After the Tears* and for our continued work together to give a voice to Adult Children of addicted families who may have lost their own.

Lorie would like to thank the colleagues and friends who have loved and supported her over the years. She would especially like to thank her "bungee-cord friends," Wynn Bloch, Claudia Black, Patsy Carter, and Jane Middelton-Moz.

And a special message from Lorie to Jane: Jane, you too led the way for so many in our field. I recall with such fondness our pioneering work together in the seven years we ran "Grown Kids of Alcoholics" workshops at Seattle Mental Health back in the late 1970s and '80s. When Claudia Black would come home to Washington state and tell us what she was seeing in the little children with whom she was working at an inpatient treatment center in California, we all became aware we were seeing a defensive adaptation developed in childhood that continued into adulthood. Out of that awareness, the original edition of this book was born.

She Was My Mother, Bless Her Soul

i sometimes sit
in the corner
in the dark
and recall my mother
with a brown bottle in her hand
or the sounds of clanking ice at 2 am
she'd call me baby if she wanted another beer
or a slut if she hadn't had enough
she'd make me cookies on Christmas
before she'd get too drunk
many nights
she would fall asleep on the floor
i'd cover her with a blanket
and put a pillow under her head
i'd awaken in the morning
to the sounds of her screaming
she wasn't an easy woman to please
most of the time
we didn't get along
but sometimes i miss her
and the loneliness

—Jane Middelton (Moz),
from *Juggler in a Mirror*, 1980

Introduction

AFTER THE TEARS WAS FIRST RELEASED in 1985. At that time, we wanted to write a book about Adult Children of Alcoholics (ACOAs) that we hoped would help Adult Children, and the professionals who work with them, make sense of the "Adult Child Syndrome" and the grief resolution process which is integral to recovery. We tried to keep professional jargon to a minimum. We wanted the book to serve as both a cognitive map and as a beacon to light the way in the journey toward health and wholeness, not only for the many Adult Children with whom we had worked, but also for many others who were trying to reconnect their feelings with suppressed memories from the past. We believed, and still do, that human beings are open systems shaped by, but not determined by, their pasts.

We were delighted *After the Tears* was successful in accomplishing what we set out to do. Although our specific audience was Adult Children who were raised in alcoholic homes, *After the Tears* could also have been written about adult children from any dysfunctional family where a major trauma is denied rather than discussed and worked

1

through. Over the years, we have heard from hundreds of adult children from alcoholic and dysfunctional families as well as hundreds of professionals who have found *After the Tears* useful in beginning, validating, providing hope for, and guiding a healing journey.

Our knowledge and awareness of the issues facing adult children of alcoholic and dysfunctional families have changed a great deal since 1985. We know far more about post-traumatic stress disorder (PTSD) and the effects of inconsistent attachment on the developing minds of children. When we decided to re-release *After the Tears*, we knew we wanted to include new scientific evidence while maintaining the "personality" of the original book so enjoyed by readers. We also solicited feedback about changes and additions from a sampling of Adult Children who read the original book.

Because of that feedback, we have kept much of the original text and have added chapters on Adult Children in intimate and sibling relationships, as parents, in the workplace, and caring for elderly parents. We have added chapters on resiliency, acceptance, forgiveness, and spirituality. And at the suggestion of many who attended our early workshops, we added two lists: "Common Characteristics of Alcoholic Families" and "Characteristics of Adult Children of Alcoholics." These were developed in our early work with Adult Children.

These characteristics are defined in the appropriate chapters in the body of the book. Each one is viewed as both an early survival mechanism that originally protected ACOAs, as well as a defense that later began to negatively affect their well-being and relationships. We end this introduction with both lists as "user friendly" references and a jumping-off point to the body of the text.

Common Characteristics of Alcoholic Families

- Focus on alcohol by all family members: alcohol is the central member around which all interaction revolves.

- All family members are shame-based: "No matter what I do, it will never be good enough."

- Inconsistency and insecurity: Parental responses, discipline, and rules change depending on the stage of alcohol intoxication and/or the codependent's response. Promises made are often not kept.

- Denial of feelings and/or addictions.

- Looped, indirect communication and double messages: "It's not your fault, apologize to your father." "There's nothing wrong here, and don't talk about it."

- Repetitive emotional cycles of family members: fear, anger, guilt, self-blame.

- Chaotic interaction or no interaction: Interactions change depending on whether or not people are drinking, or the stage of alcohol intoxication.

- Hypervigilance and hypersensitivity: Children learn that survival depends on being alert and aware of the behaviors of those around them.

- Unspoken rules: "Don't talk, don't trust, don't feel."

- Doubting own perceptions: "There's an elephant in the living room but no one acknowledges it's there, so I must be crazy."

- Fear of normal conflict: Conflict in alcoholic families frequently leads to emotional or physical abuse and is rarely resolved.

- Broken promises: "Dad promised me he'd go to my game. He's not here; he must be drunk."

- Family members develop survival roles and coping mechanisms: caretaker, adjuster, pleaser, scapegoat.

For an in-depth description of these characteristics, please see Chapter 1.

Common Characteristics of Adult Children of Alcoholics

- Fear of trusting
- Debilitating guilt
- Loyalty to a fault
- Hyperresponsible or chronic irresponsibility
- Need to be perfect
- Counter dependent/Fear of Dependency
- Need to be in control/difficulty with spontaneity
- Guess at what normal is
- Difficulty hearing positives and difficulty with criticism
- Please or defy others
- Overachievement or underachievement
- Poor self worth or shame
- Compulsive behaviors
- Continual trigger responses
- Addictions
- Living in anxiety and fear
- Need to be right
- Denial
- Fear of conflict and normal anger
- Chaos junkies
- Fear of feeling
- Frequent periods of depression
- Fear of intimacy
- Repetitive relationship patterns
- Fear of incompetence
- Hypersensitive to the needs of others
- Fatalistic outlook
- Difficulty relaxing or having fun
- Discounting and minimizing pain
- Resiliency strengths

For an in-depth description of each characteristic, please see Chapter 4.

1

The Bomb in the Basement and the Bomb in the Attic:
Common Characteristics of Alcoholic Families and Survival Adaptation of Children of Alcoholics

Over time, attempts to suppress or avoid
painful feelings or memories become like a pot of
water put on boil—though feelings, like the cold water,
are initially calmed by avoidance, eventually all the
painful and conflicting emotions, thoughts, and memories will
build up and start getting hotter and hotter and
may even boil over to the point it feels like you
have no control over the situation.

—*from* Finding Life Beyond Trauma
by V. M. Follette and J. Pistorello

WE HAVE OFTEN HEARD THAT CHILDREN need *roots* and *wings* in childhood to become confident, secure adults who are capable of forming healthy, fulfilling relationships. Unfortunately, many children of alcoholics have not been given a secure base from which to venture into the adult world. The focus on addiction in their families, rather than on the developing needs of children, often causes children of alcoholics to feel shameful and anxious rather than confident and secure. These children learn to *adapt* to life rather than learning how to *live* their lives. Without connection to an empathetic and nurturing other, children of alcoholics frequently feel like imposters, often hiding their insecurity, fear, and lack of self-worth behind a mask of confidence. Many live out the legacies of their childhood years feeling fearful, unlovable, out of control, and unworthy. They lick their wounds in silence, often feeling like children emotionally after feeling thirty and hyperresponsible at the tender age of five.

The Alcoholic Family

When we think of an alcoholic family, we think of a family with an alcoholic in it. A more accurate definition, however, is a family where all members are affected by parental alcoholism and codependency. The alcoholic parent is addicted to a substance and the codependent parent is addicted to the abnormal behavior of the alcoholic. The focus is on a substance, not the developing needs of children. The entire family learns to function in a system of alcoholic denial. It is like living in a home with an elephant in the living room; nobody acknowledges it is there. The elephant is fed and cleaned every day. Sometimes it is quiet, funny, loving, and pleasant. Then, without warning, it loses control. Everyone works to quiet the elephant, and each family member feels responsible for its behavior. No one acknowledges that the elephant exists, or talks about what it is like to live with it. Children grow up in pain, doubting their own perceptions. They experience tremendous guilt for not caring for the elephant properly, for not learning to control it and somehow make it happy. When they are older, they think they see an elephant in the living rooms of their own homes. The elephant is never discussed .. . maybe it isn't there. As therapists we have heard a variation on this experience from hundreds of Adult Children of Alcoholics (ACOAs); Peter was just such an Adult Child who came to us for help.

Like many ACOAs, Peter was a high achiever, happily married and successful in his profession. All of a sudden, seemingly out of nowhere, he began feeling the bottom fall out of his life. He had graduated in the top of his class from a prestigious law school. He was on the fast track for partner in his law firm and was married to his college sweetheart, Mary. He had three children: a son age eight, a daughter four, and a son six months old. He was doing everything "right," everything he thought was "normal." Then one day, at the bottom of his driveway, he had the first of many panic attacks.

> I really felt like I was going crazy. I just couldn't make myself drive up the driveway. The cell phone kept ringing and I knew it was Mary on the phone, worried, wondering where I was. The panic wouldn't stop. The harder I worked to control it, the worse it got. I was frozen, yet my heart was racing and I was covered with sweat. I thought for sure I was having a heart attack. The doctor says there isn't anything wrong with my heart. I feel like I'm going crazy. Am I going crazy?

Peter began feeling detached from his wife and he would be angry at her for no apparent reason.

> I felt like I was falling out of love with her. I thought we were close and then realized that I didn't really know Mary. We led separate lives. I worked; she took care of the kids. I felt like I was living my life as an imposter—doing the right things, going through the motions of what I thought was "normal," not connecting with anyone.
> I remember that first time I saw you; you asked if I was happy in

my marriage. I don't know "happy." I didn't even tell Mary what had happened in the driveway that day. I told her that I didn't answer the cell because I was preoccupied with work. I didn't want her to make a big deal out of it. I thought I was having a heart attack for God's sake and I didn't tell anyone. I just made an appointment with my doctor. I kept my fears to myself. I guess I don't know what it would feel like to let someone in. I've always taken care of things myself. I didn't want to worry Mary or tell her how scared I was. I thought I was going to die. Good thing I didn't tell her. She'd really think I was going crazy.

Early in therapy, I asked Peter to describe what it was like growing up in his family.

Both of my parents were alcoholic when I was younger. They both sobered up after I left for college. When they were still drinking, living in my family was like living in a war zone with a bomb in the basement and another bomb in the attic, and I never knew when either bomb would go off. But they are sober now. They are okay, good grandparents.

When I asked Peter how old he felt that night at the bottom of the driveway, he immediately said "Eight," then seemed shocked by his answer. I asked him to describe what it was like to come home from school when he was that eight-year-old boy.

Most of the time it was okay, I guess—well, except for Mondays. Mom and Dad usually were drunk on the weekends and would often take Mondays off "sick." We never knew what we would find when we came home on Mondays. Sometimes they were still in the "happy drunk" phase, sometimes they would be passed out, sometimes they would be in the "angry drunk" phase and would be yelling at each other.

Peter continued as if he was talking about someone else's life—removed and distant.

> I remember one Monday, it was around Christmas time, and we were supposed to go to town when we got home from school and see Santa Claus. My sister was six and I was eight. We were really excited. We came running into the house, excited to go to town. The house was a mess, the tree was down, and the ornaments were broken. Mom and Dad were yelling at each other and didn't see us come in. I took my sister by the hand and ran into my bedroom. I hid with her under the bed. I remember hearing the screaming and yelling for a long time. I don't know how long we were under the bed. The fight seemed to continue for hours. When it was silent for a while, I knew they had passed out. I made my sister stay under the bed while I went to check stuff out.
>
> My mom was bloody but she was breathing. Dad was passed out next to her. I knew better than to call anyone. I would have really gotten into trouble if I called someone. I just went to the medicine cabinet and got disinfectant and stuff and took care of her the best I could. I tried to put her to bed but she was too heavy. I remember thinking that she might die or something. But they woke up the next morning and went to work. Mom said she had fallen down putting the tree up. Dad didn't say anything. It used to happen a lot I guess. Mondays—well, the weekends too, I guess—weren't that great. I don't know why I'm thinking of this now. It was a long time ago. As I said, Mom and Dad sobered up a long time ago. Everything is all right now."

In a well-functioning family, emotions are openly expressed and the household runs fairly consistently. In an alcoholic family, day-to-day expectations are inconsistent and unpredictable. A child grows up with many parents: the drunk parent, the sober parent, the parent with a hangover, the parent preoccupied with the thought of the next drink, the funny drunk, the angry drunk, the parent who has passed out or is just not there physically or emotionally. The loving and attentive parent is "present" far too rarely. Both parents may be alcoholic, as was the case in Peter's family, or one parent may be the alcoholic and the other parent may be codependent, focused on the ups and downs of the alcoholic, busy denying the alcoholism, and unable to focus on the needs of children.

The impact of childhood trauma on Peter was too much for his developing mind to process. He shut down painful feelings in order to insulate himself from the horror he was going through. His feelings were encapsulated within him, cut off from his awareness and protecting him from consciously feeling them, until that fateful day many years later when Peter's wife, Mary, called him at work and told him that she had decided to take the day off from work to make Christmas cookies. Mary told Peter that she and the kids would be anxiously awaiting his arrival when he came home from work so they could all go to the mall to see Santa and then go out to dinner. Peter's feelings from that long ago time flooded his awareness and he froze at the end of the driveway, the terror of the eight-year-old bursting into awareness.

As Peter stated so well, growing up in an alcoholic family is frequently like growing up in a war zone. Often, emotions are not expressed or they are expressed judgmentally with blame and projection or with violence and abuse. The child learns to distrust his environment; feelings are not safe. In a well-functioning family, needs are expressed and met; rules are consistent. In an alcoholic family, roles are confused and needs can be dangerous depending on the time of day. The father may have told his son on Friday night that he could spend the weekend with a friend but may forget the promise by the next morning. Dad gets angry and Mom, in her wish to not upset her alcoholic husband, cautions her son, "Be good. Don't upset Dad, honey."

Jennifer also suffered from anxiety attacks that seemed to come out of nowhere. After listening to a story that was similar to Peter's at an ACOA workshop, Jennifer shared her own experience.

> I must really be crazy. I have anxiety attacks too, but I never grew up with violence; no one hit anyone. My parents drank every night for sure, but they never started drinking until five o'clock on the dot. I kind of liked it sometimes because our aunts and uncles would come over on the weekends and everyone would drink together. It seemed like the only time people were happy or connected. Of course, later in the evening people would start arguing but no one hit anybody.

Jennifer's family was a "looking good" family. The family rule was "There's nothing wrong here, don't talk about it." The abuse was much more subtle but just as terrifying to a young girl. Jennifer was expected to perform at these nightly parties. She was made to play the piano and sing while everyone stared, laughed, or sang along. She hated the wet, slobbery kisses she got from relatives when they had reached the "happy drunk" stage. If she made even a small mistake, her father would yell at her and her mother would tell her she wasn't practicing enough.

In therapy, Jennifer realized that the scars she carried from her alcoholic family didn't show on the outside but she was hemorrhaging on the inside.

> I felt like a trained monkey, forced to perform. I was terrified of making a mistake. I remember once feeling so embarrassed that I started to cry. People laughed and Dad ridiculed me, called me a "baby." My dad and mom wouldn't hit me with their fists but both of them would criticize me pretty constantly, not just for missing a key on the piano but if my room wasn't spotless or if I took too much food at dinner. I had to be perfect to hold up the image of the perfect family. What was worse was everyone thought we were the perfect family. We looked good on the outside.

Jennifer's anxiety attacks came whenever she was the center of attention, when she was at a gathering, or, later in her marriage, when she felt the house wasn't perfect enough or she was afraid she would be late getting dinner on the table.

> My heart would begin to beat faster and faster and I would begin
> to sweat and have difficulty breathing. Sometimes I would yell at the
> kids if they didn't put their toys away or if they spilled something. My
> husband didn't expect a perfect house or dinner at exactly the
> same time but all of a sudden I was eight years old again. I'm afraid
> I am passing this hell I lived in to my children. I want this to stop.

Painful feelings from and memories of growing up in an alcoholic or dysfunctional family that are not processed consciously are complicated. Sometimes it can feel like this childhood legacy is no longer an issue. Then, all of a sudden, the feelings and memories begin to erupt, seemingly out of nowhere, and begin to direct feelings and behavior that cause the terrified eight-year-old in an adult body to freeze at the end of the driveway or panic when the house isn't clean.

There is little consistency for children who grow up in an alcoholic family; children can't rely on adults being the same from one day to the next and sometimes not from one hour to the next. The adult caretaker may be tuned into a child's needs and empathetically respond to their feelings in one instance, but not in the next. A promise made in the evening may be forgotten the next morning. Rules are inconsistent and discipline is unpredictable. A child learns to rely on himself and no one else for internal controls. He either learns to live his life trying to be that "extra good" kid or he gives up and rebels. The alcoholic drinks; the spouse (if not also an alcoholic) is frequently preoccupied with the alcoholism. Children in these families too often become parentlike to both parents.

Common Characteristics of the Alcoholic Family

A number of years ago, we were staying in a hotel in New Mexico and decided to go for a swim in the hotel pool. We immediately became aware of two little girls on opposite ends of the pool who were being taught how to swim by their fathers. One of the fathers was at the stage of alcohol intoxication we often refer to as "star time"; he was loud and happy, sometimes showing off, narcissistic, and grandiose. This man was obviously playing to the crowd. It actually reminded us of times when we were growing up, when being taught something by an alcoholic parent actually meant being thrown to the wolves and then being made fun of for showing fear. In our families, being "taught" how to swim by a drunk parent was actually being tossed into the water while being commanded to swim or drown, or being ridiculed for being a sissy if you clung to the side of the boat.

That day, the drinking parent was repeatedly asking his young child to do things she was afraid of doing. He would take her to the deep end and make her let go, and then berate her or laugh at her when she began to cry in fear. Then he would throw her in the water and while she would dog-paddle like mad, he would brag to his adoring audience—friends and family who were also drinking—"See, that's the way to teach her. She's swimming, isn't she?"

The sober father at the other end of the pool was also teaching his daughter how to swim. He got into the water with her and told her what to expect every step of the way. He assured her that if at any point she wanted to stop, all she had to do was say so and the lesson would end. He carefully showed her each step and when she was ready, they would both chant, "fim, fim, fim" (swim) while she dog-paddled. He was playful, making a game out of it, and was ever

vigilant to cues that she might be afraid or was getting tired and losing focus. His focus was on his daughter and her developing needs—
very different from the focus on self that the other father was
exhibiting. What is "normal" in a healthy family interaction is not
"normal" in an addicted family interaction.

Without the presence of an empathetic, trusted other in her life
who can help her integrate this traumatic day at the pool, the little
girl being taught to swim by her alcoholic father will remain imprisoned by a painful past. Years later she may be staying at a hotel with
her significant other. They may decide to take a swim in the hotel
pool. When her beloved begins to playfully splash her with water,
reaches out to hold her in loving arms, or playfully chases her
around the pool, she may become enraged, feel overwhelming fear
or anxiety, have difficulty breathing, or abruptly leave the pool, convinced that her beloved is trying to humiliate her. When the time
capsule from the past bursts open, flooding her with feelings, she
will confuse her traumatic memory from the past with her experience in the present. Painful experiences from the past, if not understood, validated, processed, and integrated with a compassionate
and trusted other, will continue to intrude on our present and form
our beliefs and expectations of others and life experiences.

Following are common characteristics in alcoholic families that
can begin to shape a painful legacy of insecurity, fear, and lack of
self-worth in children of alcoholics.

Focus on alcohol by all family members. In a healthy family, parents are tuned in to the developing needs of their children. In the
alcoholic family, the alcoholic focuses on the alcohol or the stage of
alcohol intoxication, the spouse focuses on the changes in mood of
the addicted partner, and the child focuses on "survival" and the
needs of his or her parents or siblings.

All family members are shame-based. Alcoholic families are frequently blaming and verbally and/or emotionally abusive. Some are physically and/or sexually abusive as well. As a result, many of the family members frequently feel not only guilt, but a deep and profound sense of shame as well. They may feel unlovable, unworthy, or unacceptable in one way or another. The little girl being taught how to swim by her intoxicated father will likely blame herself for her fears, not realizing that what was being asked of her was inappropriate.

Denial of feelings and/or addictions. Denial is commonplace in an addicted family. The addicted individual denies the affect of his or her addiction on other family members. The spouse denies his or her feelings and frequently trades a sense of personal power for perceived love. He or she often fears abandonment. The nondrinking parent may either deny the effects of the drinking altogether or "parentify" one of the children, placing adult expectations and duties on the child. This often includes inappropriate expectations for comfort and/or support from one of the children rather than from the addicted partner.

Inconsistency and insecurity. In a healthy family there is a sense of sameness, order, and consistency. In an alcoholic family, rules made one day may be forgotten the next. The security of the family is influenced by the stages of drinking and intoxication. Johnny might be helped with his homework on one night and yelled at the next for being a burden to his parent. The household might be nurturing and consistent one week and dangerous, shaming, and inconsistent the next.

Looped or indirect communication and double binds. Communication in this family is rarely direct, which may lead children in these families to have difficulty with healthy communication as adults, whether or not alcohol is involved.

looped or indirect communications: communicating indirectly with
   someone through a third party; inappropriately confiding in a
   child when angry with a spouse; one parent may begin to discipline a child and end up fighting with the other parent.
double bind: giving conflicting messages, with one message negat-
   ing the other.

Repetitive emotional cycles of family members. Often in alcoholic
families when the drinking and chaos have stopped, family members
wait for "the other shoe to drop" or they "walk on eggshells" for fear
of causing the drinking to start again. Emotional cycles of fear, anger,
guilt, and self-blame loop in a repetitive pattern.

Chaotic interaction or no interaction. Relationships in alcoholic
families frequently follow patterns of isolation, enmeshment, and/or
chaos. Family members may feel extreme detachment for one
another on one hand and unhealthy enmeshment on the other.

Hypervigilance and hypersensitivity. Because growing up in an
alcoholic family is frequently like growing up in a war zone, individuals in the family tend to operate on survival adaptations. Children
learn to be aware of the slightest changes in emotion, mood, or
appearance of adults. In their own adult lives they are more aware of
the needs of others than of their own feelings and needs. As children,
they needed to be hyperalert and aware of what was changing around
them. Their focus was outside of themselves rather than inside.

Unspoken rules. The unspoken rules in an addicted family are
don't talk, don't trust, and *don't feel.* Peter explained, "I knew not to
call anyone for help. I knew I would get in trouble if I did." A child
of an alcoholic learns to trust only him- or herself for getting needs
met because needing becomes hurtful or sometimes dangerous.
Feelings are blocked early because they are too overwhelming. *Don't
talk, don't trust, don't feel* becomes the norm for all relationships.

Peter didn't consider sharing his fear with Mary; the thought never entered his mind. Peter had learned lack of trust as a normal reaction to an abnormal and painful life.

Doubting of perceptions. Because growing up in an alcoholic family is like growing up with an elephant in the living room that no one acknowledges, children from alcoholic families begin to doubt their own perceptions early in life. The child could see that Father was drunk, but Mother said Father was just tired from a long week at work. The child heard the fighting the night before but was told Mother's bruises were from the Christmas tree falling down. A child in this position constantly asks himself or herself, "Do I really see what I see? Do I really feel what I feel?"

Fear of normal conflict. Life in an alcoholic family is frequently unpredictable and often based on the stages of intoxication or the codependency of parents. There is often either the threat of emotional and/or physical violence or violent eruptions. There is often the fear of "making waves" or "not being good" and enormous guilt for doing or saying the wrong thing or making a mistake. Family members rarely see or learn normal conflict resolution, and any sign of conflict triggers fear of either violence or abandonment. Later in life, the normal, everyday conflicts in the home or workplace may cause irrational fears in an Adult Child.

Broken promises. Children in alcoholic families learn to distrust promises. A parent may promise to come to Saturday's ball game but will miss it instead because of a hangover. A parent on the "rising side of a blood alcohol curve" (on an alcohol high) may promise to buy his or her son a ten-speed bike; later, when reminded (and having no memory of the earlier promise made in the grandiosity of an alcohol high), he or she will yell at the child for being "spoiled." Children learn to deal with broken promises and broken dreams and learn to trust only in themselves. They have difficulty believing they are worthy of being given to, and this can create a great deal of difficulty in their intimate relationships later in life.

Survival and coping roles. Children in alcoholic families adopt survival roles early in their lives and become defined by those roles early in development. Coping roles are necessary to bring needed stability within the family. As adults, they become unable to tell the difference between the role adaptation and the self. The child becomes buried and the "ideal image" becomes the presentation to the world.

Labeling the ACOA Survival Roles

Because many in the field of addiction and recovery have developed labels for survival roles, there is often confusion in the general public as to which role is which. Many of us have developed different names for the same roles when referring to the survival adaptation of children of alcoholics: Claudia Black's "caretaker," for instance, is the same as Sharon Wegscheider-Cruse's "family hero." We used the term "adjuster." Black called that role adaptation "lost child," and another early pioneer referred to the "withdrawn child." Throughout this book, we use the following labels (and include definitions of each role):

Caretaker/Overachiever/Hero

- The fifty-year-old five-year-old
- Usually the oldest child (or oldest daughter if ages are close)
- Goal oriented; functions in a maze of goals
- Extremely reliable; a perfectionist; hates to make mistakes or be perceived as wrong, and uses perfectionism as a defense against shame

• Feels like a failure when receiving a B rather than an A, yet would never give an A if asked to grade self

• Is disappointed in self when he or she loses

• "The Responsible One"; often assumes the parenting role

• Continually tries to bring pride to the family; attempts to keep the family "looking good"

• High achiever in academics, popularity, leadership

• Views self as good or bad

• Bases self-image on being helpful, giving, achievements, and the positive attention from others

• Replaces love and nurturing with applause or accolades, yet applause and appreciation is never perceived as genuine or warranted; does not know what self-care is and would feel guilty if not caring for others

• Has difficulty when told what to do; is a great leader but has difficulty as a team player

• Feels inadequate, not good enough

Rebel/Scapegoat/Acting-Out Child

• Draws attention to self by negative behavior

• "Milk-spiller" in the family (provides a distraction during family conflict by drawing the fire)

• Takes the focus off the alcoholic or addicted parent with own behavior

• Acts out the family stress

• May appear hostile, defiant, and angry

• Frequently the first child to engage in his or her own substance use

• Has underlying feelings of hurt and guilt

- Very sensitive child with the exterior of a "fire-breathing dragon"
- Frequently the first family member to identify and speak out on the alcoholism in the family
- Labeled by other family members as "the problem"
- Referred for professional help because of frequent poor grades and/or acting-out behavior; is one of a small percentage of children of alcoholics to be referred for professional help

Pleaser/Clown/Mascot

- Frequently the youngest child
- Uses jokes, humor, and clowning to cover feelings in self and family
- Terrified of overt or covert conflict
- Has little or no understanding of his or her own needs or emotions
- Constantly attempting to smooth "troubled waters"
- Can sometimes appear fragile, immature, or in need of protection
- May appear to be hyperactive
- Bases tastes and wishes on the needs of others
- Has little ability to tolerate stress
- Bases inner feelings on fear
- Can be the angriest of all roles but is terrified to express anger, so often is depressed and/or ill; anger comes out full blast when drinking
- Can feel terrified if others aren't happy; often attaches identity and emotional well-being to own children or partners in adulthood (enmeshment)
- Focuses own life on helping others feel better to the extinction of own identity

Adjuster/Withdrawn or Lost Child

- Frequently the middle child; tends to look outside the family for validation; is often the most social but not within the family
- Serves as a "sponge" for family tension
- Works at not drawing attention to self—the invisible child
- Extremely anxious when focus is directed on him or her
- Adjusts to outer reality like a chameleon
- Becomes invisible, quiet, introverted, shy; can be a loner
- Can watch television during family upheaval; shuts out external reality
- Often speaks in a monotone
- Makes others "disappear"
- Finds conflict terrifying
- Has difficulty at times making decisions—frequently a follower
- Absorbs self in reading, music, television, video games, isolated activities
- Frequently very creative
- Has inner feelings of loneliness and feels lack of importance
- Is often detached emotionally; can "survive any situation" without expression of feeling
- An observer who knows everything that is going on but never comments on it; stays out of the way

It is important to note that survival roles save the emotional life of the child who grows up in an alcoholic family. Each role offers strengths as well as limitations and difficulties that may cause problems later in life. Part of the healing process is learning how to recognize the strengths as well as the limitations of survival adaptation and to become aware of the importance of "turning down the volume," not necessarily turning off the music. In the next chapter, we examine the strengths and limitations of each survival role.

2

The Same but Different:
Differences in Children from the Same Alcoholic Family and Differences in Alcoholic Families

It is perhaps ironic that I have met so many adult children
of alcoholics whose brothers and sisters
are not adult children of alcoholics!

—*from* Same House, Different Homes:
Why Adult Children of Alcoholics Are Not the Same,
by Robert J. Ackerman, Ph.D.

TANYA WAS JUST FINISHING THE DISHES when her brother Paul
called, asking if he could come over later. She explained that she
would love to see him but was on her way out to an ACOA meeting.

"ACOA?" Paul questioned. "What's that?"

"Adult Children of Alcoholics," Tonya replied.

"Geez, Tanya, are you still dwelling on the past? Mom and Dad have
been dead for five years. You need to get on with your life. Besides, it
wasn't so bad growing up. They went to work every day, didn't they?"

Which house did you grow up in? Tanya thought. How could Paul have grown up in the same house and thought it "wasn't so bad"? How could he think the pain of growing up in an alcoholic family wasn't still affecting their lives? Both had difficulty with relationships. Both had suffered severe bouts of depression. Both were continually critical of themselves.

If we were able to see a movie of Tanya and Paul as children, we might understand why they have such differing perspectives on family life years later. By age seven, Tanya was the caretaker in the family. She cleaned up after drunken parties and made sure she and Paul were fed in the mornings and got off to school when her parents were slow-moving because of hangovers. She tried to keep the house running in an orderly manner when her mom couldn't. She did the grocery shopping and learned how to get the grocery money from her dad when he was "feeling good." Tanya was responsible for adult obligations, even though she was just a child herself.

Paul, on the other hand, went to his room when a drinking binge began. To drown the sounds of his dad yelling at his mom or sister, Paul would crank up the volume on his stereo. This was his method to block out the pain: he would pretend that he was being raised by model parents instead of an alcoholic dad and a mother who sometimes joined her husband in his drinking and sometimes just stayed out of the way. Paul had a sister who was able to buffer him from the some of the effects of their parents' binges and she attempted to keep the "abnormal" as "normal" as possible. He lived under the umbrella provided by his sister so he didn't get rained on in the same way.

Even though their parents had died five years before in a car accident caused by their dad's drinking on New Year's Eve, Paul still minimized the dysfunction in the family. "Dad just had a bit too much to drink; all men drink too much sometimes. It was New Year's, after all" was his justification.

As we discussed in Chapter 1, an alcoholic family isn't merely a
family with an alcoholic in it. An alcoholic family is one in which all
members are affected by alcoholism, drug addiction, and/or codependency. As Sis Winger, director of the National Association for
Children of Alcoholics (NACOA), put it:

> Some of us grew up in families where adults knew intuitively that if
> children lived in the household, then consistency, predictability, hon-
> esty, love, and support were part of everyday life. Some of us grew up
> in families where our parents were trapped by alcoholism, where posi-
> tive parenting traits were nonexistent, and where fear, embarrassment,
> and sadness were intrinsic parts of everyday life.... The people hurt
> most by drugs and alcohol don't even use them—they are the
> Children of Alcoholics.

There are also differences between different alcoholic families.
Some alcoholic families are "too hot," where there is physical, emotional, and sometimes sexual abuse within the family. Some families
are "too hard," where emotional abuse is commonplace and the
child is never able to "get it right" and is constantly put down by the
adult caretakers. Some alcoholic families are "too cold," where parents are removed and isolated, and the child feels that "if only I was
good enough, my dad would love me."

Then there are two types of "too soft" families, where parenting is
absent. In the first, children are left to their own devices and often literally raise themselves. In the second, the codependent parent feels so
guilty over the drinking parent's behavior that he or she attempts to
make up for it by indulging the wishes of the children and withdrawing needed limits. He or she may continually buy material things for
the children to make up for "last night's drunken party."

Most alcoholic families share characteristics from all four types of
families, depending on the extent of the drinking, the duration and

progression of the disease, the developmental stage of the children, and whether the family is intact, or divorce or separation has taken place. The two things that separate a family *with an alcoholic in it* from *an alcoholic family* are denial and shame; denial of the affects of alcoholism and codependency on family members, and the level of shame in all members of the family.

The perception held by Adult Children of Alcoholics of their families' dysfunction is affected by several factors—which may also influence the degree of difficulty they experience functioning later in life. These factors include the child's survival role in the family; the adult child's level of denial; resiliency characteristics inherent in the child; the developmental age of the child when confronted with parental alcoholism; and the existence of at least one adult in the child's life who can validate the child's reality and emotions.

The Child's Survival Role Adaptation

When we began doing workshops for Adult Children of Alcoholics in the late 1970s, the majority of initial attendees were the Caretakers/Overachievers/Heroes in the family, like Tanya. Predictably, many of them came to the workshops not for themselves but to help other family members. But they did come, and they began a healing process, learning that they couldn't make an alcoholic parent, spouse, or sibling stop drinking, and they couldn't rescue resistant adult siblings or lift them out of denial. They could, however, learn to care for themselves.

Each of the adaptive survival roles children learn helps them in their youth, and each one offers both positive skills and negative effects later in life. The chart that begins on the next page shows the characteristics of each survival and caretaker role, as well as the effects on Adult Children both with and without intervention and healing.

ADULT CHILDREN SURVIVAL ROLES AND EFFECTS

Caretaker/ Overachiever/Hero	Without Intervention and Healing May:	With Intervention and Healing May:
WORK AND SCHOOL	• Become a workaholic • Have difficulty delegating or being a team player • Have difficulty making a mistake and feel the need to do something perfectly or not at all • Show great leadership ability while sacrificing health	• Be able to limit workload to stay healthy emotionally and physically • Have control over caretaking "volume knob" • Be a leader as well as a team player • Accept mistakes as well as successes
RELATIONSHIPS	• Need to be right • Need to be in control • Be "counterdependent," with difficulty stating needs and wishes • Feel uncomfortable with intimacy • Marry or partner with an alcoholic or someone who "needs" him or her • Have caseloads rather than friendships	• Accept mistakes and make apologies • Feel in control even when being spontaneous • Be dependent as well as independent; ask for needs to be met • Feel comfortable with intimacy • Seek out a relationship of equality—give and take • Have friendships based on being supported and supportive
HEALTH AND EMOTIONS	• Have difficulty expressing emotions but feel his or her body "cry" with frequent illness, headaches, pain, etc.	• Be able to express full range of emotions as they are experienced • Express anger in a healthy way • Celebrate success of goals being met by relaxing and having fun

ADULT CHILDREN SURVIVAL ROLES AND EFFECTS

Caretaker/ Overachiever/Hero	Without Intervention and Healing May:	With Intervention and Healing May:
HEALTH AND EMOTIONS (cont'd)	• Deny anger; may instead be passive-aggressive or may explode when anger cannot be contained • Experience depression upon goal attainment; may move from goal to goal, surviving rather than living	• Celebrate success of goals being met by relaxing and having fun

Rebel/Scapegoat/ Acting-Out Child	Without Intervention and Healing May:	With Intervention and Healing May:
SCHOOL AND WORK	• Be in frequent trouble in school • Act out in jobs, have difficulty with success, or be comfortable with failure • Drop out of school • Act out with rebellious behavior	• Be able to enjoy successes and be accountable for mistakes and learn from them • Enjoy completion of tasks and schooling • Show leadership ability • Turn internal sensitivity and compassion toward creative ability and may be an artist, poet, or writer
RELATIONSHIPS	• Run away from home as an adolescent—acting out behavior in relationships • Partner with a codependent who will take care of him or her and continue acting-out behavior	• Build healthy relationships of give and take • Live happily without chaos • Couple with a partner who is equal and have a give and take relationship; comfortable with intimacy

ADULT CHILDREN SURVIVAL ROLES AND EFFECTS

Rebel/Scapegoat/ Acting-Out Child	Without Intervention and Healing May:	With Intervention and Healing May:
RELATIONSHIPS (cont'd)	• Be hurtful and/or abusive to partners or children • Have unplanned pregnancies	• Show caring and sensitivity to those he or she loves
HEALTH AND EMOTIONS	• Begin substance abuse early, often before teen years • Act out feelings rather than talking or showing true feelings • Feel blocked from showing compassion and have a need to be "tough" • Run away from difficulties	• Go into alcohol and drug recovery • Talk openly and honestly about feelings and show true feeling • Show great compassion and sensitivity • Face difficulties and can confront them in self and others

Adjuster/Withdrawn or Lost Child	Without Intervention and Healing May:	With Intervention and Healing May:
SCHOOL AND WORK	• Isolate—keep to himself or herself • Act out "learned help-lessness" rather than take initiative • Withdraw from taking leadership • May not achieve to full extent of talents for fear of being noticed	• Feel comfortable engaging with others in social situations • Face challenges respon-sibly; embrace tasks • Be sensitive to the power needs of others and can be a fair and compassionate leader • Achieve full potential of talent

ADULT CHILDREN SURVIVAL ROLES AND EFFECTS

Adjuster/Withdrawn or Lost Child	Without Intervention and Healing May:	With Intervention and Healing May:
RELATIONSHIPS	• Isolate—may be withdrawn in friendships and relationships • Choose partner who allows him or her to remain invisible or continue to cope as he or she did in family of origin	• Interact successfully with friends and is intimate and communicative in love relationships • Develop healthy long-term relationships and is comfortable with intimacy
HEALTH AND EMOTIONS	• Begin substance abuse to gain a sense of personal power • Continue to have low self-worth, remain shy and withdrawn, feel little control in life • Often be manipulated by others • Be unable to take action on own behalf, feel a sense of helplessness	• Feel a sense of power and control in his or her life • Have a positive self-image • Be unlikely to allow manipulation by others; independent in thoughts and actions • Take action when action is warranted—protect self from further abuse

Pleaser/Clown/ Mascot	Without Intervention and Healing May:	With Intervention and Healing May:
SCHOOL AND WORK	• Be a clown and have difficulty being seen seriously • Allow others to take credit for his or her accomplishments	• Be a leader sensitive to the power needs of others • Be creative and artistic

Pleaser/Clown/ Mascot	Without Intervention and Healing May:	With Intervention and Healing May:
RELATIONSHIPS:	• Continue a life of invisibility, becoming what others want him or her to be with little sense of personal identity • Continue to be a clown instead of facing difficult situations • Enmesh with children and partner rather than allowing them to be separate • Have difficulty setting and keeping limits • Have difficulty expressing anger and stating needs • Be dependent in relationships • Become invisible in relationships • Remain selfless but couple with a partner who is self-involved	• Develop a sense of personal identity, recognizing likes, dislikes, needs, and feelings • Continue to have a delightful sense of humor but no longer use humor to deflect feelings • Allow independence in children and partner while setting caring and firm limits and boundaries • Learn how to appropriately express anger, needs, and feelings • Be sensitive to the needs of others without losing a sense of self • Learn to receive in a healthy rather than dependent way • Couple with a partner who is equal and can give and take appropriately
HEALTH AND EMOTIONS	• Have difficulty handling stress • Drink to let go of anger; may rage or become depressed • Internalize feelings resulting in constant fatigue or health problems	• Go into recovery; learn to show appropriate anger • Express feelings appropriately rather than internalizing • Learn to care for self in healthy ways

In most alcoholic families, children may change roles when siblings leave home, parents separate, or the alcoholic stops drinking. An only child in an alcoholic family may play many roles within the family, depending on the need for stability at any given time. It is clear, however, from the differences in roles and survival adaptation why siblings in alcoholic families may have differing perspectives on the dysfunction in the family as well as differing issues in the healing process.

Levels of Denial in Adult Children

Although denial is often seen as a barrier to treatment and recovery for the Adult Child, denial is literally what saves the child's emotional life. Denial convinces everyone that everything is fine, even when it is not. One of our favorite quotes on denial comes from Robert J. Ackerman, Ph.D., a professor of sociology at Indiana University at Pennsylvania and a founding board member of the National Association for Children of Alcoholics. In his book *Same House, Different Homes: Why Children of Alcoholics Are Not the Same*, he writes, "The child may at times deny that the problem exists in order to alleviate the emotional pain or to take time out from thinking about the situation. All children in stress need 'an emotional vacation' and denial is one way to create a 'time out'" (15).

When a child grows into adulthood and leaves the family, however, the denial doesn't always decrease. In our earlier example, the adult Paul was still using his denial and minimization as coping methods. They were still protecting him from seeing his alcoholic family realistically as well as preventing him from seeking help for difficulties in his adult life. Tanya had an "active" role in the family. Her caretaking, as difficult as it had been at the time, may have given her a sense of purpose and a certain amount of self-esteem as she tackled difficult problems. She didn't need the same level or type of denial as Paul, who was in a more passive survival role. Tanya was more likely to deny her own needs and repress her feelings rather than remain in denial of the dysfunction in the family. The level of Paul's denial was frustrating to Tanya as she wondered if they grew up in the same home, and Tanya's need to address the problem was a continual irritant to Paul.

Denial and the developmental stage of the child account for the differing views of siblings as to when the alcoholism began in the family. Younger children who have not achieved developmental awareness of cause and effect will not see their parent's behavior as connected to the parent's alcohol consumption but rather as connected to the child's actions. An older child will realize that his mother or father is different when drunk compared to when sober. One sibling may state with conviction, "Looking back, I think Dad was always an alcoholic; there were always difficulties in the functioning of our family." Another sibling may insist that the difficulty in the family stemming from Dad's alcoholism didn't begin until the children left home, and another may be convinced that "it was never that bad."

Resiliency Characteristics Inherent in the Child

Are some children born with more ability to deal with the stress and adversity of living in an alcoholic family than others? There have been many disagreements in the field of psychology over the role of nature versus nurture in the development of psychological strengths or difficulties. It is our belief that both affect a child's perception and development. Many research studies have proven that children who grow up in even the most dysfunctional and/or abusive families often show the capacity to survive, whereas some children growing up with much less family dysfunction show considerably less resiliency. When looking at the differences in Adult Children in alcoholic families, one of the factors that must be taken into account is the inherent personality strengths of the individual child.

Children who have the ability to attract and reach out to other adults in their life for support and nourishment seem to display the most resilience. They also appear to have intuition and insight about what is actually going on around them, a sense of their own power, a high degree of individuality, honesty, problem-solving ability, and the appearance of being socially at ease. In his book *Understanding Addiction and Recovery Through a Child's Eyes,* Jerry Moe, Director of Children's Programs at the Betty Ford Center, tells a story that illustrates these resiliency characteristics. On the first-day meeting of his children's groups at the Betty Ford Center, he was introduced to a group of three siblings: Tommy, age twelve; Sophie, age nine; and Justin, who was only seven years old. Here is Jerry's recollection of Justin's story:

> "Let me tell you what happens in my house . . . My dad goes into the bathroom for like an hour but he never flushes. I can smell smoke coming from in there, and I start to get really scared. Finally the door opens, and a mean, crazy alien comes out in my dad's body. Sometimes he hurts my mom and she cries. Tommy runs to get help, but Dad grabs him before he can." At this point Tommy is slumped in his chair with tears streaming down his face. It looks like he wants to run, but he's paralyzed by his little brother's honesty. Sophie has buried herself in one of our female counselor's warm embraces. The words keep pouring out of Justin. "Sophie runs and hides under the bed. I go in the closet and refuse to come out until the alien is gone." Justin takes a deep breath, sighs, surveys the room, and finally locks in on me. "Hey, mister, will you please help me and my family." (11)

For seven-year-old Justin and for many hundreds of children like him, Jerry Moe will be an adult in his life who will make a difference.

Overwhelming evidence in resiliency research indicates that a child's ability to endure and rise above painful childhood adversity depends on the presence of at least one caring, nurturing adult in his life.

Developmental Stage or Age of the Child
When Confronted with Alcoholism in the Family

Children internalize the words, actions, feelings, and behaviors of their adult caregivers. A child who is repeatedly greeted in the morning by the loving and welcoming arms of a parent will internalize self-love. A child who is hurting and sees love, compassion, and empathy mirrored in his or her parents' eyes will develop compassion and empathy for self and others. It is from early adult caregivers that children develop a set of beliefs about themselves and others, and learn to trust or not to trust in themselves and in others.

Children learn different lessons at different ages. Newborns learn the most basic lessons of trust in others, and through them, the ability to trust that they can soothe themselves when they are alone. Two-year-olds learn anxiety tolerance by the way they are comforted. They also begin to experiment with very basic independence and learning skills that will be perfected in different ways until adulthood. Three- and four-year-olds experiment with autonomy, and learn pride and joy in offering to help or in giving.

A child in an alcoholic family who has experienced loss and shame throughout his or her earliest development might find a new sense of "belonging" through helping as a four-, five-, or six-year-old. This new learning may be the training ground for workaholism and compulsive caregiving later in life. This child may experience tremendous depression in adulthood when, after achieving self-set goals for education and career, he or she is laid off from work, faces retirement, or suffers rejection of his or her caretaking efforts "after I worked so hard." He or she is literally unemployed psychologically, and this undermines a lifelong coping strategy of being needed and busy.

A child raised in an alcoholic family from birth who develops as the disease in the family develops may show different developmental strengths and weaknesses than a child whose parent marries an alcoholic. This is especially true when that child is focusing on peer relationships in early adolescence. A child partially parented by an older sibling may have different skills in relationships than a child who was an only child. One child may have learned the developmental lesson that "I will be loved as long as I'm good," or "I can trust in myself but needing another is dangerous." Another child, rather than learning the healthy developmental lesson of a normal seven-year-old that "I can experiment with decision making and learn from my mistakes," may learn instead at that developmental landmark that "mistakes are dangerous or injurious to myself or those around me so I'd better be extra careful and get it right the first time." He or she may have learned the additional lesson that "if I make a mistake, I am a mistake." This child (as an adult) might be highly competent at decision making and handling crises but may have little ability to truly connect in a relationship or know how to experience normal anger or resolve conflicts. Survival adaptation is often at the expense of interpersonal relationships.

An adolescent learning the developmental lesson, "I can leave you without losing you," may be terrified to go to school for fear of what may happen at home in his or her absence. That same adolescent may be so busy supporting the family emotionally and/or economically that the experiences normal to being an adolescent simply don't happen.

The Presence of At Least One Adult
Who Can Validate the Child's Reality and Feelings

A child flourishes in an atmosphere of parental warmth, connection, honesty, protection, and belief in the child. Children who do not have the support they need in their family may find validation in a healthy and caring teacher, neighbor, grandparent, clergyman, or other role model. Children show again and again that they can build amazing strength on the foundation of one caring adult's love. In some families of alcoholics, the sober parent can provide a foundation for the child. Again, the difference between an *alcoholic family* and a family *with an alcoholic in it* seems to be the presence of a caregiving adult who can be honest about the addiction, validate the child's reality and feelings, provide a buffer from the addict's shaming and hurtful behavior, and nurture the child's growth and development.

3

Self-Sufficient in an Insufficient Way: Learning to Survive Under Chronic Stress

> Our implicit models can manifest as a feeling in our bodies, an emotional reaction, a perceptual bias in our mind's eye, or a behavioral response. We do not realize we are being biased by the past; we may feel with conviction that our beliefs and reactions are based on our present good judgment.
>
> —from Mindsight, by *Daniel J. Siegel*

BETH WAS AN EXCEPTIONALLY COMPETENT professional woman who began therapy in her midthirties because, in her words, "The bottom is falling out of my life." She graduated at the top of her high-school class and earned a scholarship to college. She continued her academic success in college, not only graduating with top honors but also winning a full scholarship to medical school. After completing her medical training, she moved to a small town in the East where she developed a highly successful medical practice. She entered therapy at the age of thirty-five after her second divorce.

Beth felt that her whole life had been a lie; she called herself a competent imposter who had fooled everyone. She worried that people would find out that she was incompetent. She worried about her career, her divorces, her past, and that her therapist would think she was nothing more than "a whining child," who couldn't even do therapy right. During one of her early therapy sessions, she reported the recurring dream that for her had become a metaphor of her life.

The alley is dark and cold. I'm sitting about halfway down the alley with a couple of shabby empty suitcases. I've pulled my coat tightly around me to keep warm, but it doesn't seem to help. I know I'm alone in the world and I also know that I've finally gone totally crazy. The only thing that I have that's mine is my diploma from medical school. I'm almost crumpling it because I'm holding it so tight. Then a figure floats up the alley toward me—a man. At first I can't make out who it is. As he gets closer, I recognize him. It's the dean of the medical school that I graduated from. He looms up in front of me and grabs for my diploma. He's furious, yelling at me, "You didn't earn this! You don't deserve this! Who do you think you are?" His voice seems to be all around me like in surround-sound and he repeats his words again and again. Then, suddenly, I wake up. I was so scared.

Then, Beth paused for a minute and added, "I'm sorry. It was only a stupid dream. You must hear a million stupid dreams," thereby discounting the terror of the dream and the reality that she never felt she deserved her medical degree or anything else she had accomplished in her life.

Beth's reaction was not a surprise; as we've already learned, children who grow up under chronic stress develop ways to protect themselves in their dysfunctional environments. Richard, whose circumstances seemed quite different from Beth's, was another

ACOA who had learned adaptation techniques.

Richard had been court-ordered to alcoholism treatment after his second drunk-driving arrest. His early life history indicated that he had struggled in school, although his teachers felt that he was "a smart kid who just didn't pay attention." He had dropped out of school at sixteen and earned his GED at the age of twenty-five. He felt that the only two accomplishments in his entire life had been earning his GED and a diploma from an alcohol-treatment facility he had graduated from before beginning outpatient therapy. After his first year of sobriety, he told his therapist:

> I'm sober and I'm really proud of it. One day at a time hasn't been easy. I've worked hard at it, but deep down inside, I feel that I'll screw up my life again, maybe this time not through drinking, but through something else. I've always been a jerk. I feel like I'm not doing this right either. It's not your fault—you're a good therapist—but I've just never done anything right. In AA they would tell me that I'm sitting on the "pity pot." Maybe that's true. It's just that things never work out for me.

Beth and Richard appear to be very different individuals with quite different paths and life experiences. Yet they shared a common history, had similar feelings and experiences of the world—and both had alcoholic parents. They hadn't grown up in the same city or gone to the same high school, but both had felt lonely, and neither one ever felt quite as good as their classmates. Despite her popularity and many friendships, Beth felt that she was never close to anyone. Richard envied those who were always surrounded by other people because he felt he could never connect and make friends. Both grew up in middle-class suburban neighborhoods with lots of kids close by, but each felt estranged and without friends.

Beth and Richard grew up in alcoholic families, but until therapy, neither one of them understood how parental alcoholism had affected their lives and development. Both talked about traumatic events from childhood as if they were talking about someone else's life, showing little feeling for the children they used to be. Both were depressed and both suffered from unresolved or delayed grief. What would account for the similarities in how Beth and Richard had detached from the trauma they experienced in the alcoholic families in which they were raised? What were they grieving for? And why was their grief delayed or unresolved?

As we discussed in Chapter 1, many ACOAs feel as though they grew up with a bomb in the basement and another bomb in the attic—either of which could go off without warning at any time. For them, the stress of the unpredictability of alcoholic parents was equally matched by the stress exhibited by the codependent parents' hyperreactivity when drinking occurred.

Under those conditions, chronic stress becomes so common that it seems normal. Individuals use denial and repression to protect the ego from disintegration. Living with both the constant unpredictability of the alcoholic parent and the detachment and/or anxiety of the codependent parent is difficult enough for an adult who has a fully developed defense system. For a child, surviving the regular assault of trauma requires massive amounts of energy. This puts the normal developmental process on hold; there is no energy left to invest in development. While other children are learning to play, to trust, to self-soothe, and to make decisions, children in addicted families are learning to survive. The end result is a child who often feels thirty years old at five and five years old at thirty.

The chronic trauma of living in any family where the focus is on an addiction, rather than on the needs of developing children, places at least three burdens on these youngsters as they grow up: first, the repeated experience of the trauma itself; second, the effects of the trauma on personality development; and third, the need to re-experience the feelings and/or memories of the original trauma in order to integrate it and work it through. The effects on personality development and the process of integration will be discussed in subsequent chapters. The remainder of this chapter focuses on children's reactions to the trauma experienced.

The Burden of Traumatic Experiences

In "Trauma, Strain, and Development" in *Psychic Trauma*, Joseph Sandler describes trauma as any experience that within a short period presents the mind with a stimulus too powerful to be assimilated or mastered in a normal way. The stimulus (internal or external) results in the child experiencing a state of helplessness. To illustrate, we return to Beth's story and a traumatic event she talked about in her fifth month of individual therapy.

Although the event was highly stressful, Beth talked about it with detachment. She began by talking about a problem she had experienced in both of her marriages. She would become anxious and she would panic any time her husband came home late or on occasions when he had to leave the house after dark. If she herself left the house in the evening, she felt fine, experiencing neither panic nor anxiety. Her "attacks" would occur only if she was left alone in the house. All of her attempts to occupy herself or sooth herself when she was alone had failed miserably. She would extract elaborate assurances and promises from her husband that he would be home at a designated time, and she would go to bed and fantasize that her husband was with her. His promises did nothing to allay her fears. When alone, she was hypersensitive to any noise she heard or thought she heard, and her "startle reaction" would be accompanied by sweats, "the jitters," stomachaches, and a constant focus on food.

When asked if she experienced similar panic after dark now that she was living on her own, she answered, "Well, no, but then there is no one to be jealous of now. I've been told so often that it is really jealousy I am feeling, but I never was jealous before I was married. I never thought the panic was jealousy, but my husbands and friends thought it was. Why would marriage, just the fact of marriage, make me jealous when I wasn't jealous in relationships?"

The therapist answered Beth's question with a question: "Do you recall being afraid of the dark at any time when you were a child?" Beth could not, but then remembered a "scary" time that had happened when she was about eight years old. A terrible storm had begun one night and had intensified the following day. It was spring-time and the river that separated her house from the town flooded and washed out surrounding roads for miles. The power was out and the telephone lines were down. Because of the flood, her father hadn't been able to get home. Her mother began acting nervous and then became angry. Beth had seen her mother like that at other times, and she later realized it was because her mother was out of liquor.

Beth said she realized that it wasn't her father being stuck in town that bothered her mother, but that he couldn't follow his usual Friday night routine of bringing liquor home. Because of the storm her father was not able to get home for almost four days, and the rest of the family couldn't get to town. Beth remembered many instances of her mother's rage and panic during those four days and that she had been the target of the rage. She recalled trying to make food for herself and her brothers out of flour and water and was proud of the "crackers" she had created.

Then she spoke of her mother's crazy behavior after the second day. Beth laughed uncomfortably as she told of her mother trying to hit at bugs that weren't there. Beth did not realize until she was in medical school that her mother must have had the delirium tremens (DTs). She also felt guilty for not taking better care of her mother and for lacking sufficient knowledge to know what to do.

When one imagines the experiences of that eight-year-old child—the responsibility of caring for younger children housebound by a storm and caring for her mother in delirium tremens— it seems terrifying. Yet Beth showed little empathy for the child she had been. She was only critical of herself because she hadn't done better. She denied feeling any anger at being placed in such a helpless position at such a young age. As other memories surfaced, it became apparent that she had had similar experiences even earlier in her childhood. But the panic and terror she had experienced as a child did not show itself until the memory was triggered for the adult when Beth was left alone after dark.

In a traumatic situation such as the one just described, a child becomes flooded and overwhelmed by emotions. The response is first to freeze in a helpless state of anxiety and then to experience a sensation of numbness, as though someone else is watching the event—a type of unreality. If the child remains flooded emotionally in that helpless state, he or she cannot continue to function. Instead, to buffer the impact of the emotional flooding, the child's ego creates an elaborate barrier of defense mechanisms to protect itself from the experience.

However, the same defense mechanisms that work so well for the child begin to have the opposite effect in adulthood. The energy needed to keep feelings suppressed is much like the energy it would take to hold a large exercise ball under water; the ball erupts out of the water with what seems like violent force when one becomes exhausted and can no longer hold it down. In Beth's case, the defense mechanism triggered was panic attacks that were misinterpreted as jealousy.

In a healthy environment, a child has parents who function as emotional buffers. They stand between the child and the trauma, acting as what psychoanalyst Margaret S. Mahler refers to in *On Human Symbiosis* as "the protective shield" (44). But what if, as Beth experienced, the parents not only function poorly as buffers, but are also the agents inflicting the pain? A soldier can focus anger on an enemy that he can rationalize as deserving of his anger. For a child to consciously feel anger toward a parent, or to recognize a parent as nonprotective, would be to feel even more helpless and face a trauma of far greater magnitude—abandonment. Instead, a child prematurely develops personal resources and defenses to feel safe and protected, thereby continuing to protect a fantasy ideal of the "powerful and protective" parent. The child learns to "shut off" the experience through detachment, and with it, her or his own developmental process.

Many different mechanisms can be used to defend an ego under emotional attack. *Repression* buries the incident as well as the emotions it generated in the child's unconscious. *Denial* can create the fiction that Mother was only a little ill and that it wasn't "that big a thing." *Reversal* puts the child in the position of taking care of the parent rather than receiving care from the parent. The child may *identify with the aggressor* and believe that he or she was the cause of the incident. Through *projection* the child may believe the parent to be stupid, but powerful. Or the child may punish himself or herself rather than consciously feeling the anger toward the parent—*anger turned inward.*

Joseph Sandler agrees with the findings of other researchers. Through his own investigation he found that extended or repetitive situations of stress in a child's life combine to create trauma to the ego even though each incident on its own might not be considered as traumatic as Beth's (166).

Alcoholic families live in a state of crisis that has become normalized. Perhaps the major pathogenic factor in alcoholic families is denial of the reality of the deviant drinking and its impact on the children. For children in these families, life is lived as a rehearsal for traumatic events. These children cannot allow themselves to feel the impact of the trauma and also maintain the ability to function with it on an ongoing basis. The survival adaptation developed by these children is similar to that of any trauma survivor, with attendant psychic numbing, restricted affect, hypervigilance, and recurrent intrusive dreams and flashbacks of earlier traumatic experiences. The home environments of these children are what psychiatrist Frederic Flach calls "depressogenic" (156). These homes lack ego support, prevent the development of healthy self-reliance, create hostility and block its release, promote feelings of guilt, and cause the child to feel lonely and rejected. Such an environment engenders a chronic, pervasive sense of loss that tends to be outside of the child's conscious awareness. It predisposes children raised in these homes to problems with depression in adolescence and adulthood.

These "depression-prone" individuals are highly sensitized to situations of real or potential loss and/or abandonment. They are often "vulnerable to loss, conscientious, responsible, ambitious, competitive, self-absorbed, strongly in need of the approval and acceptance of others, dependent upon those whom they love, inflexible, highly sensitive (especially to rejection), vulnerable to being controlled by others, and unaware of feelings, especially anger" (Flach 1, 219).

Denial is the hallmark of an alcoholic family and so it is no surprise that these families provide little or no support for children to work through the pain of the absence of parenting that would occur in a growth-fostering family. A child is not able to discern that he or she is interacting with the illness of addiction or the "mirror" illness of codependency, rather than with a parent. Because of this inability, the child tends to internalize blame for all that goes wrong and embarks on what can become a lifelong career of hyperresponsibility, perfectionism, conflict avoidance, and caretaking. This is a misplaced attempt to save the alcoholic parent and to integrate the traumatic experience through cognitive and emotional mastery of it.

A paradigm developed by Jean Burgan, ACSW, clarifies this internalization process and illustrates how alcoholism or addiction in a family is the training ground for hypervigilance in adulthood. The five stick figures here represent five states of sobriety/intoxication in an alcoholic mother.

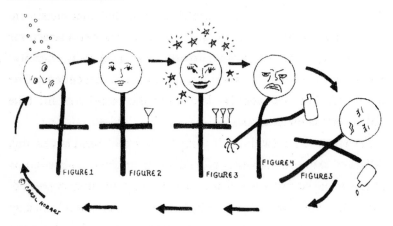

In Figure 1, the parent is in a hangover state: irritable, nauseated, wanting to be left alone. When her eight-year-old daughter asks for a sandwich, the mother responds, "Leave me alone! You always want something! Who do you think you are? Can't you see I don't feel well?" An hour or so later, the little girl returns, still hungry and determined to "get it right" this time. She asks her mother ever so carefully if she can please have a sandwich.

In Figure 2, her mother is warm and responsive, having consumed enough alcohol to alleviate her withdrawal symptoms. She offers to fix her daughter a sandwich and gives her a choice of peanut butter and jelly or bologna and cheese. The little girl feels really loved and thinks that she must remember just how she asked her mother for a sandwich the second time so that she will get the same loving response the next time she asks.

In Figure 3, the mother has had enough to drink to be on the rising side of a blood alcohol curve. She is expansive and intoxicated, and when her little girl comes back later to get the sandwich, the mother pulls her down on her lap, smothers her with wet, slobbery kisses, and tells her that since she's the best little girl in the world, Mother is going to buy her a ten-speed bike later that afternoon. This is music to the little girl's ears, especially since her interactions with her mother are an emotional feast or famine, thereby intensifying her normal needs for affection, approval, and dependency. She doesn't like the wet, slobbery kisses, but the promise of the bike makes her feel loved and special.

In Figure 4, the little girl is running back in from play, saying, "Mommy, can we go downtown to get my bike?" Her mother is now on the falling side of a blood alcohol curve and is drunk, depressed, and irritable. She snarls, "Get the hell out of my face, you selfish, ugly little brat. I can't stand you. You always want stuff." The little girl recoils, surprised and frightened. Her defense against the despair of feeling unloved and rejected by her mother is to blame herself. She decides she's stupid, ugly, clumsy, selfish, and can't do anything right. She should have been more attentive and worked harder around the house instead of playing outside. Eventually she comes to believe that because she has caused her mother's behavior—caused her to drink—she should be able to change it if she is just good enough.

In Figure 5, her mother is passed out—a state that a very small child may confuse with "dead" until she learns that mother is "sleeping" or "drunk." The little girl in our example represses the event and learns to feel powerless, apathetic, and helpless; nothing she does makes a difference. She learns to be hypervigilant, noticing even the smallest shift in her mother's speech, moods, or behavior. She is "adult" in the face of an ever-changing reality that constantly provokes a surplus of feelings and necessitates a surplus of denial on her part. She has no time to process and achieve emotional and cognitive mastery over the experience before the next stressful event takes place.

As an older child she will learn more sophisticated methods of coping with her traumatic environment, perhaps learning to ask for the grocery money when her mother is on the rising side of a blood alcohol curve, or stealing the car keys when her mother is passed out. Children who experience trauma are not capable of sorting out traumatic events or a continually stressful environment without the calming presence of an empathetic adult who can offer safety, validation of the experience, and support. The part of the brain that serves to make sense of stressful conditions, feelings, and emotions is not fully developed in a small child, and even in an older child it is shut off when the body is flooded with cortisol, a hormone that is released in response to stress.

Many of us know children who have recovered from traumatic events with little or no lasting effects on their personality development. What makes the difference is the support available to the child to work through the trauma. Any trauma can be integrated if it can be talked about, "walked through," and processed. What seems to be crucial in deciding the outcome of a traumatic experience is not so much the experience itself, but whether or not there is support provided to validate the trauma and work it through. If a child has one person in his or her life to talk to, to receive validation from, and to express feelings to, the child usually does not develop post-traumatic stress disorder (PTSD). The major difficulty that occurs when there is no caring support is the "post-traumatic state of the ego strain that the trauma engenders and the child's ability to adapt to that state" (Sandler, 168).

In *The Basic Theory of Psychoanalysis,* Dr. Robert Waelder presents an example of a child "working through" a traumatic situation with support from his environment. A little boy, six or seven, was walking through the woods with his father when his father was suddenly attacked by a stag. His father was seriously hurt and bled profusely. This is certainly a traumatic event for a young child, and the little boy stood by helplessly frozen during the attack. As weeks progressed, the little boy continued to act out the scene again and again in his play, changing its content with each new rehearsal. One day, instead of being the witness to the event and frozen in terror, the little boy became the hero who saved his father from the frightening stag. The little boy's ego won mastery of the event little by little, thus reducing its effects on his ego development because he didn't need to repress it. He had the support to remember it, feel it, and master its effects through time. This little boy had what most children in addicted families do not have: the validation and support of his father and the time and safety to work out his trauma in play. Because the stag wasn't part of his daily life and he wasn't dependent on its protection, he could act out his anger at it instead of turning that anger on himself. Children of alcoholics too often do not have supportive parents or adults who can verify that an event took place and provide the time and caring support to work through it.

Children in alcoholic homes can't be angry with the parents they depend on for care. Some children, however, have other loving adults in their lives who can validate their experiences and help them see their addicted parent as someone who has a disease. These children learn to see their own strengths and they learn to get angry at the disease and the behaviors, rather than risking anger at their parents or turning it on themselves.

Children in addicted families usually do successfully develop their own internal "buffer" to traumatic events. Events that render them helpless at age five almost seem to be taken as expected occurrences at age eleven. A little boy may have frozen in a state of helplessness at age four while witnessing his father raging at his mother. A few years later he may step into the middle of such a confrontation and take the brunt of the attack on himself. Unlike the boy who witnessed the attack on his father and then took on the stag in fantasy play, children of alcoholics become so internally defended that they take on the "enemy" in real life. As stated so well by Anna Freud in "Comments on Trauma":

> In the upbringing of children where frustration, criticism, and punishment are concerned, it is well known that the individual child tends to adapt to the level of parental handling and reacts traumatically only to the unexpected or the unfamiliar. A harsh scolding or slaps by a habitually tolerant parent may have a devastating "traumatic" effect on a child while the same treatment is assimilated in a much less dramatic manner by the children of harsh and exacting parents. (239)

The price of this "assimilation," however, is that the massive amounts of energy used in defensive adaptation are then not available for use in the often difficult process of normal psychological development. To illustrate this, we'll return to the history of Richard, whom we met earlier in this chapter. Richard recalled that he had a great deal of difficulty in school even though his school records showed that he was a bright child with no indication of perceptual difficulties. Yet there were numerous notations in the school files that "Richard just didn't pay attention." The effects of trauma on the development of his image of himself and on his ability to pay attention in school became apparent in therapy, and it was also apparent that Richard had constructed his own buffer of defenses against the trauma early in his life. This buffer was now causing difficulties in his life.

Unlike Beth, Richard's role in the family was not one of taking care of the family. He was not a child who put energy into achievement and perfectionism at an early age. Richard recalled many childhood experiences of witnessing the abusive rage of his alcoholic father, usually directed at his mother. He reported hiding in his room and trying to make the noise go away while his older sister attempted to "reason" with her parents (much like Beth). Richard, unlike Beth, was not only overstimulated, but because of his sister's partial buffering, had no active role in attempting mastery of the traumatic events in his family.

Fantasize for a moment: Take your homework assignment to a video arcade with the hope of studying and perhaps even writing a report while there. Imagine trying to shut out the flashing lights and the high-pitched beeps. Richard, like anyone who might attempt to study at a video arcade, found himself constantly overstimulated, both externally by what was happening in his family and internally by his feelings about it. As he got older, he learned to partially block out the external stimuli, but he had less success in controlling his constant internal responses to the traumatic episodes in his family. He was a compulsive reader as a late adolescent and young adult. He would come to each therapy session with a book in hand, much as someone would wear a particular type of clothing as a badge. Usually the themes of the books were "Man's Dilemma" or "The Meaning of Life." Like so many children from alcoholic and addicted families, Richard consistently tried to achieve mastery through cognitive understanding. It was as if Richard communi-cated through the symbol of the books he carried: "Perhaps if I can find meaning in this book, my suffering will have meaning; perhaps if someone in this novel shares my experience, then I will have a wit-ness to the fact that I too exist; or perhaps if I carry a book, I'll be like those other smart kids in school."

Richard said that many times as an adolescent he didn't care much about what was happening at home and he often thought his sister was stupid for putting so much energy into taking care of people who obviously didn't want to be taken care of. He would say at other times that "I am just like my old man," adding, "Yeah, all the men in my family are alcoholics." He would laugh when he talked of how stupid he thought he was and how much he had messed up his life, feeling that it was somehow his karma. Often, he could not make eye contact and would stare blankly into space. It was obvious that Richard had identified with the aggressor early in his life, per-haps to feel less helpless in a situation he could not control. He used massive amounts of energy to deny his feelings and the effects that his early life history had on him. Like so many Adult Children of Alcoholics, he was plagued by constant guilt, but unlike Beth, the only feeling he expressed was anger; he couldn't feel the tears yet.

We have both worked with hundreds of children from alcoholic families in our clinical practices and agree with noted child psychol-ogist Bruno Bettelheim, who suggested three possible emotional outcomes for survivors of chronic trauma in his essay "Trauma and Re-integration."

First, there are those individuals who literally succumb to the destructive influences of their childhoods through suicide, insanity, or by being incarcerated for much of their lives. These people are not able to establish adequate defenses for survival; they remain overwhelmed or turn the energy of the trauma against themselves. Because they lack emotional support, they are unable to feel hopeful about themselves or move beyond their self-defeating behaviors.

Second, there are those individuals who use denial, repression, projection, and other defenses to function but do so in a restricted way. They have learned how to "survive" but have difficulty "living" their lives. They often find themselves in environments that emotionally replicate those of their childhoods—environments that demand the defenses they have learned to exist behind while they attempt to achieve mastery of their pain. They have great difficulty when the demands of their environments exceed their ability to "defend," or when people in their lives want to get close to them, expect true connection and intimacy with them, and expect them to "live" and experience new things rather than merely "survive."

Third, and this is the goal toward which we can all move, there are those who are willing to re-experience the pain of the original trauma and work it through, finding their voice and gaining emotional freedom from the constraints of the past. Such working through (what we call *grief work*), is the essence of the healing process. This involves talking about how it was and how one wishes it could have been, and is accomplished with at least one caring person with whom one has worked hard to establish trust.

4

The Gift That Keeps On Giving:
Characteristics of
Children of Alcoholics

> We construct labyrinthine defenses and a moat around our
> heart to allow some semblance of safety from our grief.
> Unattended sorrow gradually displaces the joy of youth and
> adds to the diminishment of trust and hope.
>
> —*from* Unattended Sorrow: Recovering from Loss
> and Reviving the Heart, *by Stephen Levine*

JOAN CAME INTO THERAPY after several months of battling severe depression. She had been thinking daily about ending her own life and had made one suicide attempt. She showed little or no emotion as she related her painful history. Both her parents had been raised in alcoholic homes. During the course of therapy, Joan often expressed more grief over her parents' childhood losses than her own. Joan's mother had longed to be a dancer and was quite talented, but her own father's alcoholism had made it impossible for her to take lessons. From early childhood on, Joan's room had been decorated with posters, figurines, lamps, and wallpaper of famous ballerinas in graceful poses. At age four or five, when other children were out playing games, Joan dutifully practiced hour after hour under her mother's watchful eye, hopeful that someday she would be able to please her mother. She didn't realize she was supposed to be fulfilling her mother's unrealized dreams.

Joan remembered that since childhood she never felt good enough. Her mother was never completely happy with her, even when Joan's breathtaking talent won her a full scholarship to college. Joan kept working harder and harder to gain her mother's approval, and most of all, her mother's love. By age twenty-one, Joan had made her mark and was appearing as a dancer on stages all over the country. She was the object of much adoration and fanfare, and her mother was always there to see her perform. In spite of all the honors and applause, Joan felt a deep sense of loneliness as well as a nagging feeling that the applause didn't belong to her. In her late twenties, she fell on stage and injured her legs. She was told it would be some time before she would be able to dance again. To her surprise, Joan first experienced a slight feeling of relief, followed almost immediately by frightening suicidal thoughts.

In therapy, Joan drew her memories and feelings because it was so difficult for her to express them verbally. During one session, she drew a three-picture representation of herself. In the first picture, she was a beautiful, graceful ballerina with all the confidence befitting a "star"; in the second picture, she was an extremely angry young woman with a knife in her hand; in the third, she was a tiny, shaking, frightened child.

In her drawings, Joan unconsciously depicted the many conflicting feelings about the self with which individuals affected by
parental alcoholism often struggle. The first picture, the ballerina,
represents the part of the person that faces the world as the "ego
ideal," the "ideal child," the "good child," or the "acting-out child."
This part mirrors the images the child develops of the past hopes,
dreams, needs, fears, wishes, or nightmares of the parents or adult
caregivers. Her picture of the angry young woman with the knife
represents the severe depression beneath the surface of the "ego
ideal"—that is, the punitive, demanding, internalized parent who is
constantly pushing for and demanding perfection, caretaking, or
failure. The picture of the tiny, frightened child represents the disowned child's part of the self—the part that lost her voice—that
part of the ego that was never allowed the freedom of emotional

development. The child retains tears never cried, fears never expressed, anger never spoken, and the voice never heard—all of the child's normal emotional responses. Those responses have been imprisoned by a superficial image that allowed for "attention" but not true acceptance of the child—or love in the fullest sense of the word. Joan's mother needed a dancer to fulfill her own dreams.

Wounded, narcissistic parents may need a grateful child. A father who was unpopular or clumsy as a child may need an athlete. A parent afraid of his or her own anger may need an acting-out child. The real child, the child who was meant to grow and develop into a self in his or her own right, is often never seen. Even if Joan's interest had been in science or math, her mother needed a dancer—and children will make every effort to be what is expected of them.

Although the impact of parental alcoholism on child development is mediated by a host of factors, it would be fair to say that most children growing up in alcoholic homes are affected developmentally. In many cases, children raised by parents who are Adult Children of Alcoholics (ACOAs), even though they have not followed parental patterns of drinking or drug abuse, may pass on the effects of delayed grief to their own children. One Adult Child trying to raise her own children lamented the absence of what she called "the unconscious book on how to be a parent," and observed that "alcoholism is the gift that may go on giving unto the third and fourth generation."

The effect of parental addiction on child development is not the same for every child growing up in an alcoholic home; many factors need to be taken into consideration. They include:

- the degree to which the parent or parents focus on the developmental needs of their children rather than on the addiction or the effects of addiction
- delayed grief and/or trauma that has not been resolved in the parent(s)
- which parent is alcoholic and the other parent's response to the addiction
- the stage of alcoholism the parent is experiencing, and how the alcoholism or addiction is manifested
- the amount of energy that is available to the child rather than expended on repression and denial of unfinished business left over from the parent's childhood
- the presence or absence of a caring, adult caregiver who is not in denial
- the birth order and personality of the child

Five factors affected Joan's early development, which became apparent upon examining her early history. First was the effect of her mother's delayed grief from her own childhood. Early in Joan's development, rather than allowing Joan to be a freely developing child in her own right, Joan's mother made Joan an object of her unfulfilled, narcissistic desires because she had not come to terms with her own dream of becoming a ballerina.

Second, Joan had little recall of her father, a salesman who was on the road a great deal. When he was home, he was unavailable because he was either drinking or involved "in his own world," physically isolated from the family in another room. What Joan did remember were the chaotic times when her father was drunk and emotionally abusing her younger brother. The boy became the object of their father's disappointments in himself and in his own life. Although her father never vented his anger on Joan, she was a witness to her brother's ridicule, and thus, Joan was a secondary trauma victim. She felt guilty that she couldn't protect her brother, but at the same time she was secretly glad the attacks weren't aimed at her. Although she frequently tried to distract her father by clowning, her attempts were usually futile. Joan felt added guilt because her father constantly said she was "the apple of his eye." Although she had no relationship of substance with her father, his added focus on her as the "special child" caused her a great deal of guilt in light of her brother's mistreatment.

Third, both parents seemed to be focused on the repression and denial of their own early childhood disappointments. They also avoided acknowledging her father's active alcoholism and her mother's codependency.

Fourth, the family was isolated—neither parent had a network of friends—and Joan and her brother developed few peer relationships and seldom felt comfortable bringing home the few friends they had.

Fifth, because neither parent was emotionally available in the true sense of the word, Joan and her brother received very little parenting. Instead, they became the objects of their parents' needs and projections. There was little or no validation of the feelings and emotions that are necessary for the development of a real self (ego), only an emphasis on projected images (ego ideals). There was no safe place for these children to work through the traumas they faced in everyday life, let alone receive validation and support for feelings stimulated by the family's focus on addiction. There was little or no buffering or protection of these young children's developing egos. Both Joan and her brother became "adults" too early. Her brother became the "cause" of drinking and anger in the family, and Joan became the "savior" of wounded images. Their own developmental processes were put on hold.

Children such as Joan and her brother forego their own developmental processes and become prisoners to the mirror projections of their injured parents. This makes it impossible for children to develop their own true sense of self. They are unable to go through normal stages of emotional separation from their parents, either in early childhood or later in normal adolescent development.

The Child's Bill of Rights

We believe every child should be raised with the following rights:

- The right to be an object of unconditional parental love
- The right, for a time, to be the center of parental attention and to have needs met without asking
- The right to childhood innocence, and to be protected from traumatic situations and stresses

- The right to belong to a family and a community
- The right to consistency, limits, security, warmth, and understanding
- The right to be loved for what he or she is, rather than for being what others wish him or her to become
- The right to be parented and nurtured rather than falling under the weight of making up for the losses of parents
- The right to feel safe while mastering a full range of normal feelings and emotions
- The right to make decisions and learn from mistakes
- The right to become independent and find one's own voice
- The right to grieve losses as they happen
- The right to have emotional and physical boundaries

Unfortunately, children who are raised in dysfunctional families are often not blessed with a child's bill of rights. This is particularly true in alcoholic families, addicted families, or any family where the Band-Aids for parents' wounds are frequently their own children. The loss of these developmental processes is prominent in all families that share unresolved trauma and grief. They are manifested as the proverbial "elephant in the living room" and when parenting is preempted by denial, addiction, and stress. The elephant can be almost anything: addictions, depression, ungrieved losses, domestic violence, sexual abuse, unresolved separation or divorce, suffering from PTSD, or the losses associated with being the adult children of addicted parents.

Children raised in families of addiction or denial learn to repress feelings and needs, block self-expression, stifle autonomy, deny their own needs for support, lose their voice, stop trusting or learn only to trust hurtful people and painful situations, and adapt to survival rather than living. When parenting is not consistently available, children forego basic rights in exchange for mere survival.

ACOAs frequently spend the rest of their lives attempting to capture the love they so desperately lacked as children and look for it elsewhere (from their partners, their children, or their professions). They consistently attempt, through re-creation of the past, a mastery of the trauma of having never been a child.

> as a newborn, i scream as i enter the world
> a daughter, the happiest day of your life.
> hours later i scream, where are you? i scream louder
> what did i do? i don't understand. don't you love me anymore?
> i am a very shy little girl. i don't remember losing my voice.
> i don't remember having a voice.
> i crash my bike, i crash my sled.
> you don't ask if i'm ok. you laugh. you laugh at me.
> i'm not suppose to play beyond the gate. why?
> my childhood friend commits suicide. why?
> you go your separate ways.
> i don't understand. why don't you talk to me?
> you only give me rules and i can't seem to get anything right.

Kim Sebastian

Characteristics of Adult Children of Alcoholics

After working with many Adult Children in workshops and in our private practices, we developed a list of thirty characteristics we believe are common to children of alcoholics and of addicted families. It should be noted that not every Adult Child exhibits all thirty characteristics, and that other families in denial (of domestic violence, sexual abuse, and other "secrets") have children who, as adults, have many of the same characteristics.

It is also important to remember that these characteristics are used in childhood to save the child's emotional life. They become difficulties in adulthood when the survival characteristics begin to interfere with building healthy intimacy in relationships or begin causing health problems of one kind or another. The very defenses and tools children use to cope and survive often interfere with the ability to live productive adult lives. The very defenses children use for protection from painful experiences often lead them to their own substance abuse, illness, difficulty in relationships, anxiety and panic disorders, or serious depression that is often not understood.

Validating and understanding the characteristics can be a type of "cognitive life raft," allowing the ACOA to realize once again that he or she is having a normal response to an abnormal and painful life. (Learn more about the cognitive life raft in Chapter 7.) When we have grieved and healed the traumas of the past, we can live in the present and appreciate the characteristics we developed to survive while letting go of them. For instance, a certain amount of distrust can protect us from harm, but the inability to trust when trust is warranted may stop us from enjoying relationships fully or experiencing friendships based on caring and give and take. We can't trust others until we can once again trust ourselves to know the difference between those who are going to help us and those who may hurt us in ways we were hurt as children.

Fear of Trusting

Children depend on adult caregivers for nurturing and love for their survival. It is terrifying for children to feel abandoned by the parents they depend on. A child must make the parent "right" and "good"—no matter what—if he or she wants to avoid abandonment. This means that the child must take on the belief that he or she is "wrong" and "bad." When one has spent his or her childhood being "wrong," it is hard to trust in oneself as an adult. When caregiving is unpredictable and inconsistent, children learn to depend on themselves rather than others. Doubting one's own worth and believing that others cannot be depended on leads to a lack of trust in both self and others in adult life.

Debilitating Guilt

Children in alcoholic families often grow up with a sense of total helplessness. Frequently, these children gain control in their lives by believing they cause the responses and behaviors of others rather than seeing themselves as victims of the behavior. They blame themselves instead of putting the blame on the adult caregivers who raised them. (For example: "It's my fault that Mom and Dad drink. If only I was better. . . .") It is unfortunate that many ACOAs continue to blame themselves for the actions of others.

Loyalty to a Fault

ACOAs tend to be loyal even with evidence that loyalty is not deserved. They will stay in jobs or in friendships where they are taken advantage of, or in abusive relationships. They question their own feelings and simply keep trying harder, just as they did in their alcoholic families. They often believe that "change is right around the corner" if they hold out, just as they did in their families of origin.

Hyperresponsibility or Chronic Irresponsibility

Children from addicted families often take on the responsibility of adult caretakers early in life. Many children make excuses for parents who are drunk by doing the grocery shopping, listening to their mothers' difficulties with their alcoholic dads, or raising siblings when they are only children themselves. Many have told me that they failed at parenting or budgeting when they were eight-year-olds, never realizing how ill-equipped they were to handle these adult tasks. Some give up, feeling that nothing they do will ever be "good enough." As adults they may do their coworkers' jobs as well as their own, feel responsible for how the entire office functions, suffer from chronic procrastination, or blame others for their mistakes and irresponsibility.

Need to Be Perfect

Children in alcoholic families develop a fear of making mistakes, because to make a mistake is to "be a mistake." They walk on eggshells for fear of doing something wrong, or they only engage in activities that they can master. They often feel that they must do something perfectly even before they have been taught to do it. They feel foolish learning a new task or experiencing something new as those activities place them outside of their comfort zones.

Counterdependency/Fear of Dependency

Counterdependency is the fear of depending on anyone for even basic needs. When needs are repeatedly unmet by adult caregivers or are met at some times and not others, children learn to stop needing. They may actually fear normal dependency. For example, when most adults would gladly accept a stranger's offer to hold a door open, an ACOA who is carrying a fifty-pound box will decline, replying, "No thank you, I can take care of it." Children of Alcoholics stop expecting or wanting help because the continual feeling of disappointment is too painful.

Need to Be in Control/Difficulty with Spontaneity

A fear of "normal" feelings frequently leads the Adult Child to live life as a rehearsal. We know of one ACOA who opened her gifts before Christmas and methodically wrapped them back up so that she could show the appropriate emotion, rather than disappointment, when she was with others on Christmas Day. ACOAs are often extremely uncomfortable with spontaneity or surprises. The feeling that "I have to be in control or my world will fall apart" is the foundational belief of many ACOAs.

Guess at What Normal Is

Is it "normal" for a seven-year-old child to take care of younger children, or for a dad to scream at his son because he couldn't hit the ball while "playing" in the backyard? As one ACOA described it:

> I have lived my life always guessing at what normal is. I constantly guessed in relationships, and I guessed as a parent. It took me years to realize that raising children when you were a child wasn't normal. It wasn't normal to be yelled at when you made a mistake or be made fun of because you were having difficulty doing something you were never taught to do. It wasn't normal to never be told by your father that you were loved. Yet, this was normal in my alcoholic family. It took me years to learn simple things like telling my wife and children I loved them or celebrating their successes and my own. It was so easy for my wife because she'd been raised being told she was loved. She asked me once if I loved myself and I didn't know—was I supposed to? Did people normally love themselves? I didn't know. She taught me how to be a parent and an equal partner. I didn't know how.

Difficulty Hearing Positives and Difficulty with Criticism

Because of poor self-images developed in childhood, ACOAs may discount positive feedback from others, feel a sense of distrust for those complimenting them, or feel emotional discomfort and/or go into immediate denial when complimented. If an ACOA receives twenty-one positive compliments and one "need for improvement," he or she may focus on the one negative for weeks, or argue that the "need for improvement" is not warranted while inside he or she feels like a failure.

Please or Defy Others

ACOAs often develop an intense need to please others as a means to avoid hurt or abandonment. They live by the motto "whatever you want." They also feel that they are often being controlled by others when even a simple suggestion is made ("Don't tell me what to do"). This leads to an endless circle of trying to please others followed by resisting anything that is perceived as controlling. Either way, free and spontaneous choice and decision-making based on need and knowledge are often a struggle for ACOAs.

Overachievement or Underachievement

ACOAs often live in a black and white world. They may internalize early in life that they have to "earn the right to live on the earth," and continually try to gain self-worth by working harder, pleasing, or caretaking in their efforts to be loved. Some children give up, believing they can never do anything right; they stop trying, isolate, become ill, and sometimes begin their own patterns of substance abuse.

Poor Self-Worth or Shame

Children internalize others' beliefs about themselves. In alcoholic families, children often blame themselves and are blamed for the actions of their adult caregivers, feeling responsible for the drinking, emotional and/or physical abuse, or abandonment. Even a bright girl will believe she is "stupid" if told or shown often enough that she can't do anything right. ACOAs are extremely harsh in their self-judgment, internalizing the shame and fear of the abuse, neglect, or emotional distance from parents.

Compulsive Behaviors

Adult Children frequently engage in compulsive behaviors such as working, exercising, gambling, shopping, eating, cleaning, counting, spending, collecting, or sex-seeking to block feelings of pain and fear stored since childhood. They ride a familiar roller coaster of anticipation, shame, guilt, and depression, which causes a never-ending cycle of control and release. ACOAs often develop an external locus of control, believing that something outside of themselves will decrease the emptiness or the pain they feel inside. Thoughts such as "If the house is clean enough, I will be good enough" or "If I win the big one at the casino, I will be somebody important" are attempts to control blocked pain and fear.

Continual Trigger Responses

Painful feelings and memories are often complicated for ACOAs. Sometimes their painful pasts don't seem to be an issue. Then, seemingly out of nowhere, a sight, sound, gesture, or smell will trigger feelings and memories that have been safely held inside. All of a sudden, those feelings and memories begin directing behaviors. The ACOA might freeze when his or her partner walks up the driveway in a particular way, or become depressed when winter arrives. He or she might fly into a rage when a significant other has the same negative look that used to come from a parent. When a child cries, the ACOA might relive the feelings of being yelled at for showing emotion in his or her own childhood.

Addictions

Many ACOAs begin to use alcohol or drugs or develop addictions to other substances or behaviors as ways to make the pain go away. They attempt to block out memories, or self-medicate depression or anxiety to feel a sense of comfort, spontaneity, or power, or to express feelings that they have difficulty expressing. As one ACOA said, "I know that alcohol is addictive, but our family can never connect without it. People seem warm and funny for a while before the anger starts. The connection feels good even though the anger doesn't."

Living in Anxiety and Fear

ACOAs often feel fearful and anxious in situations that others may perceive as ordinary life experiences. Loud noises, dark rooms, being alone without background music or noise, traveling or leaving home or just being outside of one's comfort zone, intimacy, change, making a mistake, or being the center of attention are some of these situations. Ordinary things may stimulate the overwhelming anxiety and fear of returning to the vulnerability and helplessness that were experienced by the child.

Need to Be Right

Some ACOAs have difficulty acknowledging mistakes or apologizing if they are wrong. They need to be correct, appropriate, and "good and right," because these feelings replace the original desire to be loved. In one ACOA's words, "My wife doesn't understand that if I hear myself apologizing, it's like I've really been wrong all my life, and useless and wrong about everything I believed myself to be. I was loved because 'I was a good little boy'? I couldn't make mistakes because just being me was never enough. Doesn't she understand that inside I really feel worthless and like an imposter?" ACOAs will also remember everything ever "done to them" by a friend or intimate partner, and will not hesitate to list each and every hurtful incident as a weapon against further emotional pain.

Denial

At one time, professionals in the field of addiction and recovery believed that only the alcoholic in an alcoholic family was in denial.

Today we know denial is one of the major defenses employed by children from dysfunctional families as a means of surviving the early pain of feeling emotional and/or physical abandonment.

Fear of Conflict and Normal Anger

Because children of alcoholics and addicted families learn to fear the destructive anger or threats of violence that surround them in childhood, they often fear the normal expression of their own anger or the anger of others as adults. They may develop patterns of placation, seeking approval, or isolating when facing conflict. They may become depressed, passive-aggressive, suffer physical illnesses, or develop patterns of suppressing normal anger then raging when drinking or when triggered in some other way.

Chaos Junkies

When hurtful experiences in childhood are not resolved, feelings of anxiety, depression, fear, and painful memories may break through during times of calm. Trauma survivors frequently create chaos in their lives to continue survival adaptation and avoid feeling pain. Because of the turmoil and unpredictability in their early lives and the subsequent development of survival roles, ACOAs frequently find themselves more comfortable with chaos than with quiet times. Just like soldiers, they learn to survive in a war zone but may fall apart when things are peaceful as they wait for the other shoe to drop. They may actually encourage chaos in an effort to decrease the anxiety that comes when things are peaceful. Continual chaos, or being involved in professions where turmoil exists, allows them to numb painful feelings that have been stored since childhood.

Fear of Feeling

It is unsafe for children in alcoholic families to express their feelings because they risk abandonment or emotional or physical violence. Some children learn that normal feelings might hold the power of life or death, or lead to either drinking or sobriety. Feelings experienced in the addicted family are overwhelming to a developing child. Because many children of alcoholics learn to numb their feelings of sadness, fear, vulnerability, powerlessness, and anger, they lose the ability to identify, feel, or express emotions. Good feelings such as excitement, joy, and happiness are frequently sacrificed, as are feelings of anger, sadness, or fear. Some Adult Children can cry, but never allow themselves to have normal feelings of anger; others can express anger, but will not risk tears. In recovery, Adult Children can become aware of their feeling landscape and may regain spontaneous emotional expression.

Frequent Periods of Depression

Suffering from depression is like having your feelings caught in a rush hour traffic: anger, fear, powerlessness, sadness, and vulnerability cannot move freely. As in Joan's case, anger that is not expressed can often become depression and is often turned against the self. Some Adult Children suffer from a chemical depression that may be treated successfully in counseling and may respond to antidepressant medications.

Fear of Intimacy

ACOAs crave intimacy and fear it. They learn very early in their lives that they cannot trust others. Emotionally destructive enmeshments and triangulations in the alcoholic family, as well as inconsistency and insecurity, teach children of alcoholics that they have little ability to protect themselves with others. The trust they place in adult caregivers is frequently violated in some way. They learn to relate by caretaking, pleasing, isolating, or acting out rather than fully relating with their true and authentic selves. As a result, they feel accepted for their roles, not for who they were. Adult Children often have no idea how to have an equal partner relationship with healthy communication and normal conflict. As one ACOA said, "I feel that everyone else got a book at birth on how to live life, have relationships, and parent—and I never got my copy." An Adult Child may be stuck in the role of caretaker and feel very comfortable attending to the needs of others and solving problems. He or she may actually train a partner how to be even more "needy" and then resent the loved one because help is never needed.

Repetitive Relationship Patterns

People are usually drawn to relationships that feel normal relative to the roles and experiences lived in the past. In an unconscious attempt to work through past trauma, many ACOAs repeat the experiences of their childhoods in their current relationships. This often feels like starring in the same play again and again with new characters acting out the same old roles. Internal beliefs often become reality, and Adult Children frequently find themselves re-creating painful experiences because they are drawn to what is familiar and known. ACOAs are often attracted to others who possess the qualities that they have had to disown. For instance, a caretaking child in an alcoholic family might couple with someone who needs to be taken care of, thus creating a codependent relationship. A child who is a pleaser and is selfless may couple with a person who is self-involved. Both of these relationships may mirror the family of origin. Children from healthy families may work out childhood traumas in the playroom, while children of addicted families find themselves working out the painful traumas of the past in real life.

Fears of Incompetence

Children from alcoholic homes learn early to please and relate to the world with acceptable images and roles rather than their true selves. The discrepancy between what is felt inside and what is shown outside leads to statements such as "If others really knew me, they wouldn't like me," or "I'm just fooling you," or "I'm going to be found out." Here's how one ACOA described the fear: "I was always faking it, pretending I knew what to do when I didn't, doing things I didn't know how to do. Now, I don't know if I'm really deserving of success or just 'pretending to know what I know.'"

Hypersensitivity to the Needs of Others

Survival for a child in an addicted family frequently means constant awareness of the most minor shift in mood or behavior of caretaking adults. This leads the child to be far more aware of what others are doing and feeling than what is being felt inside. Here's how one ACOA describes that hypersensitivity: "I had to know, really know, if my dad was drinking or not, or what stage of intoxication he was in. If I didn't know, I could not protect my brother from my dad's drunken rages or myself from his wet kisses or mean words. I had no idea what I felt, but I could tell you what others around me were feeling."

Fatalistic Outlook

The powerlessness and helplessness of experiencing cumulative trauma is often experienced as a belief that bad times or even death are right around the corner, that one is living on borrowed time, or that feelings of security and success cannot last. ACOAs often expect the worst because they believe they are powerless to change things; expecting anything else will lead to chronic disappointment and more pain.

Difficulty Relaxing or Having Fun

While other children are busy learning to relate, compete, play, and develop social skills, children of alcoholic parents are learning the tough lessons of survival. Playing, having fun, or just being spontaneous becomes terrifyingly stressful. The child inside remains terrified of making a mistake, doing something wrong, or displeasing someone. Letting go means being out of control.

Discounting and Minimizing Pain

ACOAs discount the effect of being raised in a painful environment by comparing their pain to someone else's: "He was physically abused—I wasn't," or "Mom drank a lot and Dad was emotionally abusive, but it's not like we were beaten or anything." They may minimize the effect of their parents' alcoholism and codependency by concluding, "Everyone in the neighborhood drank a lot. It's just what men in our neighborhood did after working hard all week." Other ACOAs may discount the normalcy of their own behavior by concluding, "I have no reason to be anxious. It's not like I was abused everyday like others were; it was only emotional abuse. So, what's wrong with me?"

Resiliency Strengths

Resiliency is the capacity to possess overwhelming strengths when facing adversity. The ACOAs we have worked with over many decades have shown great compassion and caring even in the face of anger and abuse. They have turned their pain into creative gifts of poetry, writing, photography, sculpture, and painting. They have survived through painful situations with their delightful humor intact. They have stubbornly and tirelessly worked to heal themselves and their own small part of the world (and sometimes the broader world as well) so the abuse that they experienced is not passed on to the next generation.

Alcoholism and substance abuse are indeed the gifts that keep on giving from one generation to the next unless unresolved trauma and delayed grief are addressed and worked through. Even children whose parents don't drink or abuse drugs can be impacted by their parents' past traumas and delayed grief—if those parents are children of alcoholics themselves. In the following chapters we examine the steps of the journey to healing for ACOAs.

5

Surviving the Unimaginable: The Resiliency of Children of Alcoholics

The world breaks everyone and afterward
many are strong at the broken places.

—*Ernest Hemingway, A Farewell to Arms*

IN PREVIOUS CHAPTERS we have written about the pain of growing up in an alcoholic or addicted family, the extraordinary survival adaptations of children, and some of the difficulties these survival adaptations may cause in adulthood. No discussion of the addicted family would be complete, however, without a discussion of the incredible resiliency of the thousands of Adult Children we have met who came from alcoholic and addicted families. We have heard many heartbreaking, painful histories and stories over the years; what we find remarkable is the ability of children to survive what sometimes seems unendurable. And they more than survive—they move ahead in the world, turning enormous pain into amazing gifts and wisdom. We share one such story—the story of an amazing eleven-year-old girl.

Samantha proudly held up a piece of paper and looked imploringly at us, her green eyes hopeful and shining. "See, I got this petition signed by my teachers, the counselor in the school, our school principal, and one of my older friend's parents. My friend Amy is going to be in the workshop and Amy's mother is even on the town council. They all say I'm old enough—please let me join."

We were holding a community healing workshop that was organized following the suicide of two seventeen-year-old high school students. The workshop included adults in the community and senior high school students ranging in age from thirteen to nineteen years old. Eleven-year-old Samantha had been refused admittance to the workshop because she didn't meet the age criteria. The members of our team looked at each other, then at Samantha. The youth team leader spoke the words we were all thinking. "I think if Samantha is old enough to go to the trouble to get a petition signed, she's old enough to join the workshop."

Throughout the week Samantha's strong and clear voice proved her maturity. Although she was only eleven years old, she was a caring and compassionate leader. She spoke clearly about the pain she experienced growing up in an addicted family, crying tears that she had long held inside. She offered support to others who found their voices as they spoke of painful experiences in their lives. She shared poems from her journal that expressed both pain and hope. This strong and caring eleven-year-old helped other members of the group find the courage to speak their truths and cry their tears.

Like Samantha, many resilient children from painful environments have a unique ability in common. Mary Baures describes it beautifully in her book *Undaunted Spirits*:

> In stark contrast to the defeated, survivors are transformed by the adversity they encounter, like the phoenix, the mythical bird that is a universal symbol of resurrection, triumph, immortality, and inseparable fellowship, who, after dying, is reborn, rising magnificently from the ashes that are burnt remains of his old self. (xv)

Resilience is the ability to survive a painful family or traumatic experience with amazing grace, turning what could be a tragic life experience into gifts of creativity, spirituality, humor, tenacity, compassion, wisdom, and strength. To paraphrase Ernest Hemingway, resilient survivors of addicted families have become "stronger in the broken places."

There are many stories to illustrate the resiliency of the thousands of ACOAs whom we have met over the years, including Taylor's, which we'll share next. Their struggles and triumphs help us understand some of the key elements found in the lives of emotionally resilient children from addicted families.

Both of Taylor's parents were already alcoholic when she was born. They drank every day, but to their credit, they worked hard and rarely missed a day's work. Taylor's mother was an accountant and her dad was in middle management at a large software company. When Taylor was six, Brent was born. Taylor remembered that her mother was sick and sad a lot after Brent's birth, and she stayed in bed most of the day. Taylor remembered taking care of her brother almost from the day he was brought home from the hospital—even though she was only six. From the beginning, Brent was the apple of Taylor's eye.

Taylor would learn later that her mother's sadness had been postpartum depression, which she medicated with alcohol, leaving Brent in Taylor's care. Taylor tried but failed to block out her parents' drunken arguments. She learned that Brent was "a mistake" who was the cause of her mom's depression and that she herself was "a mistake," one that had caused her father and mother to "have to get married." She didn't understand all this as a small child, but what she did understand was that she was "bad" and she was the cause of her parents' anger and drinking. She also learned that she had to be "super good" and "super responsible" so they would be happy and maybe stop arguing.

As the years progressed, Taylor's parents were increasingly more abusive emotionally, both to the children and to each other. The arguments began in the mornings when they were hungover and continued and escalated late into the night; on weekends, the drinking usually started at noon on Saturdays and went all day and late into the night. It was often difficult for Taylor to sleep, so she would bring Brent into her bed to comfort him when the fighting began. Sometimes their parents would have friends over, and the drunken parties would keep the children awake almost all night. Their parents' friends focused drunken attention on the children, who hated the wet, slobbery good-night kisses they had to endure.

Some of their happiest times were Sundays. Even though the parents were usually hung over in the morning and sometimes grumpy, the family went to church together and often went to visit relatives afterward, or have picnics or go to movies. Both Taylor and Brent remembered kind and comforting words, closeness, and even family fun during those times. "On Sundays when there was no alcohol," Taylor commented, "we almost seemed like a 'normal' family, and I thought perhaps Mom and Dad really did love us and each other."

The drinking would usually start again after Taylor and Brent went to bed and would continue on and off until the following Sunday. Eventually the fights would start again. "The topics of the arguments were usually money," Taylor recalled, "or who worked harder, and of course us kids and who was more at fault for the 'accidents'—that would be us." Brent continued to be the target of their father's anger and Taylor was the target of their mother's. Taylor would lie in her bed next to her little brother and listen to how "awful" they were, how "stupid" they were, how much "trouble" they had caused, and how they just didn't "measure up." As they grew older, the comments got worse: Taylor was a "slut" and Brent was a "bastard." Sometimes Mom would defend Brent and Dad would defend Taylor, and then they would start fighting with each other.

When she was old enough to begin to understand the changes in her parents when they were drunk, Taylor tried to keep both herself and Brent out of the line of fire. She calmed them both with a song that she had learned in church, "You'll Never Walk Alone." She would sing it again and again late at night as the fighting continued. Taylor believed she and her brother were somehow always protected by something greater than themselves. As the years progressed, Brent developed a delightful sense of humor and he would keep Taylor laughing through the most difficult times. These remarkable children parented each other when their parents were the drunkest.

Taylor and Brent had other adults in their lives who cared about them, and research suggests this is a key factor in the development of resiliency in children. Ann and her husband Vic had a farm on the outskirts of town. Their own children were grown, and "Grandma Ann" began taking care of Taylor when the little girl was two, and then Brent when he was born, to earn a little extra money. She and Vic fell in love with these "delightful children." Taylor and Brent remembered the fun they had playing for hours outside in the woods, and the pride they felt in doing farm chores. "Grandpa Vic" always told Brent how good he was with the animals—that he was gifted and had a natural ability to connect with them. Brent eventually became a veterinarian, certainly in part because of the support and kind words he received on the farm in those early years. He experienced the success and pride in his abilities that were so important in those early developmental years. When he graduated from veterinary college, Grandpa Vic and Grandma Ann were among the first in line to hug him and let him know how proud they were of him.

From the time Taylor could remember, Grandma Ann told her how proud she was of Taylor's compassion and the loving care she always gave to her brother. She also told Taylor that she was proud of the girl's inquisitive nature and that it would serve her well in her life. "You are such a kind and wonderful child," Ann would always say. "I love your caring and your curiosity." Taylor became a school counselor and started groups for children of addicted families in the elementary school and high school in her district. Of course, her adopted grandparents were at her graduation from college too.

Grandma Ann last babysat for them when Taylor was twelve and Brent was six. Both she and Grandpa Vic held the children and cried right along with them. Grandma Ann shared something with them that both children would keep inside and cling to for a lifetime:

You know, it isn't your fault—your mom and dad's drinking and cross words. Your mom and dad love you as best they can love, but they have some deep hurts somewhere inside them. The hurts were there long before you and your brother came into this world. Their hurts are not your fault and neither is their drinking. They also have a powerful addiction to alcohol. None of this is your fault. You listen to Grandma now and remember. Okay? And also remember how much Grandpa Vic and I love you even when we won't see you often to tell you. You are a precious gift in our lives.

Until that day, Taylor never guessed that Grandma Ann knew about the drinking or had ever overheard unkind words spoken to the children. The message she gave them that day was a precious gift, and it provided a solid foundation for their future lives. Although Taylor and Brent have had their share of difficulties as adults, they promised each other that they would never become alcoholics—and they didn't. They each also promised themselves that they would never pass on to their children the hurtful words and shame that had been passed on to them—and they haven't. They have had difficulties in relationships and have sought out counseling with their partners. As Taylor said, "I'm not sure how to have an intimate relationship. I don't know how to argue and make up, but I'm learning and I will keep asking the questions. I know where to get help."

Taylor and Brent are more than just siblings; they continue to be lifelong friends. Their parents never stopped drinking, and the arguments and the shaming behavior continue. Taylor and Brent do not allow their parents to drink in their homes and have set clear limits on emotionally abusive behavior. Each is very clear that they love their parents and want to be with them. They have joint family outings on Sundays and their parents often join them. They've also made it clear that if there is any emotional abuse directed at them, their partners, or their children, they will walk out. In their individual therapy, Brent and Taylor have learned a good deal about the pain their parents endured in childhood as well as the importance of honoring both the pain and the strength of their own childhoods.

It is true that alcoholism is "the gift that keeps on giving." It is equally true that the strength and resiliency so many children of alcoholics develop, despite and perhaps because of the pain, are also "gifts that keep on giving."

As we look at Samantha, Taylor, and Brent, we see many of the

important foundations that support and are necessary for the healing process.

- Each had a person in his or her life who was an honest reflection of who
  they truly were. Children learn about themselves by the actions, words, and
  feelings of their adult caregivers. Healthy parents and other caretakers may
  be viewed as life-affirming "honest mirrors" who reflect the joys, capabil-
  ities, and sorrows of their children accurately. Those reflections become
  distorted in alcoholic families—the children learn to view themselves
  through the "dishonest mirror" that does not reflect their true selves.
  Sometimes their "honest mirror" is a babysitter, sometimes a caring
  teacher or neighbor, a friend's parent, an aunt or uncle, or a big brother or
  sister. Later in life it might be a therapist or another support group member who offers "an honest mirror" for the first time. We know that children
  build an internal world of hope and strength on the foundation of the kind
  and honest words of those who are there for them, even if only briefly.

- Each began healing him- or herself through caring for others. Each
  showed compassion and caring throughout their young lives: caring for
  siblings, for friends, for animals, and for their parents, despite the pain
  their parents directed toward them. Sometimes in caring for others,
  ACOAs begin vicariously caring about themselves.

- Each learned a philosophy early in life that is expressed in the Serenity
  Prayer of Alcoholics Anonymous (AA): *God grant me the serenity to
  accept the things I cannot change, the courage to change the things I can,
  and the wisdom to know the difference.*

- Taylor and Brent learned to take the love they could get when their
  parents were not drinking, and to take care of each other when their parents couldn't offer love or support. Samantha fought for the support,
  healing, and validation she needed from the workshop and sought out

assistance from others in her life when she couldn't get it at home.

- Each possessed great strengths: tenacity, spirituality, curiosity, a sense of humor, a willingness to work hard, creativity, and compassion.

- Each made the decision early in life to become a survivor rather than to remain a victim. Many years ago we saw a cartoon that speaks to this wisdom. An old woman who is obviously cold is wrapped in a tattered blanket and is standing in the midst of a blizzard. The caption reads: "Even though Ethel is extremely well qualified, remaining a victim is not a good career choice."

Resilient individuals deal with their anger and move past it rather than staying stuck in learned helplessness and blame. They use their anger energy to create change in their small corner of the world and in the greater world around them. Many use their anger energy to fight for the rights of children; to stick tenaciously to their promise never to parent as they were parented; to graduate from college and "prove them wrong"; to start movements like Mothers Against Drunk Drivers (MADD); or to become a caring adult in the life of another child who is in pain.

It is important that we do not forget either the pain or the gifts that we have gleaned from growing up in addicted families. Sometimes we have the volume turned up so high on the things that helped us survive as children that it becomes a detriment in adulthood—to our health and to the building of healthy relationships and intimacy. We may become caretakers to the exclusion of caring for ourselves, and we may not be able to accept caring and giving from our friends or significant others. We may become fanatical about religion for a period, focusing on dogma rather than living a foundation of spirituality. We may use humor to avoid pain or as a way to let out our anger. We may work to the exclusion of health, connection, or spontaneous enjoyment. We may lose relationships as adults because we cannot allow ourselves to acknowledge mistakes, to compromise, or to listen to another for fear of letting go of our own will or identity. It is not the compassion, spirituality, humor, hard work, or our stubbornness that is the difficulty; these strengths are lifesavers.

It would be a sad mistake to take the "care" out of caretaking, let go of a delightful sense of humor, become irresponsible, or stop honoring a power greater than ourselves. Healing takes time, and as we honor our pain and our strength, we begin to take control of our lives and fine-tune the volume knob on the strengths that helped us survive.

6

Validation of Trauma and Breaking Through Denial:
Understanding the Normal Response to an Abnormal and Painful Life

> · Triggered by a reminder, the past can be relived with an immediate sensory and emotional intensity that makes victims feel as if the event were occurring all over again.
>
> —*from "Post-Traumatic Stress Disorder and the Nature of Trauma," by Besse van der Kolk, M.D.*

BEFORE 1979 (THE BEGINNING of what was then called the Adult Children's movement), few therapists understood the concept of delayed grief in alcoholic families, and many Adult Children were diagnosed with "adjustment reactions." This term was defined in the *Diagnostic and Statistical Manual of Mental Disorders, Second Edition (DSM-II)*—(the edition available before 1980)—as "an abnormal response to a normal life situation." Dr. Timmen Cermak, the first president of the National Organization for Children of Alcoholics, was instrumental in changing that diagnosis to "delayed stress syndrome," which DSM-II defined as "a normal response to an abnormal life situation." Growing up in an alcoholic family is definitely not "normal."

The symptoms displayed by Adult Children are similar to those shown by other trauma victims, and the treatment is the same—walking back through the trauma with a trusted other. It has been our experience that the process for successful grief work and mourning has eight steps.

Step 1:   Validation of the trauma experienced in an addicted family
Step 2:   Ending the denial of past experiences and current substance abuse patterns that sometimes exist
Step 3:   Building a cognitive life raft
Step 4:   Building a relationship of trust with a therapist or a support group, thereby establishing an emotional safety net
Step 5:   Grief work, which includes walking through past trauma
Step 6:   Mourning, followed by the integration of the cognitive life raft and the emotional net
Step 7:   Behavior changes
Step 8:   Moving on, giving back, and forgiving

We'll discuss each of these steps in depth over the next several chapters.

Validation of Trauma

Triggers from the past continue to shape the present until trauma is integrated and resolved; otherwise, the trauma intrudes into daily activities and relationships without the ACOA's conscious awareness or understanding. Over the years we have treated many ACOAs who struggled to understand why they felt the way they did, until they were able to come face-to-face with their trauma.

My new client, Beth, tried to appear confident as we began our first session. "I don't know why I'm here. I feel a bit foolish. When you asked me what the problem is, I really didn't know," Beth said, looking embarrassed. She had the same type of relaxed appearance that we have seen so many times before. She had a smile on her face and her hands were folded in her lap. Her posture told me that if I pulled the chair out from under her she wouldn't move, but instead would continue the same *relaxed* position in midair. The message that she had left on my answering machine a few weeks earlier was also familiar: "I was at your workshop last week and it affected me a great deal. I don't know why I'm calling. I know you're busy working with people who need your time far more than I do. I'd like to make an appointment, though, if you have time. If you don't, I'll understand."

I explained to Beth that this first session was a time for both of us to decide whether we would continue working together. I also explained that it was often a difficult process to begin, and that I didn't expect her to trust me right away. With that explanation she truly relaxed a bit. I asked many questions regarding her history, her past and present use of chemicals, what it was like growing up in her family, and her history of losses. I asked about her past therapy experiences, her history of relationships, depression or eating disorders, and if she had been physically or sexually abused as a child.

Beth told me that she had been in therapy twice before. The first time was when her marriage had failed, and on that occasion she had been prescribed tranquilizers. The second time was when her mother died.

I was in therapy briefly when my mom died. I was so depressed, I only went for six or seven sessions. I thought I felt better. At first I was given medications to help me sleep, but I was afraid to take them. We didn't talk about my alcoholic family though, and I didn't realize that it had affected me. We didn't talk a lot about my mother or dad. The therapist just told me that the death of someone close to me was difficult and we worked on how it was affecting my daily life. It wasn't really difficult. I still went to work every day. I always have. I made all the funeral arrangements and just kept going. Except for not sleeping, I didn't feel much at all. I felt guilty because I didn't feel much. Anyway, he said my reaction was normal and I didn't need to come back if I didn't want to. He was a busy man and I was all right. I just kept feeling the loneliness I have always felt.

Therapy often focuses on the many masks of delayed grief, instead of on the frightened child inside. To be able to access that frightened child, the adult needs to feel safe enough to walk back through the traumas that were experienced. There must be a feeling of trust in another, and then a trust of self that was missing in childhood. The adult needs an *emotional net* (a healthy adult who can validate and mirror the feelings that were never allowed and assist the adult child in processing the trauma) that was not there in childhood. The longest part of the grief process is not the grief work itself, but forming a relationship of trust that eventually leads the Adult Child to validate and accept the child that he or she once was. Before the grief work can even begin, the Adult Child must receive validation of the trauma experienced.

Joan and Richard, whom we first met in Chapter 1, were each asked to complete a loss history during their first few sessions in therapy. They drew a timeline across a large piece of paper, with "birth" at the end and his or her current age at the other. They documented their losses along the line, as well as the ages at which these losses occurred. Early losses, it was explained, were not only losses of people in their lives, but also losses of childhood experiences, toys, pets, special occasions, nurturing, childhood friends, innocence, or safety. In another color, they were asked to mark when they believed they "lost their voice," meaning not allowed to speak the truth about the realities of life in their dysfunctional families. In another color, they were asked to mark at what age they believed they began to lose the expression of a feeling. In a third color, they marked the age that their own addictions and/or compulsions began and put another mark in the same color for their recovery.

Richard and Joan were able to validate losses that they originally minimized. Each was surprised at the number of losses experienced in childhood and the teen years, and each was surprised at the feelings of sadness and anger that began to emerge. For Joan and Richard, this was the first recognition of the impact of growing up in an addicted family.

When we work with Adult Children in therapy, we ask them to bring in pictures of themselves from early childhood through adolescence to use as we process their timeline together. If they have no pictures of themselves, they are asked to cut pictures out of a magazine that they believe resemble themselves through those ages. As we review the losses they experienced and note them on the timeline, we also look at their pictures at the age of each loss.

Joan remembered with amazement that she was only five when she first realized there was no Santa Claus. She had been awakened at about 3:00 AM on Christmas morning by her parents fighting over assembling her younger brother's tricycle. Her dad was drunk and was lying next to the partially assembled tricycle with a wrench in his hand. Her mother was screaming at his limp, passed-out body.

Joan realized that the magic of Christmas was lost to her at that moment. She also realized that, even then, she was more preoccupied with the fear that her three-year-old brother would wake up than with her own feelings of sadness. She had tried to help her mother fix the trike, and she felt guilty that she couldn't figure out how to help. When we looked at the picture of little five-year-old Joan, she said with amazement, "I never realized how small I was. I was just a little girl. I wonder if that is why I feel so depressed every Christmas." It was the first time Joan began to feel empathy for the child inside, and it was the first time she gave that "fearful kid" a face. For the first time she could acknowledge she had been affected.

Richard's first "loss memory" was at the age of six. It was Saturday and he was at home alone with his father, who had been drinking heavily since early morning. His mother was at work. He remembered hearing the screeching of tires outside his house. He ran to the front door to find that his best friend, the family dog, Skippy, had been hit by a car. The dog's hind legs had been broken and he couldn't move. Richard remembered screaming to his father for help, and he remembered his father's answer: "How many times have I told you to watch that damn dog?" Richard stood there when his father shot the dog "to put him out of his misery."

He remembered holding Skippy in his arms until his mother came home from work, but he couldn't remember crying. He and his mother buried the beloved pet in the backyard, and he could still hear his mother's chastising question, "Why didn't you take Skippy to the vet?" Richard related the story with little feeling, then replied, "Even at six I couldn't do anything right." I asked him to look at the picture of himself at six, standing next to his father. I said, "Look how small you were. Who was the adult?" Richard looked surprised. Later in the session, he said, "I don't hate animals. I loved that dog.

He was my life back then. I told Skippy everything. He loved me too. I have always fought with my wife about having a dog. I'd never let her get a dog and we'd always fight about it. I thought I hated dogs. I don't. I loved Skippy."

After we explore the losses on the timeline and talk about the point in time when Adult Children lost their voices and feelings, I ask them to note the people who helped them along the way and gave them hope or strength. Sometimes they have forgotten that teacher who believed in them or that neighbor who was kind. Many of the things they do in a good way today are because of the resiliency they gained from a person who cared, and they recognize that the person lives figuratively inside of them and cheers them on.

As we've discussed in earlier chapters, Adult Children from alcoholic families grow up with an elephant in the living room that they had to deny was there. Validating the traumas in their histories is especially important to the healing process. Acknowledging the trauma is the beginning of giving a face and a voice to the children they once were, often for the first time in their lives. Through validation and support they begin to construct a narrative of their lives.

Breaking Through Denial

It is not surprising, given what we learned about trauma and development in previous chapters, that denial is the hallmark of the alcoholic and addicted family. Years ago, when denial was discussed in relation to alcoholism, the focus was on the alcoholic's denial. Even at that, it was difficult for many to understand the difference between denial and lying. "Why does my uncle lie about his drinking? He just got a DWI and he is still telling us there's no problem. Does he think we're blind or stupid?"

Alcoholism is the disease of denial. Many behaviors surrounding denial are not attempts to fool or lie to others, but rather are attempts to convince the self that there is no problem. Behaviors like constructing events out of blackouts, hiding bottles, convincing the boss that it was really the flu, or sitting in a bar all afternoon without taking a drink to prove there is no problem with drinking are all ways the alcoholic attempts to deny his or her problem. Yet the alcoholic's denial comes with "protection" by many others in the alcoholic's life, including his or her family.

Denial is even less understood when family members are caught up in it. "Why does that nice person put up with her husband's drinking?" "Why doesn't he leave or set limits?" "How can he talk about how proud he is of his son's athletic achievements when he's too drunk to go to the games?" The questions must be answered with two other questions:

• If family members really acknowledge the effects of living with an alcoholic, what else will have to be acknowledged and felt?

• If a child recognizes the depth of loss and abandonment felt in the realization that parents were not always there, or feels the trauma of having to take care of younger siblings at the age of eight, what will that do to the "fantasy parents" he or she still depends on for nurturing and development?

Denial is part of the fabric of our lives and yet, for many of us, it may be one of the least understood of all survival mechanisms. Most of us experience denial nightly when watching the news. We hear that two thousand people were killed in an earthquake, but we don't put faces on the bodies—we reduce the horror to a statistic. When we hear that a hurricane has hit a few hundred miles away, we tell ourselves that will never happen in our area. If we hear of a plane crash, we convince ourselves that could never happen to the plane we will fly the next day. We deny our own vulnerability and become numb to the unimaginable, eliminate it from our minds, or distract ourselves with happier news.

Imagine for a moment that your parents died in a plane crash when you were young. What would you do to convince yourself that you weren't really alone? What would make it possible for you to get on a similar plane ten years later? Without support, some children would focus on the plane rather than the loss and never fly again. Others would panic whenever they needed to fly and never understand why. Some would become pilots or flight attendants to prove their own power and strength to themselves, rather than face the helplessness of the loss. Some would become engineers specializing in aircraft repair, driven to attain new skills in the area, yet never comprehending why they chose such a profession.

If these children had a strong support system of other caring adults, they would eventually feel anger for being abandoned so young and feel the pain and sadness at never seeing Mommy or Daddy again. They would vent anger at planes, at their parents for dying, and at life's unfairness. They would work through the tragedy again and again in their play, integrating the feelings and the event rather than repressing them. They would attach to the new adult figures in their lives—while always keeping the positive memories of their parents in their hearts. Their lives wouldn't be driven by the avoidance of air flight. They wouldn't need to become pilots, or avoid forming relationships that they might lose. They wouldn't fly into a rage because of the repressed feelings that were triggered when they saw their ten-year-old children playing with model airplanes.

Now think of all those situations in the context of the Adult Child of an Alcoholic. The losses and traumas facing children of addicted families are even greater because their traumas are inflicted by the people entrusted with their care. When those people whose lives we explored in earlier chapters first came into treatment, they had some realization of internal pain and the problems in their lives. For Peter, it was anxiety and the panic attack he experienced at the end of his driveway. For Beth, it was the panic attacks she experienced every time her husband left her alone in the house at night. For Joan, it was severe depression originally stimulated by the injury that limited her career as a dancer. For Richard, it was the recognition that he had become powerless over his drinking.

Joan's original focus was on the loss of her ability to dance. She had little idea about why she had chosen dance as a career, why her career had literally become the total focus of her life, or why the loss of a career would take away her reason for living. Richard's focus was originally on a feared relapse after a year of sobriety. He didn't believe that he could succeed in sobriety or in other things he had attempted in his life. And he didn't understand why he believed so strongly that he needed to drink to be a man, or why he constantly had nightmares about failure and trauma. None of these people had any awareness of the time capsules of pain that they carried within them. This pain could make them return to the terror of the traumatized children they once were whenever their original traumas were triggered by sights, sounds, feelings, smells, or situations in the present.

Breaking through denial for Adult Children from addicted families isn't just the process of acknowledging difficulty in their current lives, but also acknowledging the existence of the frightened child they used to be. One Adult Child pointed out that he really began the grief process in therapy when he visualized a tiny child within himself. He described it "as though a part of me was frozen." He didn't feel the pain of the child inside or have clear memories of the traumas he went through as a child in an addicted family. He just had a feeling of a frozen state. He acknowledged the existence of a part of himself for the first time.

The process of coming out of denial and healing the wounds of the past involves validating the existence of the hurting child, recognizing the effects of living in an addicted family, experiencing the pain of the original cumulative trauma without feeling helpless, gaining an understanding of how the past is affecting the present, and realizing that helplessness and vulnerability belong to the past.

It is important to understand how the feelings of the child become "encased in ice" in the first place. Let's imagine observing a little five-year-old girl on her way to kindergarten for the first time. She is timid and tearful, frightened and excited. We see her leaving the door of her house. She's begging her mother to come with her and crying because she is afraid. Her mother becomes more and more frustrated with her daughter's crying, and she tells the little girl, "You're acting like a baby. You're a big girl now and big girls don't cry and they don't need their mothers to take them to school." The little girl continues to cry but begins to be embarrassed by her tears. The mother becomes angry and yells, "Can't you see I'm busy with your brother and your dad is sick? You're making me so angry!" With that, her mother shuts the door and the little girl takes a deep breath, dries her eyes, and begins to walk to school. The child is fearful of her first day at school, and her tears are a normal, healthy reaction. After her mother's reaction, the child becomes more afraid of her mother's disapproval and anger than she is of her own fears. She is determined to gain her mother's approval and be a "big girl," so she puts away her fear.

Now let's imagine that this little girl gets a similar response whenever she is afraid. She grows up and begins to have tremendous anxiety whenever she has to face a new situation. The adult may never link her anxiety to the fearful child. When she is asked in therapy, "Were there times as a child when you were fearful?" the determined woman will say no, wanting the therapist's approval. But the little girl inside will hear the question, and she will still feel frightened. She will still not trust that someone will be there for her or that she won't be shamed for her feelings.

When a trusting connection is established with the therapist, when she is certain someone is really there, she will be safe enough to relive the feelings and memories of the child.

Asking questions and modeling feelings that weren't modeled by hurting parents is one way a therapist can assist in this process: "How did you feel? You must have been frightened all by yourself in a strange new place." The therapist can also assist by setting limits: "You cannot use drugs or alcohol during the therapy process. I care about you, and alcohol and drugs change feelings, just like they did in your family"; or by acknowledging boundaries and personal space: "I don't expect you to trust me during the beginning of this process. Trust is developed, not demanded."

Coming out of denial takes many forms with Adult Children. For some, it is recognizing the frightened child; for others it takes seeing the sad child; and for still others, it is acknowledging the angry child. In Richard's case, expressing his anger was far less difficult than releasing his tears. Anger had become a fire-breathing dragon that gave him a sense of false protection; yet, at times, the dragon would turn on him and spit contempt at the child within.

For some Adult Children, coming out of denial also involves recognizing the long-term addictive patterns of drinking or drug abuse, or long-term compulsions like gambling or eating disorders. In creating the timeline, many see the connection between their cycles of addiction and/or compulsions and the loss of their voice and feelings. It is important for the therapist to show concern for the individual by confronting the addiction/compulsion cycle. For example, if an Adult Child has a long-term pattern of bulimic behavior, it is important for the therapist to show concern for the child within by stating, "I will not treat you unless you are also willing to be under a physician's care."

It is difficult for the Adult Child to come out of denial if the person they go to for help is also in denial. The therapist or care provider can become an extension of faulty mirroring if he or she is afraid to ask the difficult questions and validate the multitude of feelings that the child experienced (love, fear, anger, sadness, loss). This can happen if the care provider has not yet cried his or her own tears or dealt with his or her anger. Adult Children from addicted families need an "honest mirror" because they have been looking at a cracked and faulty mirror throughout their lives.

The care provider must show awareness of the pain a child experienced while growing up in an addicted family, begin discussions about how the survival adaptation is affecting the Adult Child's life today, and validate the child's feelings. If the ACOA doesn't feel safe or understood, it is important for him or her to seek out a therapist who understands the impact of growing up in an alcoholic or addicted family. Adult Children seeking therapy must ask therapists if they have a background working with the effects of childhood trauma, and if they have an understanding of the impact of growing up in a dysfunctional family. Only with the help of a trusted other can ACOAs safely relive their trauma and begin to build healthy lives.

7

Building a Cognitive Life Raft:
Developing an Intellectual Understanding of the Effects of a Painful Life

The first step in dealing with trauma is to recognize its impact . . . It can impact your feelings, thoughts, relationships, behaviors, attitudes, dreams, and hopes. It can also be a way to find a new direction and purpose in life.

—*from* The PTSD Workbook: Simple, Effective Techniques for Overcoming Traumatic Stress Symptoms, *by Mary Beth Williams, Ph.D., and Soili Poijula, Ph.D.*

MANY CHILDREN OF ALCOHOLICS and addicted families feel like failures in the outside world. The relationships they establish outside of their families often make them feel as incompetent and crazy as they always feared they were. These Adult Children need a *cognitive life raft*—that is, an intellectual understanding of the emotional impact of growing up in an alcoholic and/or addicted family. It is important for Adult Children to understand the characteristics they developed to survive, and that those same survival tools that worked so well in childhood may be having negative effects in their adult lives. They need to understand—first intellectually and then emotionally—that they are not crazy; they are having a normal reaction to what was an abnormal and painful life. They need validation and a road map to use as a guide as they begin to work their way through the pain they have kept inside for so long.

Lily felt there was something very wrong with her and decided to come to us for therapy. She told us that she began her first job when she was just ten years old. She bussed dishes at a local restaurant after school and during the summers. She was proud of the fact that she was promoted to waitress by the time she was fourteen. She gave her salary to her alcoholic parents, but her tip money was secretly sent to her trusted favorite aunt who put it in the bank for her. Lily dreamed of going to college someday, and her aunt wanted to help her realize that dream, even though Lily's parents laughed at her "wild ideas." Lily thought of this bank account as her "getaway money," her ticket to freedom. Her aunt, who was also a waitress, added to the account even though she had little money herself, because she believed in Lily's dreams. Whenever the chaos in her home became too much, Lily would go to her room, lock the door, and unlock her "dream box," where she kept a statement of her growing bank account and magazine articles about "normal" families—like the ones she hoped would be hers someday. She said, "That dream box was my life raft during those depressing days."

Lily went to college three thousand miles away, feeling, as do many Adult Children from addicted families, that if she got far enough away she would be able to leave the pain behind her. But the first night alone in her dorm room, Lily felt familiar anxiety. She felt helpless, afraid that she might fail, and terrified that something was going to happen to her aunt or another member of her family. She took advantage of her weekend and late-night cell phone rates to call home every week. She was afraid she was a failure after all; perhaps her parents had been right, and the straight As and the accolades she had received from teachers in high school weren't good enough. Even when Lily continued to receive straight As each semester and was elected president of her dorm in her junior year, she still didn't feel she was good enough.

> I began to feel, as I always had—that there was something dreadfully wrong with me; that I was crazy, really crazy. I'd feel uncomfortable at school functions, terrified, not knowing what to do or say. I felt I was an imposter—popular because I was fooling everyone. I'd watch other kids talking so easily, building relationships, having boyfriends, and I just couldn't. I knew how to solve problems, how to listen when people were hurting, but I didn't know how to make small talk, or

what to do on a date. I was pathetic. I joined the crisis drug squad in
the evenings instead of dating. I'd go out on calls and help kids who
were depressed or having a "bad trip." I always knew what to do
then; I had learned about drug abuse, even though I'd never taken
drugs. I had promised myself as a kid that I never would drink or use
drugs.

Many children of alcoholic and addicted families leave home only
to seek out new relationships that are just like the ones they left
behind. For example, *adjusters* and *lost children* may seek out relationships that require little of them, whereas *caretakers* may find
people who need to be taken care of, thus continuing the familiarity
of survival roles. Lily experienced that, too.

I started dating one of the boys I had taken care of on a bad
trip. I married him, and the anxiety for the most part went away. He
needed me and I was good at taking care of him. It wasn't until
years later that I realized that I had brought along with me the
same elephant that had lived in my childhood living room.

In many families, Adult Children return to the safety of the familiar and to the roles they filled as children. They return to their childhood home or live close by and continue to take care of their
addicted parents. When asked, "What do you think would happen if
you moved out of the house?" or "What would it be like for your
parents if you left?" there is often an uncomfortable silence. This is
usually followed by a statement that affirms their fears that their
parents would somehow not be able to survive: "They'd divorce,"
"Dad would beat Mom," or "They'd die." One Adult Child responded,
"My dad would lose his job, my mom would go crazy, they would be
hurt, and there would be no one at home to protect them." For some

Adult Children, loyalty to the home is a life-or-death matter. Even a geographical move away from addicted parents does not allow them enough freedom to separate from their feelings of responsibility for the family.

Children from addicted families are often told they are the reason the parents stay together. Some become the buffer in emotional or physical violence. Others become a pseudopartner for one of the parents. Boundaries have little or no meaning for their parents; these are the children that parents confide in inappropriately, expecting the child to be a confidant, a problem solver, or an ally in a war against the other parent. Consequently, as Adult Children they are frequently violated emotionally or sometimes physically by others in their lives; or they may identify with the aggressor and emotionally and/or physically violate others, never knowing why.

It isn't until these Adult Children receive a cognitive life raft in workshops, support groups, or in therapy that they realize what is wrong: they never developed healthy emotional and/or physical boundaries and had little understanding of them. If a child, like Lily, has never been able to develop a sense of self apart from a role played in a family, then leaving home becomes no more than a cardboard fantasy. Lily felt tremendous anxiety when she was not taking care of someone else, so she was attracted only to those who "needed" her. In Lily's words, "If my husband was unhappy, I was unhappy. I couldn't tell where his emotional boundary stopped and mine began. If he was anxious, I was anxious. I was as hypervigilant with him as I had been with my alcoholic parents. Keeping them happy was my survival."

"Love" in the addicted family means giving oneself away or continually being hurt. As a result, ACOAs tend to do one or more of three things: they do what is expected regardless of their own feelings; they stubbornly rebel, always doing the opposite of what others suggest; or they pretend that no one can affect them, going out of their way to show that they just don't care. An ACOA frequently feels like there is no sense of a self apart from the wishes and/or demands of others.

Many children of alcoholics build their hopes and dreams of freedom and a future life on what they see on television, in movies, or in books. They believe that "normal" will magically fall into place once they pass beyond the doorstep of their addicted family. But television characters aren't good role models and cannot provide the nurturing necessary for a child to develop the self. Once the process of grief work has been completed, the traumas walked through, and the child inside allowed to grow and integrate the traumas of a painful past, those TV characters appear to be poor imitations of real life. Adult Children find that the characters against which they judge themselves are not representative of the ups and downs, joys and sorrows, healthy conflicts, fears, and peace of normal life.

In workshops and in therapy we often ask Adult Children to do continuum-of-life drawings. Frequently the drawings that depict their lives at age eighteen are of birds flying away or paths leading to mountaintops, suns, or rainbows, and have little relation to normal life. Their drawings at age twenty-five (next in the sequence) are often of black clouds, tears, or drug and alcohol abuse. These are reflections of the pain felt when the artists realized that the fantasy of freedom or of "normal" life hadn't magically appeared after the physical emancipation from a childhood home. Here is how Lily described that pain:

> I didn't feel that anything I could do would change how miserable and anxious I felt or the fact that I had no idea what "normal" was. I felt as helpless when I wasn't taking care of others or working as I had

in my family. Becoming a "free" adult living 3,000 miles away from home didn't make me feel more at ease or better about myself. I felt that maybe my parents were right all along—that I didn't have any business with ambitions or dreams. I was really as inadequate and crazy as they said I was.

When my husband, who I was supporting emotionally and physically, began putting me down, calling me "stupid," and treating me like I was useless, it initially felt normal. Then I began feeling like the man in the Kafka novel that I had read in high school, who was put on trial for something he hadn't done, was forced to defend himself when no one would tell him what he was being tried for, and then was sentenced after being found guilty. I had been guilty all my life and I didn't know what I had done. I kept trying harder and harder to be a "good girl" and it didn't make any difference. I was found guilty anyway.

A cognitive life raft and a trusting relationship are needed for an Adult Child to feel safe enough to dive into emotional waters and make sense of childhood experiences in an alcoholic family, create a life narrative, and recapture the "true self" that was meant to be.

Grief Work and the Cognitive Life Raft

Allowing the child of the past who experienced the trauma to have a voice and develop compassion and love, rather than contempt, for the child he or she was, is the essence of the grief-work process. Walking through the trauma with the guidance of a supportive other, and feeling the pain, tears, and fears never expressed when younger, is often a frightening process. It is a necessary one, however, if the Adult Child is to move beyond survival adaptation to the spontaneity of living.

The cognitive life raft becomes an intellectual guide—an understanding of the beginning, middle, and end of the process of healing wounds of the past. Understanding the experience of growing up in an alcoholic or addicted family and developing coping mechanisms that serve as security can relieve, to some extent, the terrifying anxiety of not knowing what to do or of feeling crazy when emotions begin to surface. This life raft of understanding is much like reading the last page of a terrifying novel. When one knows the ending, it often allows a sense of control in the frightening middle. Adult Children need the sense of safety that was never there when they were children. They need to believe that painful, repressed feelings will not be so destructive when they are expressed and felt. They need to experience the safety of a new relationship, one in which trust has been painstakingly built. Childhood relationships that condemned the expression of feelings and did not allow the child a voice were a source of pain and fear, whereas a new relationship of empathy, trust, and respect can become a source of empowerment.

Perhaps the most important part of the cognitive life raft for Adult Children is that it normalizes the necessary survival adaptation to a painful childhood. It is important for Adult Children to understand they not crazy as they have always feared, but instead are suffering the complications of delayed trauma and grief. Alcoholism or addiction can span three or more generations for many families, and this leads to generations of lost childhoods, deaths from alcoholism, suicides, divorces, medical complications, misdiagnosed nervous breakdowns, emotional detachment, and other losses too numerous to mention. In some families, addictions came after financial collapse, world wars, immigration, cultural genocide, sexual assault, or death of children and family members that could not be grieved in a healthy way.

We often ask Adult Children to complete family maps (called "genograms") that span three generations and to color code them for trauma. Unlike a timeline, which offers an understanding of one's own life, a color-coded genogram offers the ACOA the perspective of generationally transmitted trauma. ACOAs ascribe a uniquely colored dot for each trauma, such as alcoholism, depression, suicide, world war, sexual assault, cultural oppression, immigration, domestic violence, and any other traumas that may have affected their families. Then we ask them to put the colored dots next to the individuals who experienced each trauma in each generation.

When the color-coded genogram map is complete, many Adult Children have, for the first time, the emotional and intellectual awareness of the pain that has been passed down through their families. They have a visual aid to help them understand why their parents may have had difficulty with parenting. As one sixteen-year-old boy told us, "This is the first time I really understand that the drinking in the family was not my fault. My parents never recovered from the war. It had nothing to do with me."

Almost thirty years have passed since we began doing workshops for Adult Children of Alcoholics. These workshops began as trainings for professionals on the effects of growing up in addicted families. In those days it was our belief that the reason alcoholism and drug abuse were frequently missed by human service professionals was because a large majority of those professionals were themselves children from addicted families and were still caught in the web of denial. While conducting professional training on alcoholism, addiction, and depression, many participants would come up to us during a break and whisper, "I grew up in an alcoholic family but have never found a safe place to discuss it."

We found that 95 percent of the professionals who attended our first workshops were from alcoholic and addicted families. They didn't want training per se, but rather information—a cognitive life raft and a safe place to talk about what it meant to have grown up in addicted families. The participants told us that it became clear that they were the survivors of generations of victims who had never had the opportunity or support to heal the wounds of the past. After learning the characteristics of alcoholic and addicted families and the roles and characteristics of Adult Children, they felt (for the first time in their lives) like survivors of trauma instead of failures. They realized that they weren't crazy; they felt less unique, more connected with others, and more hopeful about their lives and their families. They believed that with work they could end generational grief, and that the unexplainable internal chaos and depression they had felt all their lives did not have to be passed on to their children.

During the workshops, participants learned what "normal" was in their alcoholic families. They learned that "people who lean on people who lean on bottles fall over," and that the focus in an alcoholic family is on an addiction rather than on the developing needs of children. They also learned that all members of the addicted family live in denial—not just the alcoholic—and that the extreme insecurity and inconsistency leads to the development of survival roles.

Workshop participants who were survivors of sexual abuse in their alcoholic families learned that they, too, were not alone, and felt enough validation—some for the first time in their lives—to tell the secrets that had been eating them up since childhood. They began to understand their confusion around nurturing and sexuality, their sense of always feeling like objects, their secretive compulsive lies, their sexual identity confusion, and their poor sense of boundaries, as the result of pervasive boundary violations in their childhoods. They learned that it was possible to feel nurtured and abused at the same time, and that the abuse wasn't their fault. Most of all, they said they finally felt "a sense of safety," a sense of belonging rather than the rejection they always feared if they "told." Participants who were the targets of abuse in their families began to make intellectual sense out of their fear of normal conflict, their fear of trusting, and, for some, the patterns of repetitive abuse in their adult lives.

Almost thirty years later we continue to find pervasive feelings of shame in Adult Children who seek understanding and healing. This story, told by a workshop participant, could be a metaphor for the feelings held by many Adult Children:

> A year or so ago, I was skiing with some friends when I lost control and fell down a steep embankment. I lay there for some time and then I could see the ski patrol starting to come down the hill to rescue me. I looked down at my leg, which was split open and bleeding, and felt an overwhelming sense of embarrassment and protectiveness for those on the ski patrol. I yelled up at them, "You'd better not come down here right now; it's a mess down here."

Most Adult Children report that they have always felt that they were a "mess" deep down and have protected themselves and others from the embarrassment of seeing or feeling that "mess." They have felt alone in a crowd or isolated all their lives. They have taken care of others compulsively, but never let others care for them. They have sought out relationships where needs weren't possible, or intimacy could never be achieved. Children of Alcoholics tend to have caseloads, not friends, and feel that they have to work harder than anyone else—to be more perfect, tougher, or more independent and in control. They feel they must hide the craziness they feel inside, and they must earn the right to have relationships or merely live in the world like everyone else.

The workshops, the education, the self-help books, and the cognitive life raft are not ends in themselves but the beginning of a process. Providing a cognitive life raft is a way of transporting that small child, so locked in the prison of the ideal self, to the place where feelings of fear, anger, joy, sadness, and normal anxiety are understood—first intellectually and then, with work, emotionally—not as dangerous, bad, or crazy, but rather as part of what it means to be human.

Until grief is processed, attempts at changing behavior become just one more expectation of an ideal self. If we had a nickel for every Adult Child who had spent vast amounts of money on behavioral training, self-help workbooks, and workshops designed to help them be more assertive, have more self-esteem, learn to express anger, or work out conflicts in marriage, we would be wealthy people. Adult Children who have taken classes to change behavior without working through the feelings of the frightened child inside not only have difficulty following through with expected changes, but also add new failures to the feelings of failure stored long ago. As one Adult Child put it: "I felt like a failure every time I couldn't say no or couldn't stand up for myself. I felt even more helpless, and I saw the instructor as that punitive parent who would look at me as a failure, so I began to lie about what I could do. I felt even worse."

A cognitive life raft comes with an intellectual validation of the feelings of the child, a lessening of pervasive shame, and a normalizing of responses that had always felt uniquely crazy. A workshop participant summed it up when she said: "I always felt . . . that I couldn't complain, that no one would ever understand, or that I couldn't dishonor my family by telling the secret. I realize now that the story is mine to tell, and no one here is judging me or my family. I have to tell my story to heal myself and become a better parent to my children."

It is important for us to honor and respect the amazing strengths—and sometimes even the compulsions—that got us through our childhoods. Alcoholism knows no boundaries. We need to honor the gifts that helped us survive in our individual oceans of pain. Gradually, as we become more confident, more loving, more tolerant of our humanness, and more caring of ourselves, we can applaud our survival strengths while we slowly take control of the "volume knob." We can work toward balance and find the perfect volume level. As Confucius put it, "Our greatest glory is not in never falling, but rising every time we fall."

An ACOA was in the middle of an ocean, surviving with just the life vest he was wearing. It seemed as though he'd been struggling in the middle of this ocean for a long time and he was tired. Out of nowhere, he saw a boat in the distance moving toward him. When the boat was close enough, he heard the words from his would-be saviors: "Come on, climb in! We've heard your cries and are here to save you." This was music to the ACOA's ears and he quickly started climbing the ladder. "Wait," said one of his rescuers. "You have to take off the life vest before you can come aboard."

The ACOA was devastated. Though he tried over and over to unhook the life vest, he just couldn't do it. The fear of drowning was too strong. The boat went on without him, and he continued struggling for survival. Soon he was exhausted and felt more helpless. Then he heard a helicopter in the distance and began waving and yelling for help again. The helicopter came closer and dropped a ladder. The ACOA started to reach for the ladder, then pulled his arm back. "What's the matter?" asked one of the rescuers. "Reach up, you can do it. Just a few steps on the ladder and you'll be inside."

"I'm sorry. I can't," said the tired ACOA. "I'm so tired of struggling, so tired of surviving. But I can't take off the life vest. It's all that's kept me afloat all this time."

"You don't have to take off the vest now," answered the rescuer. "Just climb up the ladder and take it off later when you feel safe enough. We have faith in you."

Sometimes, well-meaning family members, friends, and even therapists or support group members are like those on the boat who insist that the life vest be taken off prematurely. Many well-meaning and well-intentioned caseworkers, family members, or therapists want the Adult Child to immediately remove the "life vest." The Adult Child who has survived by caretaking, overeating, overworking, or using other compulsive behaviors may need to continue these behaviors for a time, but they will stop as he or she feels increasingly safe in the healing process.

8

An Emotional Safety Net:
Building a Relationship
with the Child Within

Therapy begins with connection. Filled with the heroism
of a journey into the unknown, patients join therapists in
exploring the past, living fully in the present, and becoming
the creative authors of the future chapters of their lives.
Connections then emerge beyond the therapeutic dyad,
freeing the patient to explore new avenues of authentic
living within the mind and with others. By making sense
of our lives, we become free to join with others in
creating emerging layers of meaning and connection.

—*from "An Interpersonal Neurobiology of Psychotherapy: The
Developing Mind and the Resolution of Trauma," by Daniel J. Siegel*

WE LEARNED IN EARLIER CHAPTERS that when a child is
raised in an alcoholic family or in a family whose major
foundations are built on denial, there is frequently a huge gap
between the real self and the ideal self or image. The child learns at
an early age that to be who he or she is—to speak the truth, to

express spontaneous feelings, or to ask for needs to be met—is to be rendered helpless or abandoned.

Adults who are focused on their own pain or addictions are not consistently available or nurturing to their children. These parents often violate the psychological (and sometimes physical) boundaries of the child, and they are often not capable of supplying love or structure, or of setting healthy limits. They can only accept the child as a mirror image of what they wish and need the child to be. The result is the development of a looking-glass child: a child who satisfies the parents' unmet needs but whose own needs are not met by the parents. In the end, the child's true self is "encased in ice."

It is not surprising, given this developmental process, that it is not the true self whom the therapist meets in early sessions, but rather the looking-glass self. Most Adult Children originally seek help to improve their images or their ability to cope with isolation, not because of empathy for themselves or to deal with the pain of childhood losses. They want to lose weight, get a better job, or get rid of depression. They want to figure out what they need to change about themselves so they can fix an isolating or abusive relationship. They want to learn how to be an even better need-satisfying object for partners, parents, friends, or siblings. They want tools to add to the enormous tool case they already carry, more self-help books to be an even more acceptable person, or a therapist's help in the construction of an even stronger mask. The Adult Children who empathize with and care for others frequently have contempt for their own true selves. We often see the Adult Children who are so well described by Dr. Alice Miller, author of *The Drama of the Gifted Child:*

> They recount their earliest memories without any sympathy for the child they once were, and this is more striking since these patients not only have a pronounced introspective ability, but also are also able to

empathize with other people. The relationship to their own childhood emotional world, however, is characterized by lack of respect, compulsion to control, manipulation, and a demand for achievement. (6)

Building a Bridge

Part of the role of the therapist is to help the Adult Child construct a bridge between the "looking-glass self" and the true, unrealized child of the past, who was never given a voice, using materials from both. The therapist also provides safety and validation for the frightened child and for the adult, aids in the construction of internal psychological and physical boundaries, and helps the Adult Child become an honest mirror for the true self, rather than for the image. Sometimes the therapist serves as a protective buffer between an internalized abusive parent and the abused child. Other times the therapist helps provide a map for the Adult Child to safely walk back through childhood trauma as well as the support he or she needs to feel safe enough to reconnect the memory of the experiences with the repressed feelings. Such support and reconnection help the Adult Child release the pain, fear, healthy anger, sadness, and "voice" so long held hostage.

One of the survival mechanisms of children raised in alcoholic families is an awareness of parental needs and feelings and of changes in parental moods and behavior. The Adult Child often makes a full-time occupation of mind reading with partners, friends, employers, and therapists. As a consequence, they earn a Ph.D. at the age of six in observing the behavior of others and assessing parental needs—but are in elementary school at age thirty, trying to learn to assess, label, or communicate their own needs and feelings.

To further understand the bridge between these two worlds of the Adult Child, we will return to Beth, whom we met in Chapter 6. Before making a telephone call to request a therapy appointment, Beth had already decided that her needs were less important than those of the therapist. She had taken the therapist's busy schedule into consideration and prepared herself for one more disappointment, telling herself, *You really can handle this if she's too busy with others who are more in need than you are.* By discussing the telephone message with Beth during our first session and, with humor and sincerity, assuring her that she did not have to take care of the therapist too, I began to build a bridge between her neglected child of the past and counterdependent woman she expected herself to be, as well as provide the safety and acknowledgment she needed. Beth's feelings of fear, abandonment, shame, and low self-esteem became focuses in her therapy.

In our first session, Beth attempted to use a forced, relaxed appearance, her apparent lack of concern, and her detachment from the pain of her abusive childhood memories to protect the therapist from the insecurities, fears, and emotions of the child—just as she had learned to protect her mother. As we've discussed earlier, children in alcoholic families become need-satisfying objects of parents, and develop bond permanence to them and other parental substitutes, including partners, therapists, and, frequently, their own children. It is difficult to be available to friends and partners if you can't trust your ability to protect yourself from the feelings, thoughts, and needs of others. As internal boundaries develop, so does the ability to establish trust in relationships.

New research into the neurobiology of attachment helps us understand the healing that can take place in a therapy process. Healing on the deepest level of the mind begins to occur when there is connection, compassion, consistency, and continuity in the therapy process. The therapist is able to make sense of and respond empathetically to the Adult Child's verbal and nonverbal communication as well as provide an emotional safety net when the Adult Child is experiencing intense emotions. The Adult Child may connect to the therapist in a way that he or she couldn't to the wounded and/or addicted parent.

Many Adult Children have difficulty verbally expressing their feelings, or they have used intellectualization throughout their lives as a defense against feeling. With these individuals, the use of art or symbolic representations of history prove far more effective in building a relationship and an emotional safety net in the process of healing. Sometimes tools like continuum-of-life drawings (mentioned in the previous chapter) aid the child within to express feelings and memories. Seeing the progression of drawings from ages five to sixty-five assists an Adult Child in understanding the powerful effects of childhood pain in mapping future life directions. Many who have difficulty telling their stories verbally can tell them in pictures. Rose was just such an Adult Child; early in her healing she could express through pictures what she couldn't verbalize.

Rose's father was alcoholic and her mother was codependent. Rose was the youngest of seven children and remembered having very little contact with her mother. She was left alone in the care of brothers and sisters who were frequently abusive to her. Her drawings of herself from three months to three years of age showed her tied to a crib. The drawings depicting her life from ages three to five reflected Rose's feelings of being the scapegoat of her brothers and sisters. She remembered being locked by them in a bee-filled shed. In her drawings, Rose was cooking the family dinners at age eleven while her mother worked. She remembered the awful dinner-table scenes where no one was satisfied and her dad was drunk and made fun of her cooking. Her drawing of herself at sixteen showed her happiness as her brothers and sisters left home, as well as her first romance. Her drawings of age eighteen reflected her decision to enter a convent when she completed high school, and she began a life devoted to God.

Rose remembered both the pain and joy in her early years in the convent; joy because of the isolation and prayer, and pain from her continual worry about her mother, who she rarely saw because of the discipline of the religious order she had joined. Her father died of alcoholism when Rose was twenty-five. Her mother remarried, and her new husband (also alcoholic) was far more physically abusive to her than Rose's father had been. Rose worried constantly about her mother and begged the order to let her go home. Her mother died of a heart attack when Rose was twenty-eight, and Rose felt responsible. She said her mother's death had been caused by abuse and that she should have been home to care for her mother.

Rose left the convent shortly after her mother's death and began drinking. She worked in a hospital as a nurse during the day and drank all night. Rose said nothing seemed to matter anymore. She became involved with many men, all of whom were alcoholic, and she married a man who was psychologically abusive. She kept a wall between herself and others. When she discussed the years that followed her mother's death, Rose frequently said, "I was walking around making the motions of living every day and drinking every night, but it was my mother that had my heart."

Rose's feelings of guilt about her mother's death protected her from feeling the helplessness of the abandoned child. It also protected her from the rage caused by being tied to a crib and placed in the care of her angry and abandoned brothers and sisters. Rose's anger began to emerge toward the end of her first year in therapy. She was angry at everything, but especially at people who had let her down: friends who didn't call right back after she left a message, auto mechanics who made her wait for her car, and her therapist who wouldn't give out her home telephone number.

It was important for the child in Rose to understand that the feelings of rage, sadness, loss, and fear were real and valid. In therapy she began to understand that she had lost a part of childhood to which she had a right. It was important for the child inside to cry the tears of early trauma and to separate the childhood feelings from the feelings of current adult disappointment. The pain of the childhood loss of that special part of life, of being the center of the world to healthy adults, is valid—and that is the pain that frequently emerges when triggered by adult disappointments. It is the right of the child to expect to be the center of parental focus and enjoy unconditional love, but it is not realistic for an adult to expect to be the central focus of partners, friends, employers, or other adults.

Part of the role of the Adult Child's support system (including the therapist) is to help construct an emotional safety net by developing a relationship of acceptance. This allows the Adult Child to build a bridge to the child within and to begin to heal. Now the child within has a face. Tears can be cried, and fear and pain can be felt. Instead of repressing the pain of the past, which leads to unhealthy adult behaviors, the fear and pain are processed in a healthy way. After the tears, a new bridge can be constructed to build peer networks of support and to regain the choice and spontaneity imprisoned within the frightened child of the past.

The process of coming out of denial and healing the wounds of the past involves validating the existence of the hurting child, recognizing the effects of living in an addicted family, and gaining an understanding of how the past affects the present. The next step, grief work, is the painful but necessary process that allows the Adult Child to regain his or her voice and experience the pain of the original, cumulative trauma without feeling helpless—while coming to the realization that helplessness and powerlessness belong to the past.

9

Grief Work:
The Pain That
Begins to Heal Itself

An old Chinese proverb talks about a man that was
so disturbed by the sound of his footsteps and so bothered
by his shadow that he tried to outrun both. No matter how
fast he ran, his shadow effortlessly kept up with him and when
he put one foot down there was always the sound of another
step. He believed his failure was because he wasn't running
fast enough, so he ran faster still. Finally, exhausted, he
became very sick and finally died. He never realized that if
he had just sat down and rested in the shade, his shadow
would have disappeared and there would have been a quiet
time without the disturbing sound of footsteps.

—from ChuangTzu, Taoist philosopher (400 BC)

Much like the man in the proverb, Adult Children from
addicted families often try to outrun their grief and are rarely
satisfied with their "footsteps"—never feeling good enough and
always trying to be better. Joan tried to be the perfect ballerina,

hoping to receive enough applause to fill the empty space inside. Richard tried to convince himself that he was "a no good guy who just didn't care." Peter tried to work harder and harder, endlessly busying his life. Beth wanted to be self-sufficient enough that she wouldn't bother anyone with her presence or her needs.

When we attempt to run away from our grief, we actually intensify our pain and deaden a part of ourselves in the process. Delayed grief narrows our options in life, causing us to continue surviving rather than living. Joan had little life outside of dance. Richard couldn't allow himself to be successful. Peter and Beth both focused their lives on work, work, and more work. Neither could ask for help even when they felt they were emotionally drowning.

We must complete our psychological business with the past before we are ready to move on and form new attachments. For Adult Children, grief work may involve facing losses that have been denied for years. Four tasks must be accomplished when working through the grief of growing up in an addicted family:

- The first task of grief work involves naming the loss and accepting that it has taken place.

- The second task is feeling the emotions associated with the loss, including both sadness and anger.

- The third task is to adjust to an environment in which "that which had been lost…is missing" (Worden, 14–16). It is important to own what has happened and take responsibility for the behaviors resulting from delayed grief.

- The fourth task is to withdraw emotional energy from that which is lost and reinvest it in other relationships (healthy friendships and intimate relationships) and begin changing behavior that has been associated with delayed grief, including unhealthy anger styles and health issues.

Validating the Losses

Before one can grieve, one must first acknowledge that a loss has taken place. Joan, Beth, Richard, and Peter all felt something was wrong with them early in their counseling. They were unaware of the reality that they had sustained significant losses while growing up in addicted families. They didn't know they were stuck in unresolved grief and were having normal reactions to abnormal and painful childhoods.

Accepting the losses sustained in alcoholic families means facing the real or threatened losses of attachment, safety, childhood innocence and spontaneity, trust, the ability to play, to make mistakes, and to learn from those mistakes, and the ability to learn healthy skills in conflict resolution.

Adult Children frequently present themselves as poised and self-assured while they dispassionately recount symptoms of acute or chronic depression and/or anxiety. They explain that others had much worse childhood experiences than they did. They believe they had "normal" childhoods when, in fact, they sustained multiple losses. They have difficulty in reconciling panic attacks or depression. Until their denial is interrupted, they lack a context for disconnected feelings. They will not be able to walk through grief and integrate losses until they are able to acknowledge and validate them.

Individuals not only grieve the actual experiences they have had, but also the developmental experiences of which they have been deprived. A major deprivation for children in alcoholic families is the loss of a sense of a safe, consistent, growth-promoting family. Alcoholic families tend to be either enmeshed "super glue" families (Reid) or detached "blown apart" families made up of isolates with little interpersonal connectedness and concern.

Children being reared in both types of families experience loss—loss of autonomy in one, and loss of connectedness in the other. Enmeshed families are those in which children feel that normal individuality is the same as betrayal and abandonment. In detached families, children feel that no one cares enough to even notice if they drift away, and they do not believe that anyone will pull them back into the family to keep from losing them. In some families, one parent is enmeshing, placing emotional needs on the child that are inappropriate, while the other parent may be emotionally and/or physically abandoning.

Children in addicted families also lose healthy role modeling for intimacy and parenting, and this results in more losses later in life. In healthy families, parents have their own system of support, relying on each other for love, nurturing, and support in the day-to-day tasks of running a home and raising children with love and limits. When one parent develops an addiction, the intimacy and connection with his or her partner is replaced by reliance on, and connection with, a substance. As the scenario unfolds, the codependent partner increasingly takes up the slack left by the addict's inability to function as either a partner or a parent. One parent becomes more and more inadequate as a partner or parent, while the other becomes the overinvolved *responsibility assumer,* always in pursuit of a solution to the addicted partner's bad behavior while continuing to pretend that everything is normal.

This might be acceptable if there were only two people in such a family. The two players in this example, however, have children for whom they serve as role models for intimacy, marital relationships, and parenting. The children sustain one developmental loss after another, and later in life, Adult Children tend to have difficulty with healthy relationships and parenting. They swim in a sea of confusion and loneliness, having little idea what normal is, and often sustain more losses in the process. Some Adult Children go out of their way to do things in a completely different way than their early role models. One Adult Child told me, "I'm never going to be like my dad." When I asked him how he would be instead, he looked confused and said, "I don't know. Just the opposite of him, I guess."

Many Adult Children report always having felt different, as though everyone else received a book on how to be a healthy partner and parent and they never got their copies. As an ACOA told us in therapy, "I feel I'm making it up as I go along. I'm trying to play a role, but I'm missing connection and intimacy in the process of trying to be a 'good man,' just as I tried to be a 'good boy.'"

Over the years, we have worked with countless Adult Children who have mourned the loss of many relationships. They have mourned the missed opportunities of celebrating developmental milestones and normal activities with their children. What is tragic is that for these Adult Children, grief is truly multigenerational: they could not be effective life partners or parents because they did not have healthy role models. Until this pattern is interrupted, loss after loss is experienced in each succeeding generation.

Many Adult Children choose to forego forming intimate relationships and lead isolated lives; others choose not to have children, fearing that they too will pass on unhealthy parenting skills. They fear either being withdrawn, inadequate, or abusive like their parents were. They may believe that they are simply so ill-prepared by their own childhood experiences that they can't allow themselves to take a risk. Other Adult Children forego bearing children out of a clear sense of still being children themselves, and they not are not willing to be pushed aside again for someone else.

For Adult Children from addicted families, grief work is literally a double whammy. Acknowledgment of painful losses in childhood is followed by enormous grief for the losses in adulthood. Because of the defenses put in place in childhood, the adult can suffer loss of relationships, loss of playful times with children, losses brought about by addictions, losses of health, or the loss of merely enjoying life in a spontaneous way.

Sometimes Adult Children blame themselves for having been inadequate at parenting or as healthy partners in relationships. For Adult Children, it is a sign of beginning recovery when they are able to interrupt their self-rebuke, redirect their anger away from themselves, and allow themselves to experience the anger and the pain of childhood losses that they were not able to experience as children.

Feeling the Pain

Naming the loss and acknowledging the reality of it, rather than continuing to minimize or deny it, is the first task in grief work. However, to name a loss is not to heal it. It takes both time and external support to feel the pain and integrate the losses. The second task of grief work is allowing ourselves to feel the feelings associated with the loss. Often Adult Children experience the feeling of "What's wrong with me? Why am I not over this?" They need to be reassured that they are *not* broken human beings—Humpty Dumptys whom all the King's horses and all the King's men cannot put together again. Adult Children have great personal strength, and grief work takes time.

Suppression and denial are the keystones to the survival adaptation for children in alcoholic families. These defenses cannot alter the child's external life circumstances, but their use allows the child to protect him- or herself emotionally in the face of circumstances that seem, and often are, intolerable. Children need to experience the feelings associated with loss as they grow up, and they need at least one person with whom the experience can be processed and shared, otherwise loss cannot be integrated.

"Unresolved grief is like a low-grade fever. It flows in peaks and valleys. Sometimes it spikes in almost overwhelming emotions, sometimes it lies dormant, nearly comatose, just beneath the surface," explains Stephen Levine in his 2006 book about grief, *Unattended Sorrow: Recovering from Loss and Reviving the Heart* (5). The key to understanding the spikes is to understand the triggers inside us. Triggers are the experiences in the present that bring up feelings and memories associated with unresolved grief and trauma of the past.

A number of years ago, I went shopping with my friend Paula. I had occasionally spent brief amounts of time with Paula at her father's house, which was also Paula's childhood home. Although Paula was a strong and competent woman and was highly respected in her career, she often turned into a silent child around her father. I was stunned by the way he still treated her, criticizing her work or shaming her if she was five minutes late bringing him his supper. On this particular day Paula had borrowed her father's truck. It is important to understand that Paula's dad was in his seventies and no longer drove the truck. While we were shopping, Paula was clearly anxious. When I suggested we have lunch at a local restaurant before we went home, she became extremely agitated. "I can't!" she shouted. "I told you, I have to get the truck back to Dad soon. I am already late. He told me to bring it back soon and we've been gone for over an hour."

When I asked if her dad was going to use the truck, there was fear in her eyes as she replied.

"No, he just wants it back."

"How old do you feel right now?" I asked Paula.

She stopped and thought for a minute, let out a deep breath, and then replied, "Eight. I feel eight."

At that moment, when triggered, Paula *was* an eight-year-old child again, fearful of her father's disapproval.

Unless we work through grief and trauma they will live inside us for years. They become locked inside time capsules of memory and feelings, cut off from our awareness, until sights, sounds, smells, or other prompts in the present cause the capsules to break open and flood us with feelings and memories from long ago. A large part of feeling the pain of past grief and trauma is allowing ourselves to experience other associated feelings that are often blocked by self-defeating behavior when our triggers go off. When triggered, the Adult Child will sometimes bypass these feelings. Instead, they will eat, rage, clean, go into a depression, medicate the feelings with drugs or alcohol, work, start a fight with friends or significant others, isolate—anything rather than feel the feelings.

When we work on triggers with our clients, we ask them to take time out, journal about the triggers, and then seek support to feel their emerging emotions instead of using negative behaviors (like those mentioned in the previous paragraph) to block feelings.

Paul grew up with a father who was alcoholic and was always putting his son down, particularly when the father was drinking. As an adult, Paul was triggered whenever his wife innocently asked him a question. His journaling revealed the original pain.

PAUL'S TRIGGER JOURNAL

What was the trigger that set off the feelings from the past? My wife asked me if I had fixed the heater in the basement yet.
How old did you feel? Six.

What did your body feel like? I felt really tense and tight.

What did you do? I got really mad at her, told her I could only do one thing at a time, and listed everything I had done that day.

What were the feelings emerging from the past that you may have blocked by your behavior? I think it was the fear, shame, and powerlessness of that little boy. I wasn't doing it right again, and I was going to get in big trouble.

What was the original loss or trauma from the past that was triggered? When my dad was drunk, hung over, or unable to get a drink, he would jump on me. There was nothing I could do right. I got the wrong tool when I was helping him. I didn't do things fast enough. I was worthless, not good enough.

Whom did you go to for support? After journaling, I realized that I had been triggered and that my wife was just asking a question. She wasn't criticizing me. She just wanted to know if it the heater was fixed so that she could decide whether to do the project she was working on downstairs or upstairs. She wasn't judging me at all. It was my dad's voice I heard. I was able to apologize to her. I was able to talk to her about the powerlessness and shame I felt when I was young. It was really great because in the past, I could be angry and silent for the rest of the day and I never could apologize.

In 1984, Dr. Timmen Cermak gave a presentation at the Children of Alcoholics Conference in Seattle, Washington. In "Children of Alcoholics: The Power of Reality and the Reality of Power," Dr. Cermack characterized the Adult Child syndrome as an example of post-traumatic stress syndrome (PTSD) or delayed grief. The following is a list of symptoms of PTSD that are common to many children of alcoholics:

- an intermittent, partial breakdown of denial

- emotional freezing

- intrusive, recurrent memories or "flashbacks" of suppressed childhood experiences

- disturbing nightmares

- emotional hyperreactivity or startle reactions

- a wish to avoid anything that could lead to an emotional re-experiencing of the trauma

When Adult Children begin to accept the reality of their losses and feel the emotions associated with those losses, they begin to take charge of their lives instead of reacting as captives of a painful past. Therapists can function as attachment figures or as emotional support, helping Adult Children to develop *affect tolerance* (the ability to tolerate feelings and emotions) or *psychological muscles* as they allow suppressed memories and feelings to surface gradually. There is no coercion in the process. The therapist must respect the Adult Child's defenses and recognize that he or she may feel like a terrified animal who wants to bolt off to a place that feels safer emotionally. The Adult Child's pace in therapy also is respected; there is no simple prescription for how he or she ought to be working through grief and trauma. The therapist waits patiently for the story to unfold along with the once buried emotions. There is no therapeutic big bang that leads to instantaneous resolution. The Adult Child gradually develops psychological strength, a new vocabulary, and understanding for his or her feelings and for the meaning of a once submerged life experience, which slowly surfaces into conscious awareness.

Adjusting to Loss and "Owning It"

There are many losses to which an Adult Child must adjust: loss of normal childhood experiences, loss of self-esteem, loss of memory, loss of self-respect, loss of normal childhood development, loss of relationships, and other losses. According to William J. Worden, in his book *Grief Counseling and Grief Therapy: A Handbook for the Mental Health Practitioner, Second Edition* (14–16), the next phase of grief resolution is the acknowledgment of that which has been lost. If the Adult Child has adequate support and ventures forth (in manageable doses) to feel the feelings associated with the loss and then accepts the loss, healing can begin.

For instance, the Adult Child will never be a warm, secure, loved four-year-old with a happy, healthy mommy and daddy. But there *can* be an understanding that the only repair of the past is in the present, and this allows him or her to have experiences now that were missed then. This journey is made with the awareness that no amount of reparative experience will completely erase how it was "then." As adults, we are in the driver's seat of our own lives. We are the authors of our present and future realities.

There is a bumper sticker that sums it up nicely: THE TRUTH WILL SET YOU FREE, BUT FIRST IT WILL MAKE YOU MISERABLE. In effect, a person becomes willing to relinquish his or her sense of entitlement to reparations for wrongs done in childhood. He or she realizes that although it was unfair that some essential experiences in childhood were missed, the rest of the world does not owe the debt. It is unfair that things happened as they did, but by finally letting go and no longer attempting to extract his or her emotional needs from others, the Adult Child is in a position to be in control, sometimes for the first time in his or her life. During this process it is important to understand the difference between being a victim in childhood and victimizing oneself as an adult. Being a victim is simply not a good career choice. After the tears, we regain ownership of our own lives, our choices, our emotions, and our responsibilities.

Children raised in alcoholic and addicted families who have not worked through their own delayed grief are emotionally blind. Joan, for example, thought she loved to dance, when in fact, she danced because she was seeking the love, acceptance, and nurturing she so desperately needed from her mother. Individuals with such an emotional impairment do not know that they live with such a disability until they are offered the opportunity to see life through corrective lenses.

Making a choice to safely enter the process of walking back through pain is choosing to regain emotional vision. Frequently, the grief process involves experiencing the grief of several generations as well as the losses of one's own childhood. For Joan, the ballet dancer, that meant not only experiencing the pain of her early childhood memories of practicing dance while other children played outside, but it also meant experiencing the pain of her mother's unfulfilled fantasies and dreams. Taking back one's life from the chains of bond permanence to one's parent (the enmeshment referred to earlier between Joan and her mother) is an emotional challenge. It involves feeling the pain of being held captive while other children played freely, feeling the fear of abandonment, and feeling the parent's fears, anger, and pain. Like a sponge absorbs water, the child absorbs a parent's fears and losses. Joan cried tears for her mother's life first, and then she was able to cry tears for the child within her who had been held captive by her mother's pain. It was her mother who had grieved the loss of dance her entire life, not Joan.

As Joan retrieved each memory from the past, she was able to separate her mother's pain from the pain she herself experienced. As each painful memory returned, and was worked through, she was able to actualize more of her own unmet dreams and regain control and choice in her life. In one session she was able to experience the anger of the years lost in trying to attain her mother's dream: "I can't believe I almost committed suicide because I injured myself and couldn't dance when I really didn't want to be a dancer in the first place. I almost killed myself for my mother's pain."

Taking the Next Steps

The final task of grief resolution is to be willing to withdraw emotional investment in that which has been lost and move on to form new attachments. For Adult Children, this step often comes after they have been able to see their parents and their family from a multigenerational perspective. In looking back three generations, familiar patterns often emerge and help to explain the life circumstances with which one's parents and grandparents wrestled. It is difficult to hang on to blame, anger, and disappointment when the Adult Child sees that his parents were themselves burdened with the unresolved grief of their own parents or with unresolved trauma and loss.

Full grief-work recovery also entails recognizing that many of our parents didn't stock their emotional shelves with what *we* needed because *they* never received essential supplies from their own families. In recovery, Adult Children begin to recognize that only they can create the reparative life experiences that make some restitution for the past. Rather than railing at their parents to give them something they never received, or demanding that needs be replaced by their children or significant others, Adult Children become their own "good parents," providing themselves with the self-soothing, self-care, and self-respect they have longed for. They learn to provide for themselves—not in defensive ways as in the past, but with a sense of empowerment—knowing that they have choices and knowing that it is their own responsibility to create optimal life circumstances for the adults they have become. They become willing to move on and attach to life. They feel sadness, not despair, about the past. The emotional wounds of the past begin to heal when they begin to name the losses, feel the feelings connected to the losses, and own the defenses and behaviors associated with delayed grief. Just as a festering wound begins to heal once it is treated, grief work is the pain that begins to heal itself once an Adult Child takes the time and finds the support to nurse the wounds of the past.

10

Mourning, Then Behavior Change:
Moving On and Giving Back

It is never too late for the child within to benefit
from finally gaining a sympathetic ear.
It is as though the child you were has waited patiently inside,
never giving up hope that someday
someone will be there to listen. Once you develop
a willingness to listen compassionately to your own story,
an entirely new relationship with yourself is possible.

—*from* A Time to Heal: the Road to Recovery
for Adult Children of Alcoholics, *by Timmen L. Cermak, M.D.*

A NEW PROCESS OF MOURNING comes after the process of grief. It is not possible to mourn the real losses of others until you have become a separate self. *Grief work* is the process of taking back your life; *mourning* is the process of feeling the sadness of the loss of others.

In Chapter 4 we met Joan, the ballet dancer who came into therapy after suffering from severe depression for several months. As she went through the grief-work process, Joan began to grieve the losses she had experienced in her childhood years. As she examined those traumas one by one, she was able to understand how cumulative trauma in childhood affected the adult she had become. Arriving at each new understanding allowed her to gain perspective on the story of her life, like adding pieces to an unfinished puzzle. After the tears, Joan regained choice in her life. She allowed herself new experiences that led to an expansion of her choices. She realized that she had never made the choices to remain single and childless, and that the choices that she had once believed to be her own had, in reality, been the desires and unmet needs of past generations. Joan grieved the loss of childhood play, the toys she never had, and most of all, the pain of never having the unconditional love that every child deserves. As she separated emotionally from her mother, Joan came to a new awareness that she had never wanted the applause—she had only wanted to be loved and nurtured. She realized that the applause would never have filled the emptiness of a lost childhood. As she put it:

> I have lived my life trying to give my mother a life so that finally she would love me. Now, at the age of thirty-two, I am grieving the loss of me and just beginning to see my own life before me. Now that I have myself, I feel this strange sadness at never really having a mother in the true sense. It's as if she has died. I'm mourning her death and in that mourning, accepting the mother I really have. I can receive what she can give rather than being angry at what she can't.

Mourning

When an Adult Child has given a face to the child held hostage within and freed that child from emotional bondage, he or she can also give a face to others in his or her life. He or she begins to see alcoholic parents as real men and women with pain and history, rather than demons or "perfect" people on pedestals. The Adult Child can begin to mourn the loss of healthy relationships with brothers and sisters who may be lost to their own addictions, or are still distant and in denial. He or she can begin to recognize the experiences that siblings had in the family without feeling responsible or guilty for their pain or loss. When others in the family can be seen as separate individuals, it is possible to develop new relationships with them, taking into account who they really are, not who they are expected to be or desired to be.

It is both freeing and sad to realize that an alcoholic parent or sibling may never recover from alcoholism or addiction to drugs, or that a codependent parent may never achieve the freedom of living his or her life. In seeing significant others in our lives as real people with real faces, we are also able to see that the decisions they have made in their lives are their choices—not our responsibilities. Sometimes their choices involve further losses in our lives: the loss of shared experiences, family holidays, or of quality time with our children or with grandparents, aunts, or uncles. With each loss there is more grief work and mourning, but there is also the freedom of choice—both ours and theirs.

Freedom of choice may mean seeing parents only when they are sober, and therefore, seeing them less frequently. It may mean fewer phone conversations if we make a decision to eliminate our exposure to shaming or alcoholic conversations. We are sometimes asked by those who are new to the grief-work process, "Will there be a time when I won't feel sadness and disappointment?" The answer is no. By seeing life as an emotional world of color, rather than as a sterile fantasy projection of black and white, we regain the ability to experience spontaneity, to rejoice in the joyful and nurturing moments of life, and to allow ourselves to feel sadness. A span of colorful feelings does not mean a life without pain and sorrow. It means the ability to feel the full range of emotions in the present.

After the tears, Adult Children of addicted families begin to experience new balance in their lives. This often means new experiences of play, alone time, quality time with children, and new feelings of spirituality. It frequently means the ending of old relationships and the beginning of new ones.

Changing Unhealthy, Grief-Based Behaviors

Behavior change is the final step of the grief-work process. Working through grief allows the self, once held hostage, the freedom to live life rather than being held captive by the unmet needs and expectations of others. It allows spontaneity and the choice of living in the present, rather than in the past or the future.

As we have said before, alcoholism is the gift that keeps on giving. Often Adult Children who have not worked on the cumulative trauma of growing up in an addicted home find themselves repeating many of the same patterns in their new family systems—with or without alcohol. They often feel distanced from their children or they see the development of the same chaos that existed in their families of origin. Some attempt to raise "perfect" children in "perfect families," and see their children as evidence that they are doing well. Some, rather than distancing or living in similar chaos, *enmesh* with their children and find it difficult to set and keep limits. Their children's tears become their own, and they withdraw any limits they might have set. In an effort to avoid repeating past patterns, ACOAs are often much too permissive and raise children who constantly push for limits. To grow into healthy adults, children need both love and limits. Because they fear hurting their children as they have been hurt, these parents deprive them of much-needed limits. Many ACOAs have difficulty tolerating normal emotions, and overly permissive behavior is also frequently fueled by delayed grief. Children become controlled by their parents—not because of addictions this time, but because of unresolved pain.

Before grief work, Adult Children often lack spontaneity and choice. They frequently lose the joy of experiencing their own children's development, just as they didn't experience the joy in their own childhoods. One ten-year-old boy told us of his experience when he was on vacation with his parents, who were both Adult Children from addicted families:

> It is no fun going on trips with my mom and dad. They saved up to take us on a trip to the Grand Canyon. We were so excited until we realized that the goal of the trip was getting there and seeing everything on a list they had made. We saw it and checked it off the list. When we were done with the list, we came home. It was really a drag.

This little boy was denied the playful spontaneity of childhood because of his parents' need for control. They were doing what they had always done, but now their defensiveness affected not just them, but the next generation as well.

Moving On to the New Normal

Janet was on her way to the grocery store with her four boys. It was a beautiful summer day. When they reached the entrance to the store, Janet saw a line of children waiting to ride the brightly colored merry-go-round horse. Her thoughts went back to the summer days of her childhood. She remembered watching other children jump on similar horses and wait while their parents dug into their pockets for dimes. She remembered the children giggling with delight when the coins were put in the slots and the horses jerked and moved up and down. Janet's eyes filled with tears as she remembered that her alcoholic parents were rarely there on such summer days. If they were, they were usually in a hurry to get home to drink and they would never take the time to let her ride. She remembered one day when she was four and had begged her dad for just one dime. She was slapped, and she never asked again.

Janet stood and watched the children, almost in a daze. She wondered if the grief would ever completely go away. Then it occurred to her that she was now an adult and in charge of her own life. "Why not?" she said out loud. Janet reached into her pocket, found a coin, and got in line. Her four sons looked at her in amazement. The oldest said, "Mom, you're not going to, are you?" "Why not?" she replied. Her boys all laughed. They were enjoying this new, fun-loving mother. The boys remembered times in the past when they thought their mother was a bit too serious and hard working. Now they were delighted with these times when they would all play spontaneously, laughing and teasing each other. One of the boys saw a friend and yelled, "Would you believe my mother is riding a merry-go-round horse?" His friend, a frequent visitor to their house, was not surprised. He answered, "Yeah, that's just like your mom. She is really something else. She's a real kick."

Janet, like many Adult Children from addicted families, had not always been "a real kick." Prior to working through her own delayed-grief process, she had been extremely serious—a perfectionist in need of control, frequently depressed, sixty pounds overweight, and suffering from headaches and back pain. She felt, as many Adult Children do, that "My world will fall apart if I am not in control of myself and everything else at all times." In the evenings after her children went to bed, Janet's exhaustion and loneliness were fed by a big piece of chocolate cake. She was so worried about raising her children correctly, cooking only the healthiest food for them, keeping a perfect house, and being the best she could be at her job, that she was exhausted and had little or no time left to enjoy her sons as they were growing up. Like many ACOAs, Janet didn't know what normal was. She constantly read books on child rearing and took many parenting classes, yet she felt she was a bad parent.

Confidence in parenting skills, healthy relationships, weight loss, or the joyful experience of living life instead of merely surviving it, cannot be found in self-help books or through practicing behaviors listed in articles on the Internet. The effects of early childhood trauma cannot be "cured" by adding more information about perfection to an already overtaxed ideal image. Adult Children have experienced enough pain in childhood to encase their spontaneity in ice. With the freezing, they often lose their ability to make healthy choices and live in the present rather than be bound to a painful past.

Behavior change in Adult Children is the end result of the grief-work process. There is no master plan that can be designed and memorized to attain a more perfect self. Our caseloads are full of individuals who have gone through many programs to stop addictive and/or compulsive behaviors without success, or have successfully stopped one behavior only to replace it with another. The process of all addictions is the same, regardless of whether it is an addiction to drugs or activities. The word *addiction* comes from the Latin word *addicere*, "to be given over unto." Addictions and compulsions are attempts to soothe pain. Mate Gabor stated it succinctly in a lecture: "There is a continuum of addictions in our society; some are highly rewarded like workaholism and caretaking. All addiction is self-medication. The question we should ask is not 'why addiction,' but 'why the pain that is being soothed?'"

Those who have tried for years to stop addictive behaviors often find their addictive or compulsive behavior decreases after grief work. They find themselves more capable of assertiveness in relationships and in their professional lives without consciously practicing elaborate skills. Those who have been compulsive caretakers find that saying yes or no now comes from a place of internal comfort rather than from a place of anxiety and fear.

Some Adult Children have lived their lives with caseloads rather than friendships. They are often able to begin setting limits after completing grief work. Sometimes this results in angry responses from those who cannot handle relationships where there is an expectation of two-way traffic. Some individuals cannot accept a relationship of equality because of their own unmet dependency needs. For others, behavior change may mean a change of career based on one's own needs rather than painful generational legacies. Like Joan the ballet dancer, many ACOAs have not chosen a career but have followed a script influenced by their parents' painful pasts.

After grief work it is possible to follow one's own dreams rather than someone else's. For most Adult Children, behavior change includes leading a much more balanced life. The graphs on page 143 reflect the changes in the balance of Joan's life after grief work. The first graph represents the way Joan spent her time before grief work, the second her life in greater balance after the tears.

After the tears, Adult Children regain spontaneity. They free the child inside from the bondage of past generations and with that freedom, they regain choice. Janet, the mother we met earlier, realized

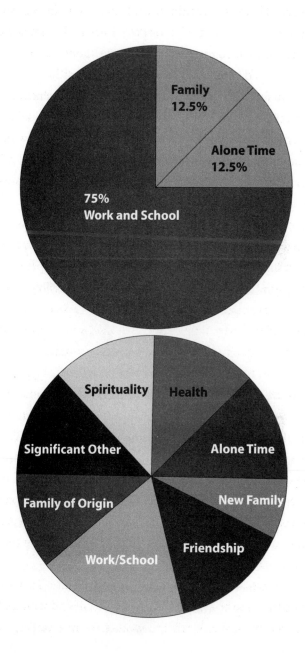

that losses in the past can never be completely regained in the present. Janet was not able to ride a merry-go-round horse at the age of five, nor was she able to experience many of the joys that are normal for a five-year-old. She realized, however, that although five was gone forever, she could enjoy some childhood experiences in adult life and part of the experience could be reclaimed through her new-found freedom and spontaneity. It is not possible to retrieve the lost experiences of childhood—we can never be five years old again—but we can develop a range of experiences as adults that were not possible in childhood.

We can never go back and be loved unconditionally, but we can *ask* for nurturing as adults. We can begin new rituals for this generation and future ones. After the tears, we can open up to a life of touch, warmth, and spontaneity that was not possible when the child inside was encased in ice.

Giving Back

As we move forward in our healing journey, the painful legacy of growing up in an alcoholic family can be turned into compassion and empathy for others who have gone through similar painful life experiences. The National Association for Children of Alcoholics (NACOA) was founded by those who wanted to reach out and help children growing up in alcoholic and addicted families.

We have been struck by the number of Adult Children in our workshops who continually reach out to other Adult Children, empowering them in their healing process and offering support and compassion. Sometimes the smallest gestures can have the most impact, as they did for Ann.

Ann and her husband, Bob, attended a workshop for Adult

Children of Alcoholics. Both experienced pain throughout the day as they realized more and more of their childhood losses. The next day, instead of forcing herself to go to work, as would have been her pattern, Ann decided to allow herself the time and space to experience some of the sadness she was still feeling after the workshop. Bob was supportive of her decision to "take the time she needed and be good to herself."

The first thing Ann did on her day off was to call her best friend, who was also an Adult Child. She sobbed over the phone and told her friend, "I realized that I will never be an eight-year-old again." She asked her friend to come over and spend the day. Her friend soon appeared at Ann's house with popcorn, coloring books, crayons, peanut butter and jelly sandwiches, and "jammies with feet." Ann's friend didn't tell her that her feelings were inappropriate or the expression of them made others uncomfortable. She didn't put Ann down for taking the day off. Instead, she held Ann and let her sob as Ann grieved the loss of an important time in childhood. Then, Ann put on the "jammies with feet" and had fun with her friend as they ate popcorn and peanut butter and jelly sandwiches, and lay on their stomachs on the floor and colored in the coloring books.

With the support of Bob and her best friend, Ann realized that those experiences from childhood couldn't be regained, but she could experience the reparative joy of being a forty-five-year-old eight-year-old, and most important, she could allow herself to feel the warmth, caring, and nurturing of a understanding friend and a loving husband. While she could never reclaim lost childhood moments and experiences, she could open her heart and life to new experiences of play, joy, and nurturing after the tears.

11

I Want You, Want You Gone, Want You Back:
ACOAs in Intimate Relationships

Intimacy means that we can be who we are in a relationship,
and allow the other person to do the same. Being who we are
requires that we can talk openly about things that
are important to us, that we take a clear position
on where we stand on important issues, and that we
clarify the limits of what is acceptable and tolerable to us
in a relationship, allowing the other person to do the same.

—*from* Dance of Intimacy, *by Harriet Lerner*

A COAs OFTEN DON'T KNOW who they are outside the survival roles they have been required to play. It was not acceptable to take a strong position on most things in their birth families,
nor were they allowed to set limits on inappropriate behavior. Most
ACOAs did not learn these tasks developmentally, nor did they witness primary role models who emulated healthy intimacy. Many
begin relationships believing a fantasy of intimacy found in popular

146

love songs or storybooks. "And they lived happily ever after" provides an ending of a story without the plot line. The fairy tales and love songs do not address the speed bumps that will have to be negotiated along the path to "happily ever after."

In couples' therapy, Grace told us that meeting Paul was "the answer to my prayers." They'd met in college. Grace described her dreams for herself with Paul. They were much like those described by many Adult Children of Alcoholics—a fantasy found in a fairy tale where Prince Charming or the loving princess takes us away from all the pain. In that dream, we will live happily ever after—but we don't have the remotest understanding of healthy intimacy and the hard work that goes into relationships, so the dream can sometimes become a nightmare.

Grace sobbed, remembering her wedding day:

> It was perfect. He was perfect. I felt so loved, so protected, so cherished by him. Seeing him at the end of the aisle that day waiting for me, I just knew that he was the man that lonely kid in an alcoholic family dreamed of finding someday. He was someone who would love me and take care of me, and we would make a wonderful family together.
>
> Even though I begged my dad not to drink that day, he had been drinking anyway. I prayed he wouldn't embarrass me. I was literally holding him up as we came down the aisle, just like I figuratively always had. But I knew, as soon as Paul took my hand, that he would be the rock my dad never was. He would love me and hold me during difficult times just as I would him. I would feel the security with Paul that I had always dreamed of.
>
> Now, only two years later, it seems like we fight all the time. He never apologizes and he rarely says he loves me anymore. We have been separated for a couple of weeks and I am so lonely for him, that man I married. It's like after we'd been married for

a few months he became somebody else: self-righteous, opinionated, always wanting his own way, letting me handle everything myself. I just want the man back who loved and cherished me. I want him to be the man I married.

Psychoanalyst Erich Fromm wrote in *The Art of Loving* that children from addicted families often ". . . take the intensity of the infatuation, being 'crazy' about each other for proof of the intensity of their love, while it may only prove the degree of their preceding loneliness" (6). Paul and Grace connected in their pain and loneliness. Grace's father was an alcoholic and her mother spent her life trying to prop him up, all the while denying that he had an addiction. Grace grew up hearing excuse after excuse: Dad was just tired or upset because something happened at work, or he was just celebrating, or he'd just had a couple of drinks. On her wedding day she was told, "He's just celebrating his little girl's special day. It's not every day a man's daughter gets married."

Grace continued to describe her childhood:

Mom and Dad didn't have much of a relationship that I could see. While Mom worked to take care of everything and prop up my dad, I took care of a lot of the household things she didn't have time for, including taking care of my little sister. We all just pretended we lived in Pleasantville and that Dad's drinking and bad moods were normal. When he'd call us names, it was because he was tired. When he drank too much and embarrassed us in front of our friends, it was because he was "a bit grouchy." I always wanted Mom to stand up for us, but she never did; she just made excuses.

Paul also came from an alcoholic home where both parents were alcoholic. He had been the target of his dad's rages, and his sister had been the target of his mom's emotional abuse. His sister, like Grace, had been the caretaker in the family. Paul was the lost little boy and his sister had done her best to take care of him. Paul, too, talked in early therapy sessions about his feelings that Grace had been his ideal partner.

> From the very beginning, we were best friends. We began talking to each other when we were both in a psych class and there was a guest speaker on alcoholism in the family. When the speaker asked if any of us were raised in alcoholic homes, we both raised our hands. It was like we were magnets, immediately attracted to each other. I had never felt so comfortable with anyone. I had never met another person who understood what it was like growing up with alcoholic parents. We connected to each other's pain and were immediately an "item" on campus. We were inseparable. We never fought and now all we do is fight. She was not only my wife but also my best friend—and I want my best friend back.

Shame: The Fuel That Drives Unhealthy Relationship Behavior

Adult Children like Grace and Paul often come into relationships expecting their partners to heal the wounds of a painful past. It's a bit like the alcoholic described by Harriet Lerner in her book *Dance of Intimacy* (17–18), who lost his keys in the alley but insisted upon searching for them by the lamppost because the light was better. Too many times we look for healing outside of ourselves—in our children or our work—when the key to healing our wounds of the past can only be found inside us.

Grace and Paul both came from homes where they felt abandoned in one way or another. Adult Children who feel the pain of abandonment often idealize others in their lives while continuing to diminish their own sense of self-worth. They feel the Other can finally fill the emptiness inside them and provide a sense of security that they have never felt. Since the Other simply cannot supply them with a sense of self and security (because we can only do that for ourselves), the anxiety grows as does the dissatisfaction with a partner who is not their *rescuer* after all. When there are unhealed abandonment issues in the past, any loss in the present will cause old wounds to reopen. The Other is blamed for the feelings of unworthiness and emptiness, and the anger experienced in childhood is aimed at the relationship partner. The partner creates distance upon having the anger directed at him or her and emotional separation follows.

This becomes a vicious cycle. When childhood feelings of abandonment are triggered by the partner leaving or creating distance, the Adult Child once again idealizes the partner and directs the anger and resentment back at him- or herself, giving more power to the partner and less power to the self. The longing for the idealized partner begins once again, creating a yo-yo-like experience in the relationship: "I want you gone. I want you back." In this dance, Paul and Grace were equal partners. Without focus on self, this pattern could continue repeatedly with each other, or with new partners, throughout their lives.

Adult Children project an external image that "all is well," but internally they are bound by shame. "I'm okay, fine, competent, tough, happy, right, and here only to meet your needs." Sometimes, as a defense against the shame, they convince themselves it is the Other who can't handle intimacy, not themselves. They may become more controlling and righteous, demanding the Other to "fix yourself." They may keep the defensive thoughts and feelings that support their denial inside: "There's nothing wrong with me. I want to get close. If only he/she would fix himself/herself, we could finally get close."

For healing to take place, the "in control" mask must be gradually moved aside to allow the true self to be healed and accepted. The feeling behind "if you only knew that I really am (afraid, insecure, vulnerable, frightened, angry), you wouldn't love me," is the shame that stops true intimacy and connection. The mask is used to hide the belief that "If you truly knew that I'm not as tough, secure, or in control as I appear, or if you saw my anger, you wouldn't love me. If I showed my true feelings, you would recognize that I am as unlovable as everyone else in my life has found me to be, and you'd abandon me, too." This protective mask is the barrier that prevents the building of healthy relationships for Adult Children.

Identifying and staying connected to one's true feelings allows for connection to another. Otherwise, one is relating to the world through the protective mask rather than as one's true self. The ACOA believes that it is the mask others find acceptable, not the true self and all the secrets hidden behind the mask. Secrets fuel shame and shame fuels secrets. Secrets create isolation and disconnection in relationships.

Some Adult Children may be attracted to partners who are emotionally inaccessible. Others seek partners who are as emotionally abusive as the alcoholic parent was because hurt and abandonment seem so normal; it is healthy attraction that is suspect. As comedian Groucho Marx once said, "I would not want to belong to a club that would have me as a member."

Psychotherapist Susan Anderson discusses the study of brain chemistry and the power of stored feelings and memories from childhood (emotional time capsules) in *The Journey from Abandonment to Healing*: "Your amygdala-driven emotional memories are triggered, arousing your deep-seated desires: your desire to be loved, nurtured, and accepted. People who can set off this sense of deep longing are pushing your love buttons, the emotional triggers established by childhood attachments . . . This complex process is what you have come to feel as an attraction" (241).

The chemical release created by fear of abandonment may have created a feeling that was confused with "love." Once a relationship that evokes the feelings of past shaming or abandonment has been formed with a partner, some Adult Children may focus on changing their partners into "someone warm and caring who will finally love me"; in trying to heal feelings of earlier abandonment and shame, the cycle is repeated.

Trigger Spirals

Triggers are the sights, sounds, smells, touches, tastes, feeling states, holidays, gestures, and any other prompts in today's environment that open the time capsules inside us and cause an unconscious release of unprocessed memories and emotions from the past. We can be triggered by other things, too; for example, every age our children turn has the potential to release the emotions and memories of the child we were at that age. When the time capsules are triggered, fragments of strong emotion or pieces of memory spill out, frequently orchestrating unhealthy behaviors. A trigger spiral is when one person in a relationship is triggered and their behavior or response triggers their significant other, and that response triggers the first person, and so on.

Jason and Jennifer met in a support group for ACOAs. Both were caretakers in their families of origin. Both of Jennifer's parents were alcoholic binge drinkers who got drunk several weekends a month. Her parents were emotionally and physically abusive and her uncles, who were often at her parents' drunken parties, were sexually abusive. Jennifer spent much of her early life taking care of her younger brother and sister, making sure the house ran smoothly, keeping her sister safe from her uncles' and father's rages, and trying to ignore her mother's hurtful words. She also did her best to keep her mother safe when her dad was in a drunken rage. Her mother was emotionally abusive to everyone in the family when she was sober and passive when she was drunk. Her father was passive when he was sober and violent when he was drunk. "I used to try to be a little scientist," Jennifer said, "watering down my dad's drinks and putting more liquor into my mom's."

Jennifer was also, as she put it so well in an early ACOA group, "a poster child for hypervigilance." She described her role when her parents were on a binge.

> During drunken parties at my house, safety depended on my ability to accurately read the stages of alcohol intoxication, to know just when my dad and mom were about to get combative and when violence was about to happen. I had to get my brother and sister under the bed and out of harm's way and then make sure that my mother would live through my dad's physical rages. I also had to move fast enough to avoid my uncles' wet slobbery kisses and yucky touches.

Jason grew up with a dad who was an alcoholic and a mom who was overly controlling. He was, like Jennifer, the caretaker in their family, helping his mom run the household and take care of his younger brother.

> For the most part, my dad just drank in isolation, although at times he was emotionally abusive to me, my mom, and my younger brother. I didn't realize for years that my dad's drinking and shaming didn't affect me as much as my mom's constant attempts to control my life. I was, as she so often said, "the apple of her eye, her good boy."

I remember feeling proud of helping things run smoothly in the family and yet also felt smothered by my mom's praise and attention. It was like I just couldn't breathe.

For many years, until I began going to support groups, I didn't realize how much my mother's need to control my life affected me. I thought it was just discipline, but I couldn't get away from her— either her continual uncomfortable praise or her interference in my life. She would even call my employer or school principal when I was a teenager if she didn't think they were treating me fairly, and she was a constant interference in my relationships. Even when I was in college, she called the girl I was dating and told her she should leave me alone because she was a "tramp." I was mortified. We finally broke up because she couldn't take my mother's calls anymore. I really loved her. I still think about her today.

To get a bird's-eye view of a trigger spiral, let's visit the home of Jason and Jennifer one Saturday afternoon after they started couple's counseling. They had cuddled in bed until midmorning, then enjoyed a leisurely breakfast, which they prepared together. They sat on the couch after breakfast deciding what they would each do that day. Jason said that he wanted to get some things at the hardware store so they could spend the next day completing the deck they were adding to the house. He was also expecting a call from an out of state colleague who would be coming to town on Monday

In their previous therapy sessions they had learned to ask each other for "gifts" of time and tolerance. Jennifer knew that Jason didn't especially care for reggae concerts, so she was careful in her wording. "The reggae band I have been so anxious to see is playing a matinee concert at the theater this afternoon," she began. "They will only be here today, and I really want to see them, but I want to spend time with you, too. I know reggae isn't your favorite music but the band has gotten great reviews and I would really like to see it. Would you give me the gift of going to the concert with me?" Then she suggested that they could go to the hardware store on the way and still make it to the theater on time.

Jason, not altogether delighted by the suggestion, still wanted to please Jennifer. He made a face, sighed, and said he'd go.

"No, it's all right Jason, I can tell by your face that you don't want to go."

"Look, we're going, okay?" Jason reached out and put his arm around Jennifer and both agreed on the plan for the day.

The concert, as expected, was exciting for Jennifer; she loved the music, yet at the same time she was distracted. As she watched Jason, she became concerned that he looked bored.

"Are you okay?" she kept asking.

"Yes" he said. As Jennifer continued to ask the same question, Jason began to get irritated.

First I give her the gift of coming to the concert, now I have to enjoy it as well? he thought. *I wish she would quit asking me.*

He really doesn't want to be here, Jennifer thought. *He's not enjoying it. We shouldn't have come. He's going to get sulky and spoil the rest of our weekend.*

As they left the theater, Jason turned on his cell phone and realized that he had missed the call from his out of state colleague. "Damn," he said in irritation, "I missed his call." Jason feared he'd missed the small window of time when his colleague would be able to speak on Saturday, as the man would be out of the service area for the rest of the day. He quickly dialed the number of the missed call and got an answering machine.

"Damn, damn, damn," Jason said, abruptly putting the cell phone away.

"I'm sorry, Jason," Jennifer apologized. "You probably shouldn't have come. I'm sorry."

"Will you quit saying you're sorry, for God's sake? It isn't your fault that he can't be reached. I'm just frustrated," Jason said.

"What did you need to talk with him about?" Jennifer asked, hoping to move into a more conversational area and out of the tension that seemed to be building between them.

"Just stuff," was his abrupt reply.

"You don't have to be like that. I'm just trying to have a conversation!"

"Well, this doesn't concern you. Let's just get home."

"My work doesn't concern you either, but we talk about it. You're angry. I apologized, for heaven sake. I thought we were going out to dinner."

Jason abruptly turned the car around, fuming.

"Forget dinner. You don't have to act like this, damn it," Jennifer said as she folded her arms, pulling away into silence.

"Don't tell me how to act. I'm taking you to dinner, aren't I? What's wrong with you now?" he asked angrily.

"No you're not. Just take me home. I'm sick to death of your moods and I'm not going to sit across the table from you in silence."

Jason stopped the car. "*My* moods? Just get off my back and make up your mind. Are we going to dinner or not?"

"Why don't you just tell me you're angry and we can talk about it?" Jennifer asked, reaching over to touch his knee.

"Damn it, I'm not angry. Quit telling me how I feel!" he answered, pulling his knee away.

Jennifer stared out the window in silence, tears falling down her cheeks.

"Answer me, damn it. Which way am I directing the car. What do you want?"

His question was met with silence.

"All right, don't answer me. We're going home." Jason turned the car around again and stepped on the gas. When they returned home, they both got out of the car, slammed their respective doors, and headed to their own spaces where they stayed for the rest of the weekend.

Trauma triggers in Adult Children are frequently set off in significant relationships because the original attachment figures (parents or parent substitutes) are the source of the emotional pain in alcoholic families. Jason and Jennifer had entered a trigger spiral as a family reunion of ghosts made an entrance into their lives. When Jason's facial gestures indicated that he clearly didn't want to go, Jennifer was triggered. She found herself right back in her family with an elephant in the living room, feeling guilty over someone putting himself out for her. She tried to soothe him, take care of him, and apologize to him as she had done with her alcoholic parents when she'd worked to avoid the possibility of violence. But violence was part of her childhood years, not her present life with Jason. She was upset by his refusal to validate the reality of what he was actually feeling. She became hyperalert, scanning the environment for the slightest changes in mood or behavior. In her alcoholic family, safety depended on knowing what was coming.

For his part, Jason didn't want to go to the concert, and on this particular weekend, he really didn't want to give Jennifer the gift of his time and patience. He didn't want to tell her that, so at the point of acceptance, he became triggered. He was being a "good boy" again, putting his needs on hold. When he was at the concert, he didn't want to tell her that he was preoccupied with the phone call that he needed to take care of that weekend. His facial gestures expressed what he couldn't say verbally. When Jennifer began to ask him questions, he felt smothered like he used to with his mother. He was caught in the conflict he'd always felt growing up. He was caught between trying to be good, which meant not having his own thoughts and feelings, and trying to protect himself from being completely controlled and smothered.

For the rest of the weekend, they both did what they had learned in their respective families—they disconnected, felt shame, then isolated and disconnected even more. The patterns continued as they retreated behind masks of stubbornness instead of asking for and receiving comfort from each other, which is what they really wanted. When Jason and Jennifer could talk in their couples therapy session about what they were really feeling and both could accept responsibility for their part in the dance, they were able to come out of their respective corners and support each other. They were then able to become closer and more supportive in the knowledge of the other's feelings, rather than disconnecting and needing to create more distance.

When Talk Is Not Possible: Affect Dysregulation

Many Adult Children of addicted families have lived in chronic stress their entire lives, and they have had to be constantly on guard and alert for emotional danger in their environment—always prepared to fight, flight, or freeze. This repetitive release of stress hormones has serious effects on the Adult Child's ability to accurately read danger cues. In an adult who does not suffer from post-traumatic stress, incoming information —such as a sight, tone of voice, or gesture—is transmitted to the thalamus (the central relay center of the brain) and then onward to the neocortex (the thinking brain). Information is organized and assigned appropriate meaning, which triggers an appropriate emotional response.

In an Adult Child who has been continually exposed to cumulative trauma in childhood, any given stimulus may be experienced as dangerous, given the association to an earlier memory. These stimuli can be such simple things as tone of voice, gestures, internal feelings of anxiety, fear, powerlessness, or even silence. The amygdala, the danger response center of the brain, is activated and it hijacks the process, broadcasting distress and disaster, triggering hormonal flooding, flight or freeze responses, or outbursts of verbal or physical rage.

Life feels like continually living in a time warp for these trauma survivors. As a child of eight it may have been extremely important to read a father's facial expressions to accurately gauge when to get brothers or sisters under the bed before an alcoholic rage began. Or a child may have felt abandoned by a mother who left for the store and didn't come back until the next morning because she stayed out drinking. For an adult, before the traumas of childhood have been processed and healed, a similar expression on a partner's face might be read as a potential threat, causing an ACOA to fight, isolate, or freeze. A partner who comes back from shopping later than planned might trigger old feelings of abandonment or powerlessness in an ACOA, sending him or her into a jealous rage.

When a child in an alcoholic family is continually exposed to trauma and stress, his or her neural network becomes oversensitized to stress. In these cases, Adult Children may have lost the ability to accurately determine whether something is truly emotionally or physically dangerous. He or she may be on guard persistently, alert for the slightest change in a partner's tone of voice or facial expression, or to the slightest indication of potential powerlessness or abandonment. "People with PTSD go immediately from stimulus to response without being able to first figure out what makes them so upset. They tend to experience intense negative emotions (fear, anxiety, anger, and panic) in response to even minor stimuli. This may lead them to either overreact and threaten others or shut down and freeze" (van der Kolk, McFarlane, and Weisaeth, 13).

Remember the amygdala, the danger response center of the brain? When the behavioral response to a trigger or trigger spiral is rage, it is important to note that an individual's higher thinking capability has been hijacked by the amygdala. Talking about issues is not productive until there is some form of emotional rebalancing. It is important for Adult Children to recognize their own physical and emotional reactions to a potential emotional escalation, so both partners can take time to rebalance their neurophysiological states and interrupt a nonproductive or abusive interaction. (See "Taking a Break: Dealing with Trigger Responses" below.) More productive communication can occur when both partners have their feet firmly planted in the reality of today rather in traumatic times of childhood.

Taking a Break: Dealing with Trigger Responses

It is important to believe that you have control over how you respond to triggers. You can discipline yourself to interrupt potentially destructive interactions such as blaming, judging another's intentions, a buildup of jealousy, name calling, or anger beginning to spiral out of control. This can be accomplished by taking a break and practicing one or more of the following techniques every time you feel you are beginning to spiral into unhealthy responses:

Deep Breathing

1. Sit comfortably in a chair or lie down with pillows under your head and knees.

2. Place one hand on your chest and another on your abdomen.

3. Take in a deep breath to the count of six, making sure that you are breathing deeply enough for the hand on your abdomen to move, and then deeper still for the hand on your chest to move.

4. Let out the breath and begin again.

Continue this deep breathing until you feel relaxed. While you are breathing pay close attention to those areas of the body that are tense and need to relax. Adult Children are often shallow breathers because of the many times in childhood when they attempted to remain invisible.

Deep Breathing with Healing Light

Follow the steps given earlier in DEEP BREATHING, only this time close your eyes.

1. With your first indrawn breath, picture with your mind's eye a large circle of healing light forming in front of you.

2. When you breathe out, picture yourself stepping into that circle of healing light. Imagine it surrounding you.

3. As you breathe in again, inhale the magical healing light that is now surrounding you.

4. As you breathe out, let go of your tension, worries, and negative thoughts.

5. As you breathe in again imagine this light traveling from the crown of your head, down your spine to your tailbone, and back up again.

6. As you breathe out again, imagine the tension leaving the areas that have been flooded by the healing light.

7. As you breathe in again, imagine the light suffusing your inner organs: lungs, heart, stomach, and so on.

8. As you breathe out, imagine the tension leaving your inner organs.

9. As you breathe in, imagine the healing light in your bones and muscles, hands, arms, legs, feet, toes, and every cell of your body.

10. As you breathe out, feel the peace as tension leaves every area of your body.

(from The Ultimate Guide to Transforming Anger: Dynamic Tools for Healthy Relationships, *by Jane Middelton-Moz, Lisa Tener, and Peaco Todd)*

Visualization

Another addition to your deep breathing exercise is to imagine yourself going to a place in your mind that is absolutely safe. This place might be a cabin in the woods, a place by a stream, relaxing on an island, any place that you can feel is absolutely safe. As you are relaxing in your safe place, pay close attention first to the sights around you, then to the smells around you, then to the sounds around you. Relax in your safe place until you feel a sense of calm.

Cognitive Refocusing

Sit in a chair with your feet flat on the floor. Notice and verbalize five things you see, five things you hear, five things you smell, and five things you feel. Repeat the exercise counting four things you see, four things you hear, four things you smell, four things you feel, then repeat with three, then two, then one. Make sure you complete from five through one.

Healing in the Embrace of Another

Years ago when I (Jane) was working hard to heal the wounds of growing up in an alcoholic and abusive family, I came home from a particularly painful counseling session and found my husband waiting on the porch with a cup of coffee for me. I took in his comforting embrace and the loving gesture—and burst into tears. I felt cherished and loved, and I had progressed enough in my healing to experience being loved rather than putting up barriers against it. Hundreds of broken promises and toxic childhood relationship experiences had taught me to only depend on myself, because expecting anything from anyone was too painful. After healing the wounds of the past, I could allow nurturing and intimacy in the present rather than distrusting and fighting being given to. I was also learning to allow and enjoy being taken care of on occasion; previously I had only been comfortable when taking care of others. Counseling, hard work on myself, and a relationship of mutual love, give and take, and healthy conflict resolution allowed me to heal and restore my human beingness

As adults, we need healthy attachments—those significant others in our lives who give us sustenance, whom we can support and receive support from in difficult times, with whom we can celebrate successes and life transitions, and who can bear witness to our joys and sorrows.

Dr. Tian Dayton puts a finer point on it in *Emotional Sobriety*: "The presence of regular relationships in our lives actually has a stabilizing effect on our nervous systems because the nervous systems of all humans and even all mammals are interconnected . . . Our limbic systems connect and resonate with those of others, and this resonance helps us to stay in balance" (Dayton, 123).

In Chapter 10 we met Bob and Ann, who referred themselves for marital therapy after reading an article on Adult Children of Alcoholics. Before coming into therapy they had read countless books on fair fighting, marital communication, and child rearing, as well as attended countless workshops on these subjects. They had been excited by each one and had believed they had found the answer to having a happier marriage and a more fulfilling life. They had studied hard and practiced techniques, yet after a time they fought even more about the other's unwillingness to follow the methods outlined. Bob and Ann had read the characteristics of Adult Children of alcoholic families and had made an appointment searching for yet another answer.

There was a lot of humor in the first session, and they appeared to be entering therapy with the same degree of perfectionism that they had when facing other things in their life, like marriage and child rearing. They were told, "You won't get an A in here. You sound as if you wanted to come to therapy to get rid of the characteristics of being Adult Children in two and a half weeks. Do either of you ever let up on yourselves?" They presented examples of their disagreements and talked about the techniques they had used unsuccessfully to solve problems.

Throughout their counseling it was apparent that most of their difficulty stemmed from injured feelings that were out of proportion with reality. Ann regularly felt attacked by Bob, and she felt that he never approved of her or respected and appreciated what she did. Bob felt that Ann *never* responded to his needs, although it was clear that he rarely stated them. Both attempted to read each other's minds and carefully processed responses to questions and needs without ever stating them, then accused the other of lack of sensitivity. They each made statements like, "But you never asked," "I never

said that. You're angry at me for something I don't even feel," or
"You never said you needed that. How am I supposed to know?"
Most of their communication was heard by their respective injured
children of the past, and most of their accusations to each other
were the words never said to abusive, critical, or abandoning parents. The bond permanence to their demanding, shaming parents
had been substituted with bond permanence to a new spouse.

We all need healthy relationships that can assist in our healing
rather than complicate it. Here are some additional suggestions that
might be helpful in continuing to build healthy relationships.

- Let your partner know when one of your time capsules has been opened.
  Take a break if your emotions begin to escalate. Work to understand your
  triggers and be in charge of them—don't let them be in charge of you.
  When you glean new understanding, communicate it to your partner;
  this will strengthen connection between you rather than strengthen
  disconnection.

- Learn to turn to your partner for comfort and understanding, rather
  than licking your wounds by yourself as you learned to do in your childhood years. In his article "The Healing Power of Relationships," author
  Daniel Goleman quotes John Cacioppo, director of the Center for
  Cognitive and Social Neuroscience at the University of Chicago who
  addresses this crucial need for connection:

  > The emotional status of our main relationships has a significant
  > impact on our overall pattern of cardiovascular and neuro-
  > endocrine activity . . . In short, my hostility bumps up your blood
  > pressure, your nurturing love lowers mine. Potentially we are
  > each other's biological enemies or allies.

- When processing conflict, listen to your partner with your whole being. Don't expend energy preparing your defense like an attorney.

- Beware of mind reading. As we've discussed many times in this book, children in addicted families needed to be hypervigilant in order to survive. It was often important in childhood to guess at an adult's needs and wishes and attempt to fulfill them to avoid further emotional, and sometimes physical, injury. Unless you live in an abusive relationship, the need for hypervigilance has passed. Asking questions, believing the answers, and asking for needs to be met strengthens communication.

- Watch your language and avoid "never" and "always." It is important to work on realistic communication. "You never listen" is an exaggeration and doesn't promote healthy problem resolution.

- If you're wrong, say so. Right won't keep you warm at night. It is a big step for you, an Adult Child, to learn that you can live through sincere apology. Apologizing for hurting another's feelings or for being late, or forgetting something that is important to your partner, will no longer render you powerless or cause your entire being to be "wrong." It is okay to make mistakes. It is also useful to communication to apologize blamelessly sometimes. Saying "I'm sorry you're feeling so frustrated" with sincerity can be very comforting. It is important for each person to take responsibility for his or her part in a disagreement without blaming.

- Deal with conflict in a "good" way. It is not possible to be in a relationship without occasional conflict. It is the nature of being human. The emotional or physical violence or void we felt as children is not "normal, healthy conflict." Compromise is important for growth when there is disagreement in a relationship. If you don't like to travel but your partner does, give him or her the gift of making a trip once or twice a year. If your partner has a hobby that is not "your thing," learn about it and support it. Every once in a while, your partner may hurt your feelings or do something that bothers you. It is important that you first ask if you may speak to him or her. Then let him or her know how you feel when he or she (fill in the blank). Then, let him or her know what you need. Always end with your appreciation for his or her willingness to hear you.

- Take ownership for your own behavior. Being a victim is not a good career choice. Adults who grew up in painful and shaming environments often felt powerless. As Adult Children, we can feel that we are being controlled when we do not exercise choice. We have the power to control our lives, and that power is within us.

- Create an emotional savings account. Adult Children from addicted families often do not know what normal is. It is normal in healthy relationships to have times of joy and closeness and times of conflict and normal anger. Our relationships go through peaks and valleys, and it is helpful to have a healthy emotional savings account for difficult times.

- Too often in relationships, whether friendships or love relationships, we focus on problem areas and fail to mention or remember the acts of kindness and caring. It is important to acknowledge the day-to-day kindnesses and gestures of love from our partners and friends and not take them for granted. It is equally important to remember those gestures when the going gets rough.

Feed Your Couple's Tree

Feed the "Couple's Tree" (your intimate relationship) every so often. On a recent trip I (Jane) was eating dinner at a restaurant and noticed an older couple sitting across from me who ate their entire meal in awkward silence. They didn't look at each other or even acknowledge each other. I didn't get the sense that they were fighting but rather had taken each other for granted for so long that they were no longer connected. It caused me to remember a quote I once read from Mary Tyler Moore: "Sometimes you have to get to know someone really well to realize you're really strangers." Just as it is important to occasionally fertilize the plants in our gardens, it is also important to feed our relationships. Our favorite spring flowers can't grow in sand, and relationships have difficulty growing without tending to them now and again. Surprising each other with special treats or gifts of kindness for no particular reason, or giving the other a card that expresses your appreciation for him or her feeds a relationship and helps it grow. Doing things out of the ordinary, like taking a vacation together, seeing new sights, or trying new things together, allows relationships to expand and become richer with time. Most important, don't neglect each other or take each other for granted. It is often extremely hard for Adult Children to apologize, say "I love you," acknowledge their own needs, accept gifts from others, and go toward, rather than away, from others when the going gets rough. A wise Native American elder who was speaking about our need for connection and the difficulties in our world today mused, "We need each other and sometimes we have no idea how much we need each other."

12

Misplaced Loyalty:
The Codependency Factor

Codependency is a trauma-related loss of self
that happens slowly throughout our personality development . . .
It is fear based and is a predictable set of qualities
and behaviors that grows out of feeling anxious
and therefore hypervigilant in our intimate relationships.

—*from* Emotional Sobriety: From Relationship Trauma
to Resilience and Balance, *by Tian Dayton, Ph.D.*

CHILDREN IN ALCOHOLIC FAMILIES, particularly those children who became the caretakers and pleasers in the family, became adept at reading the behavioral cues of those around them. Their very survival depended on scanning the environment accurately for signs of danger. Many Adult Children have lost touch with their own feelings, thoughts, and needs. "Our scanning is tied in with our fear response, which is tied in with our survival response. We get scared, we freeze, we scan. It is the co-dependent dance" (Dayton, 152).

The original definition of a codependent was the partner of the alcoholic who developed a "mirror illness" because of the distorted and unbalanced thinking and behavior that surrounded the addiction. The codependent covered for the alcoholic and joined the partner's denial system, saying in effect, "There is nothing wrong here, and don't talk about it." We now know that codependency develops not only in the partners of alcoholics, but in their children as well.

Theresa developed her codependency in her alcoholic family long before she met her first husband. Theresa wears herself out caretaking for others, yet won't allow anyone to care for her because without the needs and adoration of those around her, she doesn't know who "she" is. Like many Adult Children, she appears self-confident, self-assured, rigid in her thinking, and even righteous at times. Yet she puts herself down if she makes even the slightest mistake or error in judgment. She often becomes outwardly defensive if someone disagrees with or criticizes her thoughts, beliefs, or behaviors. Yet, she will suffer internally and obsess over the imagined or real criticism for days until she can correct the other person's perception or can somehow "prove them wrong," at least to herself. She punishes herself if she isn't the perfect mother and grandmother, the perfect friend, the perfect employee, and perfect mate. She is terrified of change because when anything around her changes, she feels out of control.

In short, Theresa is exhausted from trying to balance and juggle everything in her world as she tries to make sure everyone likes her. Without the approval of others, she cannot approve of herself. Her self-worth comes from the outside, rather than from the inside. Because her children are "hers," they must also be perfect in the eyes of others, or she must suffer because of their imperfections.

One afternoon Theresa went to visit her best friend, hoping for a sympathetic ear. Her adult daughter had told her she was feeling "smothered" by her mother. Theresa felt as though the wind had been knocked out of her when she heard her friend's words:

> Sometimes, Theresa, even with what I know are your very best intentions, those of us who love you often feel overwhelmed and a bit controlled by your behavior. To be fair, let me just speak for myself. I am always touched by your generous nature, bringing me things you think I might need, taking care of my house while I'm gone, and always listening to me when I'm down. I am very grateful for your generosity. Lately though, I have been feeling that our friendship is one-sided. You have difficulty accepting things from me. You also seem to get annoyed when I don't take the advice you offer me. Last fall when I confided in you about some difficulties in my relationship, instead of just listening, you began giving me advice and then got angry when I didn't do what you suggested. You didn't speak to me for three weeks. I love you and want to be your friend, but sometimes your behavior is a bit overwhelming.

At first Theresa became extremely anxious, and then she became defensive. She felt as though everyone was ganging up on her. She had come to her best friend for comfort because she'd had a similar conversation with her adult daughter earlier that week. Now her best friend was siding with her daughter. Didn't they understand she was just trying to help? *Well,* she thought, *I just won't offer help to either one of them anymore and see how they like that.* Instead of expressing her thoughts to her friend, she said, "Thank you for letting me know how you feel. I am not angry. I don't get angry. You're entitled to your feelings and I'm sure you think you're helping. I just need to think about all this." As she left, she promised herself she would never confide in her friend again.

Theresa, like many Adult Children of addicted parents, focuses on others in her world and feels the need to manage the problems and difficulties of everyone around her. Even though her intentions are good, her focus on others is not for their sake but rather is on managing the intense anxiety she has felt since childhood. As a child, it was her role in her addicted family to make sure that everything was taken care of, which allowed her to feel safe. Her hypervigilance has continued as an adult, even though the danger she felt as a child has passed.

Relating Instead of Reacting

Children in addicted families lose touch with their reactions to what is going on around them. They cannot process their own feelings because in survival adaptation, the thinking part of the brain is not available. When Theresa gives feedback to her daughter about how her grandchildren are being raised, her daughter views it as interference. When her daughter lets her children pick out their own clothes for school, Theresa is upset because, "they just don't match. The teachers at school might think the children are not cared for." She not only does her job at work, but also covers for the alcoholic coworker who repeatedly misses work. She does this because, "the boss might think I am not doing my own work." She thinks her friend's venting about her partner means she has to do something to solve her friend's problems. *What kind of friend would I be if I didn't help her fix things?* she wonders.

Theresa also has a relationship history of being attracted to men who "need" her, and then she becomes frustrated when they don't appreciate her efforts to "fix" them. She has been married twice. Her first husband was an alcoholic and the second was clinically depressed, irresponsible, and underfunctioning. She devoted her life to "fixing" each of them, remaining steadfast and loyal. Each man ended up leaving her for another woman.

An important part of healing is learning how to identify and then express feelings. It is easy to understand what a difficult task this is for an ACOA when we hear Theresa's story.

I don't know what I thought about anything when I was a child. I don't think I ever knew my reaction to my dad's drinking. I never thought about it. I just reacted. I never learned how to relate to others, only how to survive around them. I learned to look strong even when I didn't feel strong. My survival depended on making others around me satisfied or at least not angry. Later, I marveled at how people related. I didn't know how to make small talk and I didn't know how to play. I didn't even understand the jokes my peers told. I was terrified out of my wits at the thought of dating. Then, I met my husband.

He needed me. That was a piece of cake. I knew how to do that. I knew how to be needed. I knew how to take care of him and I did. Later, when he became emotionally abusive to me, I didn't even think it was abuse most of the time. Then later, when he was emotionally abusive to my daughter, I knew what to do. I could stand up for her before I could stand up for me. I didn't even know who "me" was. All my life I have been so preoccupied with getting it right and with the moods and problems of other people, I never fully learned who I was. I don't think I even knew what color was my favorite. If someone said I looked good in orange, I wore orange. If someone else said orange didn't look good, I wore the color they liked. I used to think I was pathetic. Now I understand that I was having a normal response to a painful life and don't call myself names anymore.

Overfunctioning Meets Underfunctioning: Steps of the Codependent Dance

We are frequently attracted to the emotional qualities in others that we have had to disown in ourselves. The characteristics that attracted us are often the qualities that anger us later when we seek to control and fix the behaviors that attracted us in the first place.

An Adult Child who has grown up overfunctioning as the caretaker in his or her family of origin is often attracted to an individual who becomes childlike or dependent in the relationship. Each member of this dyad is thinking "love at first sight," but by overfunctioning, one member of a relationship can teach the other to underfunction. Our society tends to view the overfunctioning individual as "healthy" and the "underfunctioning" one as unhealthy or "sick." A friend of mine commented recently about a coworker's relationship: "That woman takes care of the kids, she works, gardens, and keeps the house spotless while pursuing her Ph.D. What's wrong with her partner? How does she put up with her?" One frequently sees the dependent partner as dysfunctional without realizing that the couple is engaged in a dance created and sustained by both partners.

It is important to note that when we are talking about codependency, we are not talking about someone who cares for others or someone who is loyal to their commitment in a relationship when the going gets rough. We are talking about an individual who has the volume knob on caretaking turned up high and no longer has control over the volume. They focus on the needs, feelings, and expectations of others to the exclusion of their own, and are more often than not attracted to those who "need" them.

Dr. Murray Bowen, founder of Bowen Family Systems, initially described overfunctioning and underfunctioning as the steps in the codependency dance, a process of interaction in a couple where one partner takes on more and more responsibility as their partner takes on less and less. This dance can also apply to relationships with siblings, family, friends, or coworkers. Overfunctioning individuals act as though they know what is right for everyone around them and proceed to take charge whether asked to or not. Adult Children like Theresa don't know how to be "team players," and they have difficulty taking care of themselves or knowing or sharing their vulnerabilities and needs. They teach family, friends, and coworkers to rely on them, while at the same time complaining that others aren't doing their share, or that they have no one to lean on.

For the codependent, the overfunctioning behavior is a defense against anxiety. This behavior, which was perfected in childhood, allows the Adult Child to remain "other focused," thereby escaping focus on self. An overfunctioner is often the one at a funeral who is taking care of all the arrangements and offering support to everyone around while remaining stoic. Friends and family members often comment, "Isn't she doing well? Isn't she strong?" In truth, the codependent is protecting herself from the pain of loss because she is afraid to break down and doesn't know how to express sadness or how to grieve. As one ACOA told me, "I'm afraid if I open the 'loss cabinet' inside of me I will never stop crying or maybe I will even go crazy."

When others compliment the overfunctioner for being strong they are feeding a beleaguered self-worth and reinforcing the codependent behavior. It becomes more difficult to change this pattern as time goes on, because it works. It is a defense against feeling and change as well as an acceptable method for allowing the individual to receive applause from others. But as Dr. Harriet Lerner explains in her book *The Dance of Intimacy,* it is based in childhood anxiety:

This rigidity exists because overfunctioning is not just a bad habit, a misguided attitude, an overzealous wish to be helpful, or a behavior pattern caused by living with a chronically underfunctioning individual such as an alcoholic spouse; overfunctioning, like underfunctioning, is a patterned way of managing anxiety that grows out of our experience in our first family and has deep roots in prior generations. (103)

Healing: Feeling the Anxiety and Letting It Go

There is an old saying that for us describes the task of healing from codependency for Adult Children: "Short-term pain allows for long-term gain." Working through the steps to healing can be a painful process, but the rewards of leading a life that is free from the chains of the past is worth the hard work.

Healing from codependency follows similar steps to the other types of healing we've described so far. You'll probably recognize the similarities.

1. Taking the risk to speak the truth.

2. Validating the losses: "I am not crazy. I am having a normal response to an abnormal and painful life."

3. Developing a cognitive life raft of understanding that you can hold on to during the pain; a cognitive understanding of the beginning, middle, and end of the process of healing the losses of childhood.

4. Building a relationship of safety with someone you can learn to trust and who can be an "honest mirror" for you.

5. Accepting the strengths you have always had and working with your resiliency.

6. Recovery from addictions and learning more about your feeling landscape.

7. Doing grief work: giving a face to the child you were.

8. Mourning and forgiveness: giving a face to others in your life, past and present.

9. Forgiving the people who have hurt you, while holding them accountable for their actions. We can develop empathy for the person regarding the baggage they may have had to carry in life, but we don't have to let them put us down or be abusive to us today. In this way, we let go of the powerlessness and anger that has served to bind us to a painful past.

10. Changing behavior and owning the behavior we have developed that has been fueled by pain. This step may also include our amends to others who we may have hurt along the way. Behavior change means understanding and owning our own triggers and being responsible for taking the time and space necessary to work through anxiety rather than allowing it to direct our behavior.

Because her overfunctioning behavior was such a normal reaction to stress in her life, Theresa would change her behavior for a period of time, only to return to old behavior when she felt increased anxiety.

I remember the terrifying feelings the first time I let go of managing the household budget and let my very capable new significant other pay the bills. The anxiety I felt was horrendous. I thought, *If I don't do it, they will take our house. I will be a bag lady on the street.*

Then I asked myself how old I felt and allowed myself to remember the anxiety I felt when bill collectors came to our door when I was nine. I rode out the anxiety and allowed myself to live in the present, risking being loved even when I didn't do

everything, risking trusting someone to actually take care of things.
I had a lot of anxious moments and checked the envelopes to be
mailed at times so I could assure myself that all the bills were
getting paid, but I eventually just trusted and that was something
really new in my life.

Stopping my overfunctioning behavior was extremely difficult
because it was the way I had managed my anxiety throughout
my childhood, youth, and early adult years. It was so easy to focus
on others, because I didn't have to face the pain of losses or the
terrifying fear of failure or the unknown.

I remember the first time I didn't cover for my coworker when she
didn't come to work on Monday morning. My anxiety built as I let
her take the consequences of her behavior. I just kept telling myself
she wasn't my mother and I wasn't eight years old. I remember she
began to yell at me for not covering for her and getting her in
trouble. In the past, this would have devastated me and I would
have thought about it for weeks. This time, I felt the briefest anxiety
and then didn't own her stuff. Her behavior belonged to her,
not me. She ended up in treatment and that was okay.

As Theresa healed she was able to gradually stop her codependent,
overfunctioning behavior. She was able to develop relationships based
on healthy connection, communication, and autonomy, fueled by
caring and concern for herself and for others.

I think the greatest anxiety I felt was the first time I apologized to
my friend for trying to direct her life with her partner, who I thought
was taking advantage of her. The realization was slow in coming that it
was none of my business and that it was her life. The realization that
I didn't always have to be right was even slower in coming. I found
myself thinking, *She could get hurt and it would be my fault. She
doesn't know what she's doing. She doesn't know what's best for her.
I do. Can't she see that I know better?* I kept returning to the feelings
of the six-year-old child who was trying to protect her sister from our

dad's drunken emotional outbursts, or the seven-year-old making excuses to the neighbors for my dad's moods. I had never apologized to anyone in my adult life and saying "I'm sorry" was frightening.

It was as though if I apologized for this one thing, I was admitting I had been wrong for everything else in my life that I had been blamed for. If I apologized, my friend would somehow take advantage of me and I would forever be in a one-down position to her. What really happened was that she thanked me for apologizing, gave me a hug, and that was it. She never brought it up again. My self-esteem didn't collapse and she didn't try to take power and control over my life. I had said I was "just fine" my entire life, only this time after working so hard on myself, I really was.

As we previously discussed, people tend to be attracted to the emotional qualities in another that they lack or have had to disown. The characteristics that we initially found so attractive in a potential partner are often the very same qualities we seek to control or change later. When we become angry and attempt to "fix" the other person's behaviors—the same behaviors we used to admire—we become caught in a self-destructive pattern of codependency. Focusing on the needs, feelings, and expectations of others to the exclusion of our own merely perpetuates the cycle of trauma from one generation to the next. By working through the healing steps we've described, the codependency dance can end and we can create honest relationships with partners, spouses, children, and parents, and create a healthy legacy for the next generations.

13

Empowering Change
in a Painful Legacy:
Adult Children and Sibling
Relationships

> . . . The legacy of the dysfunctional family is not just the emo-
> tional trauma caused by parental abuse and neglect, but also
> and significantly, a toxic disruption of the normal loving bonds
> that siblings would otherwise share.
>
> —from Sibling Betrayal and Estrangement in
> Dysfunctional Families, by Maria Sirota, M.D.

IN CHAPTER 2 WE MET Tanya and her brother, Paul. You'll recall
that although they were raised by the same alcoholic parents in
the same home, they viewed their childhoods through very different
lenses. To deal with the chronic stress of their environment, both
children learned to adapt with denial and repression.

Siblings often have completely different memories of their alcoholic families—memories that may be colored by adopted survival
adaptations, roles in the family, gender, and birth order. It can be
frustrating for an ACOA to reach out to a sibling for support while

working through painful family memories, only to find that their sibling's memory of the family is absent or is filtered through a lens of denial.

Janet was frustrated after her return from a weekend visit with her brother. As she explained to her support group, she had visited him to learn more about her childhood. She had also hoped to find a family ally in healing, but came to realize how different her brother's memories were from her own. They both recognized that their family was alcoholic, yet he didn't remember the domestic violence with the same clarity she did:

> I just can't believe my brother and I grew up in the same family. How could we possibly have such different memories? I sometimes feel like my brother was raised in a family down the street that didn't have nearly the same level of violence that ours did. I was the caretaker in the family who tried to stop the family fights when Mom and Dad were drunk, and my brother was in his room with the door shut, trying to block out the noise and pain. I was also trying my hardest to rebel against my mother's prophecy that I was "no good and would never amount to anything," while my brother was trying to escape from my mother's smothering dreams and expectations for him—she wanted him to be the next President of the United States. It was like we were raised in different families. I guess in some ways we were.

The role we played in the family, our birth order, our physical appearance, temperament, parental fears and unmet dreams, and even our names play a role in how we were treated in the family, what our experiences were, and when, how, or if we approach the recovery process. Caretakers, for instance, were often the first to come to our early ACOA workshops. They not only wanted healing for themselves, but the entire family as well.

Parental Hopes and Fears

Every child is born with some talent, but many children born in alcoholic or dysfunctional families cannot explore those talents and become what they might have been. It is often difficult for parents to see their child's developing self and support them when those parents suffer from their own trauma. When parenting tools consist of only a music box that plays the same refrain over and over—"The hopes and fears of all the years are met in thee tonight"—a child's talents may never come to fruition. For example, a little girl who may have become a gifted swimmer may never have the opportunity to explore her talents, because her mother, who almost drowned when she was a child, instilled a fear of water in the little girl from an early age.

The musical term *resonance* is applicable to this passing on of trauma. Dictionary.com defines it as "the state of a system in which an abnormally large vibration is produced in response to an external stimulus, occurring when the frequency of the stimulus is the same, or nearly the same, as the natural vibration frequency of the system." If you hold a tuning fork and play that same note on the piano, the tuning fork will resonate—you will hear the tone ringing from the tuning fork and feel vibrations running through it—even though it has not been struck.

We all have emotional tuning forks that resonate when an experience is similar to an experience we have had before. A mother may instill the fear of water in her oldest daughter without instilling it in her younger son. Instead, the son may be the gifted swimmer because he wasn't born a girl or was not the oldest child his mother had been, so the resonance was not there as it was for his sister.

Joan, the dancer mentioned in earlier chapters, was never allowed to wear her own face because of her mother's unmet dream of becoming a dancer. If Joan had a younger sister, she might not have felt pressure to became a dancer, because Joan already took that role. Instead, her sister's desires, wishes, and talents might have stayed on the back burner because of her mother's focus on Joan. Joan's sister might have felt forever in Joan's shadow, envying her sister as "the apple of her mother's eye," and even possibly even hating her for the attention she received, never understanding that Joan was no more "seen" than she was.

Physical appearance also plays a role in the child's experience in the family. The child's appearance might resemble an adored, hated, or feared relative, which too frequently makes it impossible for the child to wear his or her own face. For parents who divorced legally but never severed their ties emotionally, a child who resembles the despised parent can forever be a reminder of emotional pain or anger that has never been worked through. Children may be rejected or ignored merely because of their looks. One mother yelled at her son, "You not only look like your father, but you act like him. You are going to be an alcoholic just like he was."

In some cases, a child may be named after a person and wear that person's face and persona rather than his or her own. The name may come with a legacy that either causes the parent to overly attach to or to be repulsed by the child. Meg, for instance, was born a few months after her father's sister (also named Meg) died in a car accident. Meg remembered her father getting drunk night after night, holding her in his lap, and talking to her as if she was his dead sister—sometimes loving her, sometimes being angry at her for leaving him. When her father was sober, he simply avoided his daughter. "I don't ever remember my father looking at me," Meg remembered. "When he looked at me he saw my aunt. I was never his daughter."

Her name and the timing of her birth prevented Meg from being a person in her own right in her father's eyes. A parent's love, adoration, permissiveness, rigidity, acceptance, or lack of acceptance might resonate with the name the child has been given.

In some cases, a child's temperament plays a role in how he or she is treated in the family. When your mother's recollections include statements such as "Susan was such an easy child. She never gave us a minute's trouble," the unspoken words are that you, the other sister or brother, have been trouble from the moment you were born. A child may evoke feelings of emptiness, incompetence, failure, hostility, or resentment in a parent (or even an older, parentified sibling) because the child wanted attention and energy that the caretaker didn't have to give. He or she might be defined from infancy as a "problem child." The child's needs, although normal, may become the foundation of his or her legacy in the family. Susan, the "easy child" who was as imprisoned by her temperament and birth order as her brother, might resent the years she was forced to take care of him and believe the labels others assigned him from infancy: "Gary was always difficult, even when he was a baby. Mother couldn't make him stop crying so she gave him to me. He was always demanding attention and still is. Nothing I did was ever enough."

Birth Order

Another factor that might make our experiences in and memories of our families different from our siblings is our birth order. The firstborn child in the family is usually the serious, responsible child, often mirroring the internalized parents. The oldest child (or sometimes the oldest girl) in an alcoholic or addicted family is usually the caretaker/hero child. The caretaker in the family sacrifices his or her childhood in return for needed love and approval, which he or she rarely gets in the true sense of the words. This child is given too much responsibility at too early an age, often entrusted with the care of younger children when only a child. Adult children who are the caretakers in the family stay strong, need to be right, deny vulnerability and needs, and are often very lonely. As adults, caretaker/heroes in addicted families often develop depression when their caretaking role is no longer working as a defense against fear and anxiety.

Middle-born children are often preoccupied with "fairness." In the sibling birth order, middle children are like the back wheels of a car—they can never catch up with the front wheels. They are always fitted to those in front of and behind them, squeezed from the bottom and the top. In an alcoholic family, they are often the scapegoat children or the lost children. The healthiest among them are able to create healthy networks of support outside the family. Some, however, look for love in all the wrong places and are easily victimized by others they seek out for support and love. In alcoholic families, the adult middle children sometimes try to hold on to those born before and after them in a desperate effort to keep the family together. Others will connect to no one in the family and isolate.

Youngest children are often parented in a far more relaxed and lenient manner. The youngest arrive when most of the roles are taken: Brother might be "the smart one," Sister might be "the athletic one," and a third sibling might be "the popular, attractive one." Youngest children trying to get attention are often like hungry chiggers under everyone's skin. They try to get attention by being "cute" or "annoying." In a healthy family the youngest might become very sociable, relaxed, and funny. In an addicted family this child is often the mascot, trying to distract through clowning or trying to put out the fire by being exceptionally pleasing. As an Adult Child, the youngest might be perceived by others in the family as the most needy and never taken seriously. Mascot/pleaser/clown and scapegoat Adult Children often carry the anger for the family, and the lost child carries the sadness.

An only child literally plays all the roles in the addicted family according to the needs of the family at any given time. Life for only children is like being a piece of taffy—they are often pulled from opposite directions, and the needs and expectations of both parents weigh heavy on their shoulders. Only children are also the absorbers of parental dysfunction, particularly if they don't have other supportive adults to nurture them and to soften the impact of the trauma on their lives. When we work with only children, one of our goals is to help them understand the importance of support people in their lives and the benefits of "chosen family" for their future. As one "only" said:

> I may not have been given siblings, but I have chosen brothers and sisters along the way who are now the colorful and sturdy threads in the fabric of my life. I continually thank them for being the siblings I never had, and I honor myself as well for having the strength to reach out and make good choices. One of my choices was not to remain a lonely only.

When There Is Not Enough Love to Go Around

In the addicted family there is literally not enough love and attention to go around, and children end up competing for and fighting one another for what they don't get. It is a painful truth that parents cannot offer love and parenting when suffering from their own legacy of pain, and it is much easier to blame siblings for snatching the love of the parent from you. In some families, children blame each other for a parent's drinking. Siblings may have little under-standing of the complexity of dysfunctional family life and for fac-tors such as birth order, names, resonance in parents' lives, and other contributing factors. This leads to little empathy for the pain experienced by siblings, and often for the pain experienced in the growing-up years.

In some addicted families the children "circle the wagons" as youngsters and teenagers, offering each other protection from the hurt and abuse in the family, but they drift apart as they reach adult-hood. They don't know how to connect outside the war zone and sometimes they are angry with each other. Some children blame their older siblings for leaving them to care for the alcoholic parent when they marry or go off to school or the service, never realizing that their older siblings weren't supposed to be the parents in the first place. In other families, fighting begins when one or more of the Adult Children has "had enough," leaving another sibling to handle the emotional (and sometimes financial) burden of caring for addicted parents and/or wounded siblings who have begun their own addictions.

Dorothy's father was the youngest of four children and the only boy born to a Scandinavian immigrant family in a Midwestern town. He and all of his sisters had college educations and were the first generation to speak English. Dorothy's mother was the youngest of five children who was born six years after her next-old-est sibling. She was unwanted and grew up with a mother who hated her and was cruel to her.

Dorothy's parents met at a café in town when her father was eighteen and her mother was fourteen. Her father was attracted to her mother's beauty and said to her, "Someday I am going to come back home and marry you." He kept his promise and they were married after she was out of high school. His father's comment about his new daughter-in-law was, "Yah, my son should have married a Scandinavian girl instead."

Dorothy's parents moved six times in the seven years they were married because of her father's work. He was gone for weeks at a time, frequently leaving Dorothy's mother alone and frightened in a new town with two small children. Her father was not much of a communicator, and he prided himself on being a man's man. Her dad had tried to join the Marines during World War II but was rejected because he had a wife and two children.

While he was on one of his trips, Dorothy's mother, who was emotionally broken by both the constant moving and the lack of communication, had finally had enough and left with the children. She gave him no notice, just took them and left without as much as a good-bye. They divorced in the middle of World War II; her father finally enlisted in the Marine Corps. Dorothy was three and a half and her brother, Tom, was five. Her father was killed in the war two years later. Every member of his family blamed her mother and held it against her until each took his or her last breath. Her mother never recovered from her father's death and the family's blame and she became more depressed as the years went by and began drinking.

Dorothy and Tom were close growing up and they relied on each other for support. When Dorothy was nine and Tom was eleven, their mother married a man both of them disliked. The siblings remained close until Tom left for college. Dorothy began drinking when he left and her mother's drinking increased. Tom was bitterly disappointed in both of them. He was also angry, and he felt betrayed by his mom and stepdad, who had promised to help him financially with college expenses, but later reneged on their promise. He never forgave them, which caused a rupture in the relationship between Tom and Dorothy that remained for most of their lives.

Dorothy got sober at age twenty-seven. By then, her mother had divorced and had a string of abusive relationships. Tom continued his distance while Dorothy took care of her mother who was hospitalized time and again due to her drinking and depression. When she would call her brother for help, his answer would always be "My priest says my only obligation is to my wife and children." Although they had saved one another's lives as children and had been very close, Dorothy and her brother remained estranged for forty years.

Tom's middle daughter started them down the path of reconciliation. Twenty-three months before Tom died of a brain tumor, his daughter called Dorothy with the news that her father was given two years to live and that he loved his sister and missed her very much. Dorothy was on the next plane, and for the next twenty-three months she was with the brother she had once been so close to. After her brother's death, Dorothy eloquently summarized the painful feelings of so many casualties of addicted families:

> I felt such tremendous grief, emptiness, and sadness at the loss of my brother, not just for his death, but for all the wasted years. Before his death we both realized how much we loved each other, and the conflict between us all those years wasn't his fault or mine. It was the fault of the horrid disease of addiction and the dysfunction in our family, our legacy, and yes, our parents' legacies as well. What a waste of so many lives—literally generations of pain, sorrow, and suffering.

Hansel and Gretel Children

In some addicted families the children survive the painful war zone–like environment by parenting each other. They literally survive by taking care of each other emotionally and sometimes physically. In their book *The Sibling Bond*, Stephen P. Bank and Michael D. Kahn, Ph.D., explain it further:

> Psychotherapists meet Hansels and Gretels who have no loving or sustaining parent at home and for whom, thus abandoned, the sibling relationship is the only caring force. These siblings' relationships and identities are intertwined, sometimes for life, because they have jointly faced traumatic psychological losses at critical stages of their development. Mutual loyalty and care giving for these real-life Hansels and Gretels permit both physical and psychological survival. (112–113)

Stacy came from a family of four girls; her eldest sister was fourteen months older than Stacy, and her two younger sisters were five and ten years younger than she. These age differences meant that birth order really defined two distinct groups: "the big kids" and the "little kids." Her birth father suffered from multiple addictions, primarily to sex, gambling, and alcohol. He disappeared from Stacy's life when her mother was pregnant with the fourth baby girl.

Stacy's mother projected a competent image to the world, but her daughters knew the extent of her neediness when there was not a man in her life. It was their responsibility to fill their mother's "empty space." She could not be relied on to provide safety, support, or parenting and she often suffered from debilitating bouts of depression and binge drinking. The "big kids" were charged with the caretaking and parenting not only the "little kids," but their mother as well. In keeping with the rules of an addicted family, they were also sworn to secrecy: "There's nothing wrong here. Don't talk about it." Stacy described what life was like for the four girls:

> I still clearly remember the pressure this kind of childhood engendered. Fortunately we were all born in rural Idaho and our blessing

was the fields and animals around us. Our maternal grandparents, aunts, and uncles were faraway on the East Coast. Our paternal grandmother despised my mother and would lavish gifts and attention only on my oldest sister—the one who most closely resembled my father. Nature was our "cookie person" (nurturer) in all its variety and acceptance, from pets and farm animals to frogs and water dogs. Here we found an embrace that said to each of us: you are okay, you belong. This early pattern of sibling connection and nature quite simply saved our lives as our parental conditions steadily worsened over the years.

A year after Stacy's father abandoned the family, her mother met a man and married him. Just as her mother and father had done, her new stepfather seldom missed the opportunity to tell all of them how discouraged he was that there weren't any sons. He had marginal jobs and was prone to fits of rage that intensified when he drank. He insisted that all the girls take his name, and he moved the family to Oregon. Within a year of that move he began molesting Stacy and her older sister. Their economic situation further declined; the family knew hunger for the first time as well as the pain of no medical care. "My stepfather's rages seemed to appear out of nowhere," Stacy said. "My older sister and I became hypervigilant and very astute at reading minute indications of inflection or tone of voice in order to move the 'little kids' out of harm's way."

The "big kids" knew that violent beatings almost always accompanied their stepfather's rages. They were not, however, as astute about sexual cues and worried constantly about their ability to protect their younger siblings from sexual abuse. They were doomed to lose this battle: their stepfather eventually abused all four girls. Stacy described how nature saved them:

My mother was unable to provide any protection for us and instead retreated further into depression and helplessness. Our role in taking care of her increased during this time as well. We took care of one another and nature again became an escape. We secured food from the surrounding countryside—fish, crawdads, wild asparagus, nuts, berries, wild apples, and huckleberries. We harvested and sold night crawlers to several small grocery stores. We were embraced unconditionally by scores of domestic and feral dogs and cats. Nature had expanded to provide not only our sense of safety, sustenance, and self-worth, but now allowed us to make bigger contributions to family survival. We took long bike rides and hikes into fields and woods, seeking that much sought-after peace and serenity. We discovered medicinal cures for ringworm (from black walnut hulls) and a host of other afflictions through trial and error. We found secure hiding places for the "little kids" that we marked for future reference. We were embraced in a loving presence and we knew it.

The mental health of Stacy's stepfather and mother continued to deteriorate, which culminated in yet another move. Her stepfather's drinking increased, as did his rages. It became commonplace for him to strip the four girls from the waist down and beat them viciously. Her mother continued to refuse to intervene, fearful of losing her husband and having to "face raising these kids alone." Stacy began to feel that her life was like a murderous cloud gathering mass on the horizon around her mother and stepfather.

About this time, my sisters and I began to develop a dark sense of humor. We retreated to the woods for extended periods of time and made jokes about our stepfather. One time he took an axe to a garden hose during one of his rages and chopped it up into six-inch pieces. The next day, he went to the hardware store and bought dozens of fasteners and put it back together. My sisters and I joked in the privacy of the woods that we were the only people that had hundreds of hoses while most people only had one or two. We began to sense we were smarter than him and this drew us even closer to one another. Nature was the caregiver, the bounty provider, the hiding place, and buffer for us. It offered us trout, frogs' legs, catfish, ground cherries, blackberries, and wild strawberries. It was generous, benevolent, and predictable.

Stacy's stepfather was a hunter, so handguns and rifles were an everyday part of her family's environment. As hunting season approached, the girls were asked to stand in the yard so he could sight in his deer rifles on them. His drinking and the disintegration of his mental health continued unabated until the year Stacy turned fifteen. Her older sister was spending the night at the home of a school friend and Stacy was in charge of keeping the "little kids" and her mom from harm. Stacy tells what happened next:

> My stepfather began drinking early in the day, and by nightfall his rage was in full bloom. The "little kids" were in bed and so his rage turned on my mother for the first time. I listened from the top of the stairs and something just broke inside me. I removed a loaded Winchester .270 rifle from the broom closet and rounded the corner of the kitchen just as he was balling his fist to hit my mother. I felt myself grow cold from head to toe, and as I leveled the rifle at him I said, "One move and I will drop you where you stand." Murder was in my heart and my stepfather could read it in my eyes. He turned slowly, exited the house, and began packing his car. He left that night and never returned. My sisters and I celebrated his departure, but my mother descended even further into debilitating depression, drinking, and illness.

Over the next several years, Stacy's mother became jealous of the close bond between the girls. One at a time they were singled out as her favorite while she shunned the other three. This was never effective at separating the three oldest girls because of their age and history together. Their youngest sister, however, suffered from this alternating shunning and favoritism.

As adults, the three older sisters remained very close, just as they had always been. They all banished their childhood demons in various ways: Stacy's oldest sister found structure and success in a career with the government and as a novelist; Stacy became an individual and family therapist for many years and then turned to business management in the private sector; the third sister became a Jungian analyst and an artist. As adults, the three older sisters renewed their bond with their youngest sister, but it was not unusual for her to be uncommunicative with the older three for long periods. She fought multiple addiction issues and often had marginal employment.

> My mother's only positive gifts to us were voracious appetites for reading and storytelling. Our major gift to ourselves is our close connection with each other, therapy, and the absence of major addictions. When my mother was on her deathbed, she woke briefly from a coma, looked intensely at her four adult daughters, and asked, "Are you real sure I didn't have any sons?" The four of us belly-laughed as Mom retreated back into a coma.

My connection and love for these brilliant women continues to this day, and I feel blessed for the experience I have shared with them.

The Gift of Healing Across Generations

Part of individual healing is gaining an understanding that any disconnection and competition experienced with siblings comes from a painful past. Often the children in the family were hostages.

Too often in addicted families, there isn't enough love or nurturing to go around because the addiction has taken the place the children rightfully deserved in their parents' lives. As adults, siblings frequently continue to blame each other for the love that was not received, and they sometimes blame each other for the parents' addiction. This amounts to turning our closest lifelong friends into enemies. When a parent dies, sometimes the siblings continue to fight for the love they didn't get as they fight for the money or objects left behind. They view the objects as symbols of the much-needed validation that they were, in fact, loved. Siblings too often become disconnected in adult years, continuing to live as casualties of the addiction and the family dysfunction.

When we truly understand that our siblings are not to blame for the pain and emotional neglect we suffered, we can begin healing across generational lines. We may begin to understand that our brother or sister didn't abandon us when he or she went to college, got married, or joined the service, but left home at a normal developmental time to do so. Our parents, not that sibling, were responsible for continuing to parent us. Later, when siblings don't help with the financial or emotional care of alcoholic parents, we need to understand that they do the best they can and we, too, do the best we can.

Siblings are the repositories of our irreplaceable life histories. As Michael D. Kahn, Ph.D., and Karen Gail Lewis explained in *Siblings in Therapy: Life Span and Clinical Issues*, "This most enduring of life's intimate ties outlasts those with our parents by 20–30 years, and remains as a constant despite aging, despite divorce, and despite children growing up" (xvi).

Reconnecting with your siblings and ironing out misunderstandings and difficulties of the past (when it is safe to do so) is a priceless gift you can give yourself in your healing journey. In addicted families, siblings do the best they can to survive a childhood where there often is not enough emotional support to go around. After the tears, a new perspective on the family can allow siblings who have been alienated from one another to offer support and connection as they attempt to break a painful family legacy.

14

ACOAs Become Parents:
A Pioneering Effort

Living with addiction and relationship trauma has long arms
that wrap themselves around generation after generation until
they are consciously and methodically addressed.

—*from* Emotional Sobriety: From Relationship Trauma
to Resilience and Balance, *by Tian Dayton, Ph.D.*

WHEN JANET LOOKED INTO THE FACE of her beautiful
baby son for the first time years ago, it was love at first sight.
She never thought she would be a mother; this precious little bundle
was a gift from God. Her initial, overwhelming feeling of love was
followed by an equally overwhelming feeling of terror. *What have I
done?* she thought. *I don't know how to do this. How am I possibly
going to be a good mother? I don't know how! I don't know what to do.*

Janet knew what *not* to do. She knew not to hit, not to yell, and
not to neglect this beautiful, new little miracle in the way that she
had been neglected. She had kept her promise never to drink like her

parents had and that was a plus. Janet thought, *Everything I know about parenting are things I know I can't do. How in the world am I going to figure out what to do instead?*

Then Janet did what she had done all her life: she straightened her back, fixed a determined look on her face, and said to herself, "Well, God trusts me. I'll just have to trust myself. I'll figure it out as I go along. Knowing what not to do is a start. It's like I'm a pioneer blazing new territory—as always. I can do this."

Children brought up in alcoholic or addicted families tend to have been raised with inconsistent parenting and nurturing. They learned very early in life that some emotions were just not allowed, including anger, sadness, and fear. They learned to be serious, hyperresponsible, and strong, and they were often parents to their parents. Or, they learned how to be invisible, stay out of the way, please others, or act up to draw the fire. They didn't learn what normal was or how to be healthy and effective parents. Most didn't learn the "Ns and Ls" of parenting: *need, no, nurture, love,* and *limits.* Most set out as Janet did: to do the best possible job of parenting they could, only to end up repeating some of the same patterns with or without the alcohol.

This repetitive pattern is often evident in ACOAs. Consider life in Judy's family. Although neither of Judy's parents had been addicted to drugs or alcohol, the atmosphere in the house resembled the alcoholic families that both had grown up in. Both felt insecure about their roles as parents and often felt they had failed in their marriage. Both had many of the characteristics of Adult Children of Alcoholics, including poor self-esteem, difficulty with spontaneity, the need to be in control, difficulty having fun, overwhelming shame, and debilitating guilt. There was little intimacy or communication in the marriage, and arguments about the children occupied a space between them where alcohol had been in their parents' marriages.

Judy was late for the bus every morning. Most of the time the bus came and went without her and her mother would have to drive her to school, which was just fine with Judy. Her parents had purchased an assortment of alarm clocks, some with music, some with beeps, some in animal shapes, and some more "grown up." The alarms would sound almost in unison at 7:00 AM every morning. Judy would reach over and methodically turn off each one and wait for her mother's angry footsteps on the stairs at 7:15 AM. "Come on, Judy, get up!" she would yell, and then rush back down the stairs to finish cooking breakfast. Judy's father would come into Judy's room at 7:25 AM, screaming at her, reminding her that she had once again overslept and only had twenty-five minutes to catch the school bus. He would then go downstairs and scream at his wife about Judy's behavior. At that point, her mother would once again climb the stairs and tell Judy that if she did not get up, she would have to walk to school. Finally, Judy would get up and get dressed—albeit slowly—for school.

Judy would dawdle over her breakfast and could feel the tension in the house. She would listen to her parents' fighting and hear her brother try to distract both of them with his funny jokes. She would wait for her father's long lecture about her behavior, and she would half listen while ever so slowly eating her food. She knew that she would not have to walk to school; her mother would always apologize for her father yelling at her and then would drive her to school.

The chaos happened every weekday morning and was repeated in the evening when Judy was supposed to be doing her homework. Her parents practiced different philosophies of child rearing that they learned from books, but neither threats nor rewards seemed to affect Judy's behavior.

In working with Adult Children of Alcoholics who have become parents, we have heard many of the same statements: "I want to be a good parent. I love my children but I feel like everyone else in the world got a book on how to be a good parent and I never got my copy. I feel anxious all the time. I don't want to do what my parents did, but I don't know what to do instead." We want to offer a few helpful hints to ACOAs who are parents or are thinking of becoming parents.

Hint One: Unpack Your Baggage and Sort the Laundry

One of the biggest gifts we can give our children is our own healing. The pain and losses of alcoholic families can be imprinted on the next generation if we do not sort through baggage to ensure that we don't pass the pain on to our children.

Memories from our painful pasts can be triggered with every age our children turn. Triggers can begin the first week we bring that wonderful new person home from the hospital. The baby cries. You feed her, burp her, walk her, rock her, and still she cries. You begin to feel helpless, as any normal parent would, but your helplessness begins to trigger all the times you felt helpless in your addicted family. You might begin to feel angry, sad, or afraid. The baby's cries might tap into feelings deep inside you of all the times your love for others was not enough in your alcoholic family. It didn't matter how hard you tried, people were still unhappy, angry, or drunk.

In addition to trying to meet their child's needs, new ACOA parents often must face uncomfortable feelings from their painful pasts. It is important for parents to take the time to recognize and sort out feelings as they happen, turning to supportive adults rather than licking their own wounds as they did as children, or inappropriately turning to their own children for support.

It is important for parents to identify the behaviors in their children that trigger them and pay attention to how they usually respond when triggered. Sorting out the baggage involves several components:

1. Be aware of your child's behaviors that trigger you (crying, lying, not sharing, talking back, fighting with brothers or sisters, ignoring you). Behaviors in children that are considered normal might produce explosions in you.

2. Make sure that adult support systems are in place to assist you in working through the feelings and memories released.

3. Always be aware of how you respond to your child when triggered (you shut down, get angry, become anxious and overprotective, lecture, feel powerless).

4. Stop unhealthy responses and take a break.

5. Determine the help you need in order to disengage the trigger.

6. Plan a healthier response to the behavior that has triggered you.

One of the biggest gifts new ACOA parents can give themselves is to ensure that they have supports in place that can be trusted to help sort through the painful baggage that may be triggered in parenting. Support might be in the form of a friend who has experienced the up and downs of parenting and can be "an honest mirror," an ACOA support group, a healthy family member, a healthy elder, or a counselor who understands Adult Children. Putting supports in place before a parenting crisis arises rather than attempting to find someone to talk to in the midst of a crisis will help to ensure healthy parenting.

Hint Two: Stop Asking "Mirror, Mirror on the Wall, Who Is the Most Perfect of Them All?"

Many ACOAs truly believe that there are parents who don't make mistakes raising their children. We would like to put the myth to rest. Although children raised in healthy families have more parenting tools in their toolbox and may have fewer triggers to work through, *there is no such thing as a perfect parent.*

Parenting is often a process of trial and error. What works with one child may not work with another. We learn from our mistakes and if we make them with love and the best intentions, our children are usually forgiving. Janet, for instance, was determined to make sure her baby was healthy. She had heard that brewer's yeast was a wonderful source of vitamin B and would benefit her little angel. Janet ate brewer's yeast so vitamin B would be in her breast milk. She also put brewer's yeast in her baby's water and juice. When she found foam in his diaper, she realized she had gone a bit too far. Both she and her baby boy lived through it and, thankfully, her next child didn't have to go through the foam-in-the-diaper period. As time passed, Janet learned to be as forgiving of mistakes she made in parenting as her children were of her.

Hint Three: Model the Behaviors You Admire and Desire

No matter how much we lecture about what is right, our children emulate our behaviors and unspoken emotional signals rather than what we tell them. Richard found this out one night at the dinner table. He was lecturing his eight-year-old son about his schoolwork: "How many times have I told you not to leave things until the last minute, Craig. How can you expect to get a good grade if you don't do it until the last minute?" Craig looked at his father seriously for a moment, then asked, "Is it like when you wait until the last minute to get your taxes together and Mom yells at you? Do you get a bad grade on your taxes and get in trouble with Mom and the tax man the same as I get in trouble with you and my teacher?"

Richard was stunned. How did his son know all this? Then, he remembered the day his son was walking in front of him and he realized that his son stuck his hands in his pocket and walked just like he did. His son was copying him. Instead of continuing the lecture, Richard replied, "Yes, son, just like that. We both need to work on doing things on time."

There is absolutely no use in lecturing our kids on honesty when we are not honest with them, or in pretending nothing is wrong when something really is. Children soak up our behavior and emotions just like little sponges. They pay attention to and model our behavior more consistently than our words. They can sense the feelings around them, and they don't rely merely on the words we say. A child may pick up the tension her parents are feeling and ask, "Why are you angry at Daddy, Mommy?" Mommy's reply of "I'm not angry, Sweetheart," falls on deaf ears as the child continues to soak up the tension around her. She may even feel it is her fault her parents are angry with each other. She learns "If you're sad or angry, deny it." Instead, a child should hear, "Mommy and Daddy are having some disagreements right now, but we will work on them. Adults disagree sometimes and even get angry with each other, just like you sometimes get angry with your sister. It is between us and doesn't have anything to do with you, Sweetheart."

Because emotions were out of control in their childhoods, and they often felt responsible for that, ACOAs sometimes tend to overprotect their own children from normal conflict, healthy anger, normal grief, and sadness. Making the investment to heal the ungrieved losses and painful memories of the past not only benefits our children, but it is an emotional savings account for generations to come.

Hint Four: Leave Your Helicopter on the Helipad

Adult Children of Alcoholics often feel a great deal of anxiety when they begin parenting. Margo's parents hovered around her crib. Even after the she had been fed, changed, rocked, and cuddled, they picked her up the instant she cried. This prevented Margo from learning to self-soothe for short periods of time. Later, instead of letting the toddler Margo learn to walk, they anxiously hovered, afraid to let her fall and pick herself back up. Margo goes on to say:

> I know my mom and dad both grew up in alcoholic families where they had to spend their lives taking care of themselves and their brother and sisters. That's really sad. I can't even imagine what that would be like. But I feel they are trying so hard to do something different with us that they are smothering us. I can't do anything. I can't make my own mistakes because they take care of things before I have a chance to succeed or fail. They even want to pick my friends. I feel like they are like two helicopters hovering around me twenty-four hours a day, making sure I don't get hurt. I can't stand it and neither can my sisters. They are smothering us.

Young children need to learn to rely on themselves as well as be protected. Instead of merely stating concerns and allowing children to gradually learn to make decisions, ACOA parents often pass on their worry and anxiety to their children, undermining their child's developing confidence in self. Because of their own early childhood trauma and their lack of confidence in themselves, ACOA parents often have their hypervigilance turned to full alert, continually scanning the environment for danger and transmitting their fears and anxieties to their children while overprotecting them. This behavior prevents children from making their own decisions and mistakes, learning through trial and error, and developing the ability to protect themselves.

Children need both roots and wings. Children of alcoholics are often deprived of one or the other—sometimes both. Some feel as though they were kicked out of the nest before they learned to fly, and as a result they often feel they like they have been *faking it* all their lives. Others feel similar anxiety if they are rooted to the nest by hovering parents who never let them try their wings, or parents who give their children everything they themselves didn't have materially and emotionally. They risk creating dependency and/or a sense of entitlement in their children.

Jim was raised by anxious ACOA parents who loved him with all their hearts but couldn't separate their anxiety from his because of their own painful childhoods. When he was a toddler they hovered, responding immediately to his needs without waiting for him to figure things out himself. They didn't allow him to experience normal, healthy disappointment. They set a specific time for homework every night, then hovered over him, correcting mistakes for him, making certain everything was done properly, and often doing the problems for him themselves. They didn't let him walk to school with friends when he was a preteen. Rather than getting to know his friends, helping him learn the lessons of friendship, and being available to support him if friends let him down, they tried to pick his friends and constantly criticized those who they thought were a negative influence or who might let him down. Jim was never allowed to stay overnight at another friend's house, even as an adolescent. In short, Jim's parents didn't allow him the space to grow up, make decisions, and learn from successes and mistakes. As a result Jim was totally unprepared to leave home when he went to college. He didn't study, leaving everything until the last minute because he had never internalized study habits. He ended up partying night after night, experimenting with alcohol and drugs, and he flunked out in his second semester. His parents were shocked because he had been such a good student. What they didn't understand was that Jim had never learned internal limits and boundaries. Anxious parents create anxious children. Here is how Jim described it:

> I had absolutely no confidence in myself. I think my defense against my parents' fears was to be fearless. I didn't know my own limits. To be honest, I don't know how I lived through my first year of college. I was reckless beyond belief. I had never learned how to protect myself or make decisions regarding my own welfare. I wonder if parents can love too much.

HINT FIVE: Find the Rainbow of Colors Between Black and White

As parents Adult Children often tend to see the behaviors of their children as either black or white and their parenting as either good or bad. In their own growing-up years, their families often functioned in extremes. Their parents' view of their children as the *best* little children in the world or the *worst,* or the atmosphere in the home as either chaotic, tense, or loving, depended on their stage of alcohol intoxication or their level of frustration in living with an alcoholic. Children in addicted families frequently learn to view the world in extremes.

It is difficult for Adult Children to sort out their own emotions, let alone those of their children, and they often don't realize that there are rarely right or wrong answers to most situations. As a result, they often prematurely jump to conclusions regarding the effectiveness of their own parenting or the normality of their children's behavior. They tend to be hypersensitive to normal conflict, worry about their children constantly, and view even signs of normal development—such as age-appropriate sibling rivalry or temper tantrums, or their own normal frustrations of parenting—as reflections of themselves as bad parents. They often doubt their own perceptions and feelings; they feel they cannot trust themselves with normal interactions and they frequently parent by the book. They often respond to their children's testing of limits in an overly rigid or in a permissive manner. One parent reported that in the seven years of her daughter's life she had followed seven different philosophies of child rearing. One minute she was permissive and the next there were "charts all over the house." During one period she would allow her child to eat anything she wanted and during another the child was required to eat what was put in front of her and stay at the table until she cleaned her plate. In another phase her child was sent to her room if she pushed the limits or didn't do her chores, and in the next phase she was rewarded for positive behavior and all other infractions were ignored.

An Adult Child may vacillate between trying to get his or her children to behave by bullying, intimidation, or sarcasm, or by becoming a buddy. In some families, one member of the parenting dyad is the buddy and the other the drill sergeant. A child needs a parent, not a drill sergeant or a parent-buddy. This is confusing to children and teaches them to manipulate the system or to love one parent and feel distance and anger toward the other.

To understand that many behaviors their children exhibit are well within the normal range and frustrations in parenting are normal, Adult Children must learn about normal child development. They also need to receive support in dealing with their anxiety when faced with gray areas and learn to sort things out rather than jumping to conclusions that are premature or unrealistic. Sometimes individual, couples, or family counseling is helpful in sorting out family or parenting issues, as well as anxieties and triggers related to parenting. It is also important for parents to focus on what they are trying to teach their child—that is, what that child will need to operate in the world. Understanding the effectiveness of logical consequences rather than punishment is important in navigating the difficult and frequently rough waters of limit setting and discipline.

Hint Six: Make Sure Your Children Receive the Two "Ls"—Love and Limits

One of the most difficult areas for parents who are Adult Children is setting and following through on age-appropriate limits with their children. In our first example, Judy had learned that her parents would not follow through on their threats of requiring her to walk to school if she didn't catch the bus. Perhaps it was too far to walk to school so the threat should not have been made in the first place; a more realistic threat would be for Judy to have to take the bus whether she was ready or not. One day with messy hair, missing breakfast, or wearing clothes that don't quite match goes a long way in learning the consequences of actions. When limits are threatened without follow-through, children become "parent deaf" and on one hand don't trust what the parent says, while on another, they need to keep escalating behavior to get their developmental needs for internal control and discipline m\

Adult Children have often grown up in homes where limits were either rigidly set and punishment was abusive, or they suffered neglect where there were no limits or follow through. Many promised themselves, "I will never treat my children the way I was treated." When children test the limits that have been set, which healthy children do, these parents tend to give in and become overly permissive or overly controlling and insensitive to their child's frustration. Let's look at two possible scenarios.

A mother may tell her daughter that if she doesn't find her shoes she will be late or not be able to go to her friend's birthday party. A few minutes later when her daughter breaks down in tears, the mother may feel tremendous guilt about her child's sadness, confusing her child's tears with her own. Instead of being empathetic toward her daughter's frustration, comforting her yet all the while keeping the limit, she withdraws the limit, finds her daughter's shoes for her, and takes her to the birthday party on time.

A father may set a limit about the use of his tools with his teenage son who has asked to borrow his dad's hammer, but who in the past has not taken care of the tools lent to him. The father tells his son that he may borrow the hammer, but if it is lost or damaged, the son will have to pay for it. When the son loses the hammer and declares "it isn't fair" that he is required to pay for it, the father, rather than following through with the consequence, may go out and buy a new hammer himself and tell his son, "Just don't let it happen again."

In both cases, the child hasn't learned a valuable life lesson but has instead learned to be "parent deaf." A parent's love is shown by providing for and nurturing a child as well as by setting and following through on age-appropriate limits. It is a parent's responsibility to teach children the lessons they need to live in the world. To do this, an ACOA needs to separate his or her own feelings from those of the child.

ACOAs are also role models for acceptable and unacceptable behavior. Parents who hit their children when frustrated and yet tell them not to hit, or smoke and tell them not to smoke, or talk negatively about friends, yet lecture their children on the importance of friendship, are not serving as healthy role models. Children learn by watching and imitating their parents as well as by experiencing the logical consequences of their behavior. Parenting is not an exact science. Parenting skills take time to learn and can be implemented throughout the learning process. Remember that parenting is not black and white, and navigating the subtle and vibrant rainbow of colors in the spectrum can provide exciting learning experiences.

HINT SEVEN: Let Go and Play

Adult Children who are parents often say that one of the most difficult jobs they have is learning to have fun with their children. There can often be as much emotional distance in the families raised by Adult Children of Alcoholics as in the alcoholic family itself. These parents are often comfortable only when functioning within a maze of goals, searching for ways to be in control. They can be workaholics at work and at home, spending very little time interacting with their children. Their houses can be controlled by rigid sets of rules or no consistent rules. There can be a lack of touching and awkwardness in hugging or showing affection to children, or in showing affection to each other in front of children. One parent expressed it this way:

> Learning to have fun is work. I have so much difficulty playing games with my children, enjoying family outings, or learning the joys and intimacy of playing spontaneously with my children. I often feel

that my unresolved tears are just below the surface. I have built a wall to keep them from coming out. I want to be able to hold my children on my lap and play games with them that were never played with me, but I am so afraid to just let go.

It is important for Adult Children to heal their own discomfort with spontaneity and affection so they don't pass their need for control on to their children. Parents need to model integrity and provide healthy discipline, but children also need parents who can show healthy expressions of affection, bonding, and nurturing, be both flexible and consistent, model healthy expression of feelings, and can connect to their children through play and laughter.

HINT EIGHT: Be an Honest Mirror

One of the greatest gifts we can give our children is the honest mirror that was never given to us. During healthy parenting a baby's smile is returned by the parents' smile. When they are in discomfort, children need to see compassion and concern in their parents' eyes. They need to feel parental support as they learn through making mistakes. Children need to see the pride and joy in their parents' eyes when they take their first tentative steps, learn their first notes on a musical instrument, attempt a sport or hobby, progress through school, then graduate and begin moving away or speaking their truth for the first time.

Our children need a truthful mirror that reflects them as they are rather than as the image of what we want or need them to be. Little Joan, the ballet dancer, didn't see concern in her mother's eyes when she wished to play with other children, but instead she saw disappointment if she missed a dance step or was too tired to practice one more routine. Our children do not need to be the sad, fearful reflections of the children we were. They do not need to be the courageous heroes and images that will tell the world we are perfect parents after all; the dancer or scientist we wish we'd had the opportunity to become; the dependent reflections of our own need to be needed; or the rebellious, acting out, angry child we were never allowed to become. Our children need us to be the honest mirrors of who they are and the people they are in the process of becoming.

Hint Nine: Be Honest About Abuse and Addiction

Children raised in alcoholic homes have great difficulty in being neutral about issues of alcohol and drugs. As a result they often can't give their children an honest education in these areas. They are hypersensitive to even occasional drinking by their spouse or to experimentation by their teenagers. One father whose sixteen-year-old son came home from a friend's party with whisky on his breath angrily grounded his son for two months. Another father of a sixteen-year-old bought beer for his son and his friend and allowed them to drink it in the house where he could "keep an eye on things." Exaggerated, supported, or ignored responses to alcohol and drug use in spouses or teens can create an equally destructive elephant in the living room for the next generation.

Our children need our honesty about the family history of addiction and the impact it has had on our lives. They need realistic education about drugs and alcohol and addictions of all types. They need us to be alert and aware, consistent about our expectations, and open to honest and healthy dialogue about the differences between use and abuse. They need us to be aware of the signs of use by them and their peers, and they need us to immediately engage them in a dialogue. If we see signs that our children are abusing drugs and alcohol, we need to intervene, take action, and seek treatment for them. Our children don't need us to turn a blind eye to their experimentation with alcohol and drugs, nor do they need us to use scare tactics, overreaction, or abusive punishment. We need to talk with our children. They need our love, and when necessary, our tough love.

Hint Ten: Feeding the Couple's Tree Makes for Healthy Fruit

Sally and Tom's parents describe their relationship as a happy one. They retained their own sense of identity as each established their own professional goals while developing their own friendships and supportive networks. They support each other's development as adults, enjoy their fun times together, experience conflicts from time to time, and say that arguments throughout their history as a couple has strengthened the bond of intimacy in their relationship rather than created distance. Their relationship is one of choice rather than need, and they feel continued renewal in their original commitment as they develop as adults.

They both acknowledge that along with the joy that Sally brought to their relationship, there were also important adjustments that had to be made. Each had to make changes in their normal schedules to accommodate an infant. Sally's needs were of prime concern, and they both acknowledged that each had to take care of his or her own needs as well as pay attention to the care and feeding of their relationship—the goal was to provide a healthy environment for their daughter.

When Sally was three, her brother, Tommy, was born. Her parents listened to her excitement at having a brother as well as her wish-filled fantasy stories of a monster taking the baby away. They reassured her in language she could understand that ambivalence regarding a new brother was okay. They read her books on "a new baby in the family," and took turns meeting the needs of her new brother, Sally, each other, and their needs as a couple. They each added gym time twice a week as well as a night out for themselves every two weeks, as it was harder for them to get needed relationship time with the addition of Tommy's and Sally's developing needs.

As time went by, new stresses were added to their little family. They continued to appreciate the need for time together as a couple for fun and for conflict resolution. They recognized new needs for understanding and limits as the children developed and new experiences unfolded. They learned the magic balance of holding children close and setting limits, yet letting go at the same time. They also recognized the need for even more time together as the children grew. They worked toward increasing their effectiveness as a parental team rather than allowing themselves to be split by manipulation, such as the children pitting one parent against the other.

It is important for parents to tend to their personal needs and to the needs of the relationship. Couples who separate or divorce for whatever reason still need to put time and attention into their parenting relationship. Single parents need to ensure that they take care of themselves and are balanced mentally, physically, emotionally, and spiritually. They need to develop a system of adult support for themselves. This allows them to expend the energy necessary to continue the hard and rewarding task of being a consistent parent while ensuring that they are not requiring their children to meet their adult needs for companionship and emotional support.

After Adult Children begin the resolution of their own grief (through ACOA or Al-Anon support groups, individual, group, or marital counseling), they may able to experience new openness with their children, and their depression may be replaced with spontaneity. They may begin to feel the warmth of healthy communication and bonding with their children. They may be able to feel more trust in their own perceptions and can utilize new skills effectively. After the tears it is possible for Adult Children to see their own children as individuals rather than reflections and mirrors of the sad and frightened children they themselves once were.

15

A Pain Too Deep:
ACOAs Taking Care
of Elderly Parents

When people confront an ocean of need they feel anxiety.
Some run for their lives; others jump in and drown.
Both reactions are rooted in the inability
to stay separate and set limits in a healthy way
that balances generosity with self-preservation.

—*from* Doing the Right Thing: Taking Care of Your Elderly Parents Even
If They Didn't Take Care of You, *by Roberta Satow, Ph.D.*

BEING THE CAREGIVER for elderly parents is one of the hardest
jobs we will ever have. Navigating health-care and insurance
systems, coordinating daily activities, dressing infirm or dependent
parents, dispensing medication, toileting, driving to and from doctor appointments or the hospital, balancing all this with your own
work and personal relationships—all the while taking care of yourself—can feel overwhelming. The task can be especially daunting if
we are also dealing with parents who have remained the same, and

we are navigating a minefield of emotional hurts and abuse from the past. Granted, if your childhood was wonderful and your parents were healthy, loving, protecting, and giving, then taking care of elderly parents is stressful but it can also be an opportunity to give back and show appreciation for their parenting. Even when your childhood was spent in an alcoholic or addicted family, if your parents went into recovery in the truest sense—validating the pain their children have carried and making amends while becoming healthy parents to adult children—there is still the chance that caretaking in their last years can become a task that feels like lovingly giving back.

"How much longer is this going to go on?" Dorothy's mother asked angrily, as Dorothy compassionately fed her the rice pudding she had made for her. Dorothy had moved her mother to a nursing home close to her own home and visited her several times a week. When her mother began to decline and stopped eating, Dorothy had taken time from her job to go to the nursing home twice a day to feed her food she had made with love. "I don't know how much time you have left . . . days, weeks, or months," Dorothy replied kindly. Again her mother asked, "How much longer is this going to go on?"

Puzzled, thinking that perhaps her mother wanted to talk about her fears of dying, Dorothy asked, "I don't know. Do you have any idea how much time you have left?"

"No," her mother said angrily. "How much longer do I need to eat this damn rice pudding?"

Like many Adult Children of Alcoholics, Dorothy wanted and needed the perfect ending with the loving, appreciative mother she had never had. To this end she put substantial emotional and financial resources into taking care of her mother, hoping that she would finally be given the love and kindness for which she so desperately longed. She believed, as she had believed since her childhood, that she would finally receive thanks and appreciation for her efforts if she only did enough for her mother. The appreciative, loving mother never materialized.

Through her own recovery Dorothy had begun to understand the pain of her mother's early life, and was bound and determined to make sure the ending of her life was a good one. Her mother, however, identified Dorothy with her own abusive mother, and rather than being grateful (which Dorothy needed her to be), she would act out, doing and saying horrible things to her daughter. Dorothy tried to solicit the help of her brother, but he had washed his hands of his mother long before and wanted no part in her care—emotionally, physically, or financially. Most of the time Dorothy contained the rage she felt in response to her mother's abuse with codependent solicitousness. She would vacillate between being clingy and dependent, feeling overly responsible, and being angry with her mother. "I would feel terribly guilty when I would get angry at her. I was exhausted from caring for a mother who was often abusive to me, and I felt rage toward my brother for leaving me holding the bag."

Adult Children frequently end up caring for elderly parents who were not there for them in their growing-up years, and who were sometimes physically and/or sexually abusive to them as well. Many alcoholic or codependent parents had lives that resulted in chronic PTSD, and they often were not appropriately cared for themselves as children. As a result, many were suffering from their own developmental losses when raising their children. They may have been neglectful, clinging, dependent, abusive, controlling, ill-tempered, or demanding parents who not only were ineffective as parents but demanded to be parented as well. As a result, many Adult Children also suffered from PTSD most of their lives. Within this framework, these Adult Children are then commandeered one more time to take over the care of their parents physically and emotionally, and for some, to rescue them financially as well; all of this while being their parents' primary caregivers.

Many of the Adult Children who are responsible for elderly parents are themselves in their sixties or seventies and are taking care of parents in their eighties and nineties. For many, this is the time they believed they would finally be able to relax. They have achieved some level of financial security and career satisfaction and often have new and improved relationships with siblings and parents. Taking care of parents often triggers "going home again" feelings. This tests their limits and can cause some ACOAs to revert to earlier roles and painful interactions with both siblings and parents. While some elderly parents who need care may have gone through recovery, others may be as emotionally difficult as they were—or may even be worse.

Adult Children often feel caught between a rock and a hard place. On the one hand they don't want to assume a caretaking role again. On the other hand, they feel that taking care of their elderly parents is the right thing to do, and they experience tremendous guilt if they even contemplate saying no. Some remain in denial, and thoughts run the gamut from, "It's just for a little while, and Dad will be back to his old self in no time. I can handle this," to "That was then and this is now. I'm an adult now, how hard can it be? I'll just leave the past in the past." Others, like Dorothy, willingly take on the role, hoping to gain some closure and trying unconsciously to finally gain the love and approval they never received as a child, only to learn that they will never receive what they want so desperately.

The Wile E. Coyote Dilemma
and the Task of Setting Limits

Although they may be geographically separated from parents, many ACOAs are often still psychologically attached to them. When making decisions about care for elderly parents, Adult Children must work toward being psychologically separate. It is essential that they set limits with parents and siblings regarding what they are and are not willing to do. To attain separation, it is essential for ACOAs to see their parents as they truly are, and to examine their own childhood years realistically.

Janet was crying in her therapist's office. She was taking care of a new infant, two toddlers, and a five-year-old, dealing with a divorce, starting a new and demanding job. On top of all that, she was dealing with her alcoholic father, who had literally been dumped on her doorstep by a police officer who was unwilling to lock up a drunk old man. She was frantic with worry when her father would disappear or when she was getting calls from one hospital after another. And her father wasn't her only concern; she had just sent money she couldn't afford to a younger sister who needed rent money. Many ACOAs like Janet end up not only with the task of taking care of their parents but also taking care of siblings who have fallen by the wayside. Caregiving siblings often feel survivor guilt and they often suffer heartbreak when they can't take care of siblings they have "raised."

Janet was surprised by her therapist's confrontation:

> Your sister isn't the problem, Janet. The problem is your continued acceptance of the parenting role. Your sister is thirty. When your sister is acting needy and deprived, you feel the neediness of that little girl inside you and can't set limits with her. You aren't helping her grow up.

> When you allow the police to dump your dad off with you instead of insisting that he be taken to the drunk tank, you aren't helping him face his addiction. Your actions aren't healthy support for either of them, Janet. You caretake because that is what helps you. Continual caretaking is your own particular brand of medication against anxiety.

Janet thought about this admonishment for a minute. "Maybe I am being selfish. You're right, I'm certainly not helping them. But I feel so mean. How can I just let my sister lose her apartment or my dad sleep in the drunk tank? He's not young anymore." She began to cry. As she thought about her situation, Janet realized that on one the hand she continually responded to the neediness of her sister and father in her attempts to *save* them, and on the other hand she was angry at them for taking more and more of the emotional, physical, and financial supplies she didn't have to give.

Her therapist continued:

> You are not mean like your mother was to you, Janet. Your need to be the opposite of your mom means that you are still very much tied to her. She was emotionally abusive to you. Your sister and father have taken up the gauntlet as well when you don't do what they want you to do. You are still letting their opinions define you. You are not defining yourself.

For healthy development, children need parents or other adult caregivers whom they can trust. When children are neglected or abused, or have parents who are realistically not good enough, they create fantasy parents. The children take on the burden of being the problem so they can continue to feel safe. Neglected or abused children can't face the fact that their parents really aren't there physically or emotionally. It is a bit like the Road Runner cartoon where

Wile E. Coyote runs off the cliff but doesn't actually fall until he looks down and realizes that he's standing in midair. Just as Wile E. Coyote will fall when he realizes that he's not on solid ground, these children feel they are suspended in midair and will fall if they recognize that their parents aren't capable of taking care of them. Their parents aren't "there" for them.

Many Adult Children would rather take abuse from their addicted or codependent parents than face the painful task of truly separating from them psychologically. For ACOAs, "looking down" is truly accepting that the parenting *they* received was not good enough but they were good kids, and what happened to them as children was not their fault. In essence, children of alcoholics take on guilt and blame to save themselves. Adult Children continue to be psychologically attached to parents if they are still trying to attain parental love and gratitude, still believing that "when I take care of my elderly parent well enough, he or she will love me and finally thank me for all I have done." A caregiving Adult Child is still not separate if he or she allows emotional abuse from an aging or ill parent. Father may demand his dinner at exactly 5:30 PM, and Daughter didn't get to his house until 6:00 PM because of an unforeseen crisis at the office. If she has not fully separated, the daughter may feel guilty for her "irresponsibility" and promise herself to do better next time, or feel guilty while at the same time being angry with her father. She may panic and leave the office early the next time, all the while feeling rage at the unfairness of it all. Until she is separate, she will not set limits on her father's demands or behavior and will still allow him to define her.

When taking care of elderly parents, it is essential that ACOAs be able to define themselves and set limits. Here are some examples of self-talk the daughter above might use in defining those limits for herself and her father:

"I am a caring person and I am doing the best I can."

"I am willing to be there to fix dinner within a reasonable time frame or have dinner delivered if I cannot make it."

"I will let my father know that his abuse and rigid demands are not acceptable."

If we are not able to set healthy limits, our own emotional and physical health will be effected and our frustration may well spill over to our friends, coworkers, significant others, or children.

It Is What It Is

We both remember times in our lives when our fantasy families were alive and well. We believed that our parents would somehow materialize into the parents we always wanted them to be if only we tried hard enough. Eventually we each, in our own way, had to put that fantasy to rest. You may have to as well.

When facing decisions about what we can and can't do in taking care of elderly parents, it is important to realize that parents are not likely to change and may, through illness and age, actually get worse. Parents who couldn't make decisions and were clingy and dependent before aren't likely to be willing or able to make decisions regarding their health care and well-being when they are elderly or ill. A parent who was self-centered will more than likely be demanding; a parent who has never recovered from addiction will continue to be addicted, possibly still hiding bottles or trying to get someone to sneak alcohol into a nursing home. Parents who were abusive will more than likely continue to be abusive. Parents who have never hugged or kissed their children are not likely to change into affectionate individuals. If parents have never been appreciative or grateful for their child's efforts, they aren't likely to be when the Adult Child is their caregiver in later years. A parent who has never been able to say "I love you" isn't likely to begin when he or she is ill. Often an ACOA will have to come to terms with the fact that the way things are is the best they will ever be. One woman summed it up this way:

> My mother was never able to care for us. She never told us she loved us. Our stepfather sexually abused us, and she never protected us.
>
> I check in on her almost every day. I have done a lot of work on myself. She has never hugged me, but I hug her and tell her I love her. It's a bit like hugging a post. I do it for me as much as for her. I don't expect her to change, but I feel freedom in the choices I have made.

It is important to accept that *it is what it is* and be realistic about expectations. It is wonderful for everyone if changes happen, but if they do it will be because the people change, not because you force something to be different than it is. Caregivers who try to fix the family dysfunction will more than likely be disappointed, frustrated, and angry.

Siblings

Another trap to avoid when making a decision regarding caregiving for parents is the expectation that siblings will change the roles they had in the family. The bad news is that under stress, family members are likely to revert to old family roles and patterns, and the process will become an exercise in frustration. A younger sister who never took on family responsibility isn't likely to suddenly be willing to take on a shift caring for Mom. The controlling sibling will probably still think that whatever is done is not good enough unless he or she does it. The rebellious, angry sibling may think everyone is crazy for the efforts they are making "for people who never took care of their children," and are likely to refuse to take part. If some siblings were treated as though they were entitled to the best of everything while others were left out, or if the boys were treated differently from the girls, they likely will continue in those roles. The caretaker in the family will often seize the role of primary caregiver but may complain, be angry at those who don't help, and have unrealistic expectations if he or she has never worked on self-recovery. Again, remember that *it is what it is* and anger, cajoling, lectures, tears, and threats are likely to be a waste of energy.

When faced with a parent who is declining and needs care, a healthy approach is to have a sibling meeting and allow each person discuss what he or she is and is not willing to do. One sibling might not be willing to participate in physical caregiving, but might be willing to offer financial support; another sibling might be willing to accept the care on weekends or holidays to give the primary caregiver a break. Someone who lives far away might be willing to take a turn once or twice a year.

The good news: we may not be able to change the behavior or attitudes of our family members, but we can change our own. We can change even if no one else in the family changes. We can make decisions that we can live with, and set limits that will benefit our own well-being. We can choose different ways to respond, put supports in place to care for ourselves, and sort out emotions as they arise. We can't control what others do or say, but we can control how we respond. We may not receive appreciation from anyone else, but we can appreciate ourselves and know we are doing the best we can.

Decisions, Limits, and Choices

The Adult Child's decision to be involved in the care of elderly parents, as well has the level of involvement, is ultimately the choice of the individual. For Adult Children from some cultures or religious beliefs, the decision will almost always be to take care of elderly parents regardless of what they have or have not done. One ACOA described it this way:

> In our culture, we take care of our elderly parents and don't put them in a nursing home. I am honoring my parents because, well, I just do, but I don't necessarily like them. They were really abusive to us kids and that never changed. It has been really hard, very stressful, but I've done work on myself that I don't think I would have done otherwise. I've learned to focus on the situation, not the emotions that are coming up. Then, I attend a support group and let the emotions flow. I will never let anyone silence me again. They haven't changed but I have. I do set limits. I don't allow my mother to emotionally abuse me; I walk away. I also don't allow my dad to drink in my house. Those are the rules if he wants to live here. He drinks at my sister's and that's okay—his addiction is his addiction. I also have requested that my brother take our mother for a month in the summer, or if he can't do that, he pay someone to come in and care for them so I can take a vacation. I need to refresh myself.

For other ACOAs, decisions and choices regarding caregiving may rest on whether they are safe in that role or whether they can control themselves enough to ensure the safety of parents in their care. No matter what choice is made, it is almost certain that everyone will not agree. It is important to know what you realistically can and cannot do before making decisions. These heartfelt comments from two different ACOAs illustrate the dilemma felt by many:

I know I can't take care of my dad although I wish I could. I am still so angry and I am afraid that under stress my anger would get out of control. Instead, I am taking care of his house while he is in a care facility. I am renting it out for him so he has extra money. I go by twice a week and do the upkeep.

I wouldn't be able to live with myself if I didn't take care of my mom. I am doing it for me.

It is important to know that you have many choices; investigate all the available options before making a choice. If an Adult Child has made the decision to be a primary caregiver, it is imperative to recognize whether anger and resentment ever cross the line to abuse.

I couldn't live with my mom. I know myself well enough to know that, but I can visit her in the elderly housing apartment. I take her out to lunch twice a week and cook for her on weekends. I have set limits on her abuse, and I have told her that I won't be able to visit her as much if she continues to be verbally abusive. I think she hears me for the first time because I mean it. She was really cruel one day, and I said, "Mom, I love you, but I will have to leave now. I will visit later in the week if you are in a better mood."

The smallest trigger can cause loss of control for some ACOAs. You must seek help immediately if this becomes the case. Some who would never cross the line between anger and abuse do so under the stress of caregiving. Elder abuse is defined as lashing out physically or verbally, mismanaging finances, neglecting physical care, ignoring reasonable pleas for help, deprivation of food or water, or force-feeding. If an Adult Child was neglected or harmed physically, emotionally, or sexually as a child and hasn't received therapy, he or she may be at risk of harming a parent in his or her care under stress. If this happens, you must seek help immediately.

Make Sure to Take Care of Yourself

Even though you have worked hard on healing, it is important to understand that emotions from the past are likely to be triggered when you are returned to the position of dealing with a family under stress. You need to decide ahead of time how you will disengage your triggers and what kind of supports you will need to put in place. It is often important to focus on the situation that needs to be taken care of first, then find support to process the triggers and allow the expression of emotions that are being felt.

> I remember all my young life and into my early adult years trying to convince my dad to stop drinking. He always told me he didn't have a problem. It was really frustrating. He finally stopped drinking, but now he's really sick, and I am trying to convince him to get health care and he's having the same response he did then: "When it's my time to die, I will go." It was really triggering me so I got the pastor of our church to talk to him and got home health care. My father really got mad. That's okay. He has a right to get mad and I have a right to do my best and I did. I am proud of myself.

It is also important to get proper rest, eat well, exercise, and pay attention to balance in your life. You might make a circle and entitle it "My Week." Divide the circle proportionally into the time you spend with family, your primary relationship, self-care (exercise, support groups, therapy, meditation, sleep, and nutrition), friends, fun and recreation, work, children, grandchildren, caregiving, and anything else that comprises your day. Pay special attention to balance. There will always be times when the balance is skewed because of emergencies, but focus on whether you are maintaining balance most of the time. Among members surveyed by a National Family Caregivers Association, 27 percent of caregivers reported more headaches since caregiving activities began, 24 percent reported more stomach disorders, 41 percent reported more back pain, 51 percent reported more sleeplessness, and 61 percent reported more depression. These statistics prove just how necessary self-care is for your long-term health and well-being.

One of the most important gifts you can give yourself while caregiving for an elderly or sick parent is the gift of support. Seek out a good therapist who understands both Adult Children of Alcoholics and caring for the elderly. You might consider attending Al-Anon or ACOA support groups. There are also many websites that deal specifically with caregiving, such as www.caregiver.com, www.caregiving.org, www.caregiverwellness.ca, and www.thirdage.com; we have found supportive material on these four sites, and there are countless others.

It seems appropriate to quote the late actress Audrey Hepburn as we face the decision regarding the care we can offer to an elderly parent: "If you ever need a helping hand, you will find one at the end of each arm. As you grow older you will discover you have two hands: one for helping yourself and one for helping others."

16

ACOAs in the Workplace:
I Can Be a Team Player as Long
as I'm the Only One on the Team

The impact of growing up with alcoholism pervades every
aspect of adult life. It influences feelings of self, relationships,
and one's ability to get things done, regardless of whether
one is looking at home, social, or work environment. Since a
large portion of one's waking hours is spent in the workplace,
whatever or wherever that may be, the way one feels and
behaves in that environment is a significant part of one's life.

—*from* Home Away from Home:
The Art of Self-Sabotage, *by Janet Woititz, Ed.D.*

SUE WAS DETERMINED TO BE the perfect employee as well as
the perfect wife and mother. Like most ACOAs who had been
caretakers in their families, Sue had a high tolerance for outrageous
behavior and dysfunction. She was loyal to her boss even when she
realized that her loyalty was not deserved. She was a high-functioning
employee who often did what others would not do. Even when pre-

sented with what could be considered an impossible workload, Sue never considered saying no. She had little concept of her own needs and limits, and yet she continually doubted her self-worth.

Sue and her friend Carol left a meeting where Sue's boss, Frank, had once again belittled her in front of her staff.

"Sue, I don't know why you keep putting up with this abuse," Carol said.

"Frank's under a lot of stress, Carol. He's involved in a divorce, and he's under a lot of pressure from the board. Besides, he always apologizes, so what's the big deal? He doesn't mean it." Sue seemed resigned to the frequent abuse.

"The pressure he's under, Sue, he's brought on himself. He's an alcoholic and you're covering for him. You cover for him when he's out of the office or late for work, you make sure his work is done, and you let him treat you like crap. It's just wrong," Carol said in frustration. "You do all the work and let him take all the credit."

What Carol saw as abnormal behavior was normal for Sue, who had grown up in an alcoholic family. She was adept at making her boss look good—as adept as she had been at making her dysfunctional family appear to be high functioning. Taking care of and covering for an alcoholic boss seemed outrageous to Carol, yet it actually gave Sue a sense of emotional security. Sue knew how to take care of others; she had done so her entire life.

If forced to give it up, Sue might actually feel psychologically and emotionally unemployed. For Sue, the elephant in her childhood living room had now moved to the office.

Fred grew up in an alcoholic family, too, but his work history was quite different from Sue's. Fred was the scapegoat in his family and was frequently told by his mother and siblings that he was "a failure and screwup just like your dad." Like Sue, Fred also suffered from extremely low self-esteem. He was a hard worker, and that hard work was often noticed by supervisors—yet Fred would respond to an outstanding evaluation by being late for work the next several days or procrastinating on a job assignment, and was unconsciously sabotaging his success. He would also turn down promotions if they were offered. His unconscious motto was "If I don't care, if I don't try, I won't fail."

Unlike Sue, Fred's job history revealed a pattern of abruptly leaving jobs. He wouldn't tolerate any criticism and he would change jobs immediately if criticized. He couldn't tolerate success or praise, but he also couldn't tolerate failure or anyone pointing out his mistakes. If he was going to fail, it would be by his own hand and within his own control.

Peggy had been the mascot/pleaser in her alcoholic family. She had little sense of self-worth and applied only for those jobs that were entry-level positions, even though she was qualified for much higher-paying jobs. She was highly skilled in her career, and her knowledge and instincts were exemplary, yet she collapsed when given decision-making responsibility, asking a million questions for fear that she might make a mistake. As one evaluator noted, "Peggy is hard-working and talented. I have recommended her repeatedly for advancement in her job, yet she seems satisfied to stay at an entry-level position. When given more decision-making responsibility, even though she knows the work and often takes on more than required of her behind the scenes, she turns down promotions."

Peggy was referred to her Employee Assistance Program at work. When asked why she preferred to stay in positions for which she was overqualified, she answered, "I don't want to be in charge. I don't want to be the focus of attention or responsibility. If I make a mistake, I open myself up for humiliation. I couldn't stand that." Peggy had been protected by her caretaking sister throughout her child-hood and was still being protected by her sister as an adult. Alcoholic families teach pseudo–self-confidence in caretakers and helplessness in mascot/pleasers and lost children. This increases counterdepen-dence in the caretaker and dependence in those who are taken care of. None of the roles develop true self-confidence or a sense of being successful.

Survivor Roles in the Workplace

Adult children of alcoholics often find their childhood survival roles and the dynamics of their dysfunctional family recurring in the workplace. Dr. Joseph Kern, director of alcoholism treatment for the Nassau County (NY) Department of Drug and Alcohol Addiction discussed this phenomenon in an interview with the *Schenectady Gazette* in 1988. ACOAs, According to Dr. Kern, ". . . are some of the most productive and valuable employees. They are con-scientious, capable, and loyal and will do everything in their power to please. They can also be inflexible, over-responsible, have exces-sive need for control and approval, and have difficulty trusting others. They may have low self-esteem, use drugs and abuse alcohol, have many health problems, and may be depressed" (*Schenectady Gazette*, May 16, 1988).

Although they showed different characteristics in their work-places, Sue, Fred, and Peggy also had many similarities. All suffered from low self-esteem, felt worthless, put others first and themselves last, and were poor team players. They didn't know what normal was, and as a result had a high tolerance for dysfunction in the work-place. Each one of them was hypervigilant, frequently second-guessing the motives or actions of those around them, and each had difficulty trusting the competence of others. They felt responsible for the mistakes and/or emotions of those around them. All felt uncomfortable and undeserving of praise, yet defensive (whether expressed or internalized) when given constructive feedback, and they never felt that their performances were good enough. They had difficulty balancing their personal and professional lives and looked to their work to fill an emptiness inside themselves while continually feeling like imposters. At one time or another each one suffered from depression.

ACOAs often feel ashamed to ask for help, feeling that they should be able to do a job without learning the skill, or that they should be able to do something without being taught. Janet Woititz, author of *Home Away from Home: The Art of Self-Sabotage*, referred to the workplace as a "home away from home" and wrote about this common characteristic.

> The rationale is "I would be invading his or her space if I asked for what I need." So of course you don't ask. You take care of it yourself whether it's little or whether it's within your domain or whether it's not. One woman shared that "When I ask my boss for what I need, I feel shame ... When I asked my mother for what I needed, she would fall apart and I would feel terrible, and I would end up not only not getting my need met but feeling shameful." (42–43)

Because Adult Children of Alcoholics feel responsible for all that goes on around them, many become workaholics and are at high risk for burnout on the job. Janet spoke to this early on in her therapy.

> I always worked harder than anyone else because I felt everything was my responsibility. Even when I was working my way through

college and got a job as a waitress, I set out to make the restaurant more efficient. It was only a summer job but I often ended up doing the work for the manager, other waitresses, and even the cook who took smoke breaks that were too long. Sometimes I was the only waitress serving all the tables as well as the take-out window where we served ice cream cones. I thought it was my personal failure if anyone had to wait. The thought never entered my mind to ask for help. I was so exhausted that I got sick on my only week of vacation before school started.

It is so pathetic: I work to prove I'm okay, yet can't ever allow myself to take credit for anything. I had straight As in college until I was asked to grade myself in a class and I couldn't give myself an A. I brought down my own grade-point average and then belittled myself for not graduating with a 4.0 GPA.

ACOAs can turn a part-time job into a full-time career and they often burn out for their efforts. No matter how hard they work, their inner voice tells them, "You're not doing enough," "You're worthless," "You're an imposter," or "See, I always knew you were a failure." As one ACOA said:

I spent my life trying to put on a confident face, pushing down the feelings of failure, and wearing a mask so that no one would guess what an imposter I felt I really was. I was terrified that someone would find me out. I finally was so exhausted and depressed that I asked for help. I am so thankful I did. Now, after healing, I can just be me, warts and all. I also realize that I wasn't an imposter after all, and I wasn't a failure. I was good at my job—my only downfall was my continued caretaking and hypervigilance.

As Adult Children of Alcoholics work through the pain of the past and enter the present full-time, they realize making choices allows them to live their lives in balance. They become more creative and productive, allowing themselves to feel competent and success-ful. After the tears, they begin to approach their work in a balanced way instead of focusing on the needs of others and neglecting their own.

TEN HELPFUL STRATEGIES
FOR ACOAS IN THE WORKPLACE

1. Stop Trying to Mind Read: For an ACOA growing up in an alcoholic family, hypervigilance was survival. As children we needed to read the faces and behaviors of those around us to know how to act and how to be safe. As adults in the work environment, we frequently spend time focusing on the moods and facial expressions of coworkers or supervisors. An ACOA might see the sour look on a coworker's face and determine that something the ACOA did was wrong, then try harder to please or become defensive and angry. Negativity often feeds on negativity, and before we know it we may have created an entire drama in our head that is baseless in fact.

2. Know Your Own Triggers and Disengage Them: As we've discussed in earlier chapters, many of us grew up with our stress-response systems turned on high. Before healing we are prone to being triggered in adulthood when the time capsules of past memories open up, flooding us with feelings from long ago. The most common areas for trigger responses are in rela-tionships, with our children, and the workplace. It is important to our success in the work environment to learn to recognize when we begin to feel our bodies get tense or shut down, and when we become inexplicably confused, can't think, or begin to emotionally overreact or underreact to situations or coworkers. We need to remember that our feelings are based on painful memories rather than on the current situation. It is important to take a deep breath, focus on the task at hand, and if possible, take a break and journal the feelings and/or pieces of memory that are breaking through, putting them in their proper perspective and timeframe. Later they can be sorted through with a therapist, support group, or supportive other.

3. Don't Take It Personally—Learn to Separate the Act from the Actor: ACOAs frequently come from environments where they were abused, felt devalued, felt responsible for the behaviors of those around them, or felt pressure to continually be the hero who held up the family image. When there is so much pressure on survival in childhood, it is hard as an adult to realize that a mistake is just a mistake and a difference of opinion does not mean that someone is right and someone is wrong— it is merely a difference of opinion. It is also difficult to focus on constructive criticism and to avoid hearing a parent's voice saying, "You never do anything right and will never amount to anything." It takes focus and attention to continue to sort out *then* from *now* and learn to not personalize constructive criticism. We must learn that perfection is not attainable, and realize that differing opinions can be the kernel of creative thought that can take us in new and exciting directions in the work environment.

4. Know Your Own Priorities and Limitations: In *Home Away from Home,* author Janet Woititz also discusses how ACOAs "tend to give everything equal priority. Getting the wash done has the same priority as, say, filling out your income tax. Life consists of many chores, obligations, and projects. If each one has equal priority, it is very easy to get overwhelmed." (84) Success in the work environment often means setting priorities and sticking to them. The completion of a grant due at 5:00 PM on Friday requires you to set aside enough time during the week to make it a priority. You cannot let yourself be distracted by the needs and demands that are constant in a work environment. This may involve saying no to others, which is difficult for ACOAs. It is important to set limits on what is healthy and reasonable. Know when your work is interfering in your life, displacing your personal needs and the needs of your family. Work is a part of life, not life itself.

5. Learn to Trust and Become a Team Player: Many of us who grew up in alcoholic families gained some sense of self-worth through learning the tasks necessary to run the family or take care of siblings. We felt it was our job to make things work, and sometimes to make the alcoholic better. We became a one-person show, never trusting that anyone was there to help. As a result, we are often uncomfortable if we are not attending to every detail, project, or activity at work, and we often double-check the work of others. We feel out of control if not in charge. Sometimes we train others to be dependent by taking on more and more of the load ourselves—then becoming angry when we are alone at work at 10:00 PM. We train others to be dependent when we take on the responsibility of others' feelings and behaviors and continually "fix" things. Learning to be a team player will take discipline and a certain amount of discomfort as you experience feeling out of control and you develop tolerance for feelings of powerlessness while allowing others to make mistakes and be successful.

6. Become a Traffic Guard on Boundary Street: There are few boundaries in an alcoholic family—children frequently take care of the emotional needs of parents instead of the reverse. Parents often confide in children when they should be confiding in other adults. Children take care of children. Family members often speak in communication loops rather than directly to the person they have a concern about, difficulty with, or want something from. As a result, lack of boundaries can frequently find their way into the work environment, as in the case of Sue, who covered for and tolerated the abuse of a dysfunctional boss.

It is important for our health and productivity in the work environment to set and keep boundaries: helping a fellow employee with a task when they have a crisis is quite different from continually doing their work for them. Covering for a boss who has an emergency one day at home is quite different from constantly covering for an alcoholic or dysfunctional boss. Talking *about* others in the workplace rather than *to* others only creates negativity. A boss divulging confidences to an employee is a breach of boundaries. Become aware when you cross boundaries to get praise, self-worth, or connection. It is also important to set boundaries for what is a reasonable workload. This is often easiest when putting things in perspective: When you are thinking of saying yes to yet one more weekend at work, think of yourself in future years looking back on your life. What was really important in the long run and what wasn't?

7. Take Time for You: Children of alcoholics learn to focus on the needs of others rather than on their own. The legacy of that behavior is described by one ACOA:

> There was never time for me. I was always busy making sure the house ran properly and no one got hurt. I never learned to relax. Today, I am burning out because I am continuing to focus on the needs of others rather than on my health and my needs first. I have to learn to take time for myself, yet when I do, I feel selfish and lazy.

It might be therapeutic to leave the office for lunch, take a walk, sit in a park, or take time for yourself every day in some small way.

8. Understand that Breaking Old Nonproductive Patterns Takes Time: Many of us sought approval and gained self-worth by taking care of everyone else. ACOAs in the workplace often attend to the needs of everyone else, taking on extra work or a coworker's or supervisor's task to search for approval or self-worth. We can often stand up for injustices to others, yet we don't know how to speak up for ourselves when we are treated unfairly, when we are expected to accomplish the impossible, or when we are asked to accept a lower wage than the job deserves. When we begin our healing journey and begin to pay attention to our own needs, focus on our own work, and carry a normal workload, we may begin to feel worthless, useless, and unimportant. It is what we call feeling *psychologically unemployed* and others call normal. Recognize these feelings for what they are—the ghosts of the past—and be assured that given time, they will diminish.

9. Practice Stress Reduction: Work is often stressful. This is especially true when we are attempting to change patterns of unhealthy behavior. It is important to learn stress-reduction techniques such as the deep breathing, progressive relaxation, and the grounding techniques presented in Chapter 11.

Talking a walk or jogging during the lunch hour, eating a healthy breakfast and lunch, and practicing grounding techniques all help when dealing with stress.

10. Live Your Life in Balance: One of the most important workplace strategies is learning to live life in balance. It is learning the difference between surviving the past and living in the present. A steady diet of working ten-hour days in the workplace and then working at home is not living life in balance. Neither is spending hours on the Internet. Living life in balance means making sure that you are attending to your physical and emotional health, attending to your spirit, spending time with friends, significant others, children, and family. It also means spending time alone, time learning new things, and having fun. It is important to spend some time understanding the past and setting goals for the future, as well as always being mindful in the present.

17

Acceptance and Forgiveness:
Holding On to Resentment
Is like Taking Poison and
Hoping the Other Guy Dies

Remaining a victim is ultimately a powerless position. It gives
those that hurt you all the power because your happiness is
dependent on someone else's actions. Healthy forgiveness
does not mean absolution; it means that you have the power
to heal your wounds if you are willing.

—*from* The Ultimate Guide to Transforming Anger,
by Jane Middelton-Moz, Lisa Tener, and Peaco Todd

O NE AFTERNOON TWO YEARS AGO, Janet passed the cabinet filled with family pictures and for the first time looked,
really looked, at a picture of herself that was taken when she was
six. A little girl with a broad smile and sad eyes looked back at
Janet from inside the frame. *She was so brave,* Janet thought. *She
tried so hard.* It was not the first time Janet had looked at the picture of her childhood self in earnest, but that day, for the first
time, she *saw* the child she had been. She picked up the picture,

held it to her heart, and examined her six-year-old self.

The alcoholism in the family was in full force at the time the picture was taken. Janet remembered that she had hidden under the bed with her brother the night before, and in the morning she had cleaned up after the drunken party. For many years she had disliked that child in the picture, even blamed her for not being perfect enough, smart enough, or lovable enough for her parents to stop drinking.

Yet that day, for the first time, she felt an almost overwhelming love for the little girl in the picture. She remembered all the times her therapist had asked if she was able to love herself. She had little notion of what the therapist was talking about, but she said what she thought she was supposed to say, what she thought her therapist expected her to say, maybe even what her head told her she should say: "Yes, I think I do." Janet had tried so hard to make the feelings come but they wouldn't. She had *thought* love, she had even felt sorry for that little girl, but until the day she held the picture to her heart, she had never *felt* love.

Today, Janet held a different photo, a picture of her mother. She took the picture out of the cabinet and held it to her heart as she had done with the picture of the little girl two years before. Just as she had when she'd held the picture of her six-year-old self, Janet felt as though she was truly seeing her mother for the first time. She saw the smile on her mother's face and the sadness in her eyes. It was only then that Janet realized how much she resembled her mother.

She had been angry with her mother for so long. Now she realized how grateful she was that she had been able to accept her mother for who she was before her mother had died. Janet had been able to spend some time with her mother without expectations that she would someday tell Janet she loved her, or that she might take Janet in her arms and say how sorry she was for her cruelty toward her child. Janet had accepted that her mother would not stop drinking and become the sober, loving mother she had always wanted. In those last couple of years, she had just accepted her mother for who she was.

With acceptance came limits. Janet was able to set limits when her mother became emotionally abusive. In a firm but loving way she refused to accept her mother's hurtful words. Janet let her mother know that drinking was not allowed in her home, fully realizing that it would mean her mother would visit less. Finally being able to accept what her mother could and could not give had been a blessing.

Today, holding the picture of her mother close to her heart, Janet felt more than acceptance; she felt love and forgiveness. She recognized the same pain on her mother's face that she had once seen on her own. She realized with gratitude that she had faced the ghosts her mother had never been able to face. Her mother had been imprisoned by a past she was never able to understand, and without that cognitive life raft her mother had been doomed to repeat the past. Janet grew tearful as she remembered the mother who never felt the joy of acceptance. She felt the empowerment that comes with the freedom of genuine forgiveness. She was able to experience the love her mother never could. Her past no longer defined her, nor did it determine her present or her future.

Henry Wadsworth Longfellow said, "If we could read the secret history of our enemies, we should find in each man's life sorrow and suffering enough to disarm all hostility." Yet, as Janet learned in her process of healing, it was not possible to be open to the history of those who had hurt her until she could be open to her own history. She could not have compassion for another until she could find compassion for herself. Acceptance and forgiveness do not come at the beginning of a process of healing, but at the end. They come after the anger and resentment, and after the tears.

Counterfeit Forgiveness

There had been a time in Janet's life when she tried to forgive because she thought she should. She had been told that forgiving the family that hurt her would set her free. When she said she forgave her parents for their neglect and abuse, it sounded as sincere as if she were talking about a table and chair. Her forgiveness was forced and therefore counterfeit. Forgiving is not something you do because someone tells you that you should. Forgiving is a personal choice that you decide to do for yourself.

When you try to make yourself forgive too early in your process of healing, you deny your anger and pain and try to pole vault over the hard work of facing and accepting your past. Forgiveness takes time. It takes courage to feel your emotions and to allow the time necessary to reflect inward, allowing the wounds of the past to heal.

If you go about forgiveness with ulterior motives, you gain no benefit and might find yourself angrier, more ashamed, or more resentful than before. Although you might believe your apologies will finally help you get the validation you have been searching for all your life, you might find that the person who has hurt you becomes defensive, angry, and denies his or her behavior. It is important that we not leave the validation of our experience to those who have hurt us. It is often impossible to validate our own experiences and accept that our family members may not share our memories. They may still be in denial of their hurtful behavior, even after we are well into our process of healing.

When We Don't Forgive

An old Chinese proverb says, "The one who pursues revenge should dig two graves." Sometimes it is difficult to let go and forgive because the anger and resentment we feel toward those who hurt us is somehow validation that the hurt took place. We tell ourselves that letting go somehow means they "got away with it" or are no longer responsible for their actions. Remember that forgiveness is not absolution.

Sometimes anger and resentment are methods of protecting ourselves from further hurt. We live inside a wall of anger and resentment because it feels unsafe to risk being hurt again. When we don't trust our ability to set limits and protect ourselves, it is an indication that we are not ready to forgive. Forgiving too quickly is a way to avoid feelings, yet if we wait too long, our rage and resentment chain us to the past.

Early in her therapy, my friend Jill commented to me, "I think I am almost finished with counseling. I've decided that my parents have hurt me enough. I'm not going to be around them anymore or even talk to them on the phone. My dad's always drunk and my mom just denies my feelings and wants me to be a carbon copy of her. I've finally had enough." I thought that Jill was setting a boundary that would make it safe enough for her to do some painful grief work. Sure enough, she spent a year facing a very painful history.

A little over a year later, Jill asked me to go to lunch. She told me that she had invited her mom and dad to visit and that she had set a limit that she had been unable to set before.

I told my dad that I loved him very much and really wanted to see him but that I didn't allow drinking in my home. As usual he didn't say much, but Mom called later and told me I was exaggerating Dad's drinking problem, that he wasn't an alcoholic and that it wouldn't hurt anything to let him have a couple of drinks in the evening while staying at my house. I have never known my dad to have "a couple of drinks," ever. I didn't argue though. I just repeated my limit in a loving way. They are coming but have decided to stay in a hotel instead of at my house. I'm really nervous, but I want to work on a different kind of relationship with them. I just hope I can.

The following week after her parents' visit had ended, Jill called me again. When I asked about her visit with her parents she laughed and said:

It was good. I learned a lot of things about myself and also was able to feel closer to my mom than I ever remember feeling. I didn't protect her. I just let her be herself but I set boundaries on her talking to me about Dad. At one point we went out to dinner. Before I even picked them up, Dad had, of course, had more than a couple of drinks. When we were at the restaurant, he made some racist remarks about our waiter. Before, I would have taken him on and been really embarrassed. This time, I realized those were his opinions, not mine. I wasn't him. It was so freeing.

On the way home Mom said something to me she has been saying in one way or another my entire life. As she handed a sweater to me she said, "Jill, I'm cold. Why don't you put on your sweater." I laughed so hard and just said, "Mom, if you're cold, put on your own sweater. I'm not cold." I realized I'd been putting on my mom's symbolic sweaters my entire life and resenting her for it. I also realized I didn't have to do that anymore. Instead of arguing, I thought it was funny.

We actually had a great visit and I didn't once get defensive. I didn't get to spend a lot of time with them because my dad didn't slow down on his drinking, but Mom actually went to lunch with me alone once and it was great.

Jill had worked hard on her own healing and was able to define herself instead of depending on her parents to define her. Because of that, she could accept who they were, begin a forgiveness process with them, and gradually begin to build a relationship with them based on reality instead of fantasy. She could accept who they were and set limits that showed her acceptance of herself. In doing so, she was able to accept what they could offer rather than continue fighting them for what they couldn't give. She could accept that she wasn't responsible for her father's drinking or her mother's unhappiness. She could not force her father to stop drinking or stop her mother from being codependent—but she could change herself.

Oprah Winfrey once defined forgiveness as "letting go of the hope that the past can be changed. No one can go back and do it over again." When we don't forgive, we need to continue to keep up a wall of anger around us. We are imprisoned by the past while the present moves into the future without us.

Known more for his quotes than for his scientific research, Dutch botanist Paul Boese is famous for saying, "Forgiveness does not change the past, but it does enlarge the present." Janis A. Spring said it another way in her book *How Can I Forgive You? The Courage to Forgive and the Freedom Not To*:

> When you say no to forgiving, you define the offender in terms of the harm he has caused you and exorcise all other information about him that might rehabilitate him in your eyes. You invest in hating him, and frame him in ways that support your hatred . . . You need to see him not as he is but as you need him to be. You define him by distinguishing him from you: "I am what you are not." (89)

For some, remaining a victim can feel like a safe place. It can mean not being responsible for the healing that needs to happen. For others, it can mean the right to sit in judgment. Forgiveness is not blind, nor does it mean reconciliation if reconnecting is unsafe. Forgiveness means operating with true insight and clear sight— often for the first time.

Forgiving Is Not Forgetting

Forgiveness is not the same as forgetting, nor does it diminish the hurt that has been caused. Forgiveness is active, not passive. The choice to forgive belongs to the person who has been injured, not to the person who is responsible for the injury. Forgiveness does not necessarily mean rebuilding a relationship with the person who has hurt you. For some, connection with those who have hurt them is simply not safe. A woman who has been beaten by her husband remains a prisoner if she forgives the beatings only to take more. She can attain freedom in forgiveness only after she truly accepts the seriousness of her husband's abusive behavior. By taking action and requiring him to get help, or by leaving the abusive situation, she allows herself to heal from the pain of the abuse. Continuing to allow the abuse is continuing to be in denial.

When You Can't Forgive Yourself

Many Adult Children are held captive by a painful past because they can't forgive themselves. In community workshops, I often ask people to make necklaces that represent their lives. They use different beads to represent their strengths, the traumas they have survived, supportive people in their lives, their addictions, their recovery, and other related life issues. Some of the most difficult beads for people to acknowledge and talk about are the beads for those they have hurt prior to their recovery and healing. It is often the story behind those beads that has stopped their progress in healing.

A woman who believed she had hurt her sister when she was only a child herself had a bead that represented that painful relationship. She resented her sister, who was frequently left in her care when their parents were drunk, and knew she had misdirected the anger she felt toward her parents to her sister. It was only when she was able to accept her feelings, her behavior, and the fact that she had been a child herself, that she was able to let go of a lifetime of guilt and speak to her sister.

If you have difficulty forgiving yourself, it may be due to an injury you caused another. For instance, we have worked with many children of alcoholics who themselves became alcoholic and hurt their own children in the process. Accepting what you have done and asking for forgiveness does not mean letting yourself off the hook. It was what it was. Acceptance means learning from mistakes, carrying the wisdom of that learning, and moving on. Blaming yourself for the injury you have caused your children and believing that you are therefore responsible for their poor choices creates more guilt, and this guilt causes you to make further mistakes—overindulging your children, enabling their addictions, or allowing them to use emotional blackmail to continue learned helplessness. Indulging is not healthy, nor is it acceptance.

Accepting the hurts we have caused others and the imperfections in ourselves, and then getting on with the business of living, is part of healing and forgiving. Taking responsibility for what we have done wrong can lead us to be more mindful of our actions in the present and can motivate us to do things in a different way. Without acceptance we can become lifelong victims of our own imperfections, bound to a painful past, blaming others, needing to be right and in control, or punishing ourselves again and again rather than changing, growing, accepting, forgiving, and moving forward.

Forgiving When the Person
Who Injured You Is Not Present

Sometimes it is not safe to forgive someone in person nor is it respectful to pressure someone to hear your apology if listening to that apology is not acceptable to them. You can forgive another person or apologize to someone you have hurt even if that person is no longer alive.

It is often helpful to express everything you have to say in a letter. It is important to understand that this letter is a vehicle for you to release feelings that have held you captive. It is not meant to be sent. It may be written over a period of time or all at once, and then witnessed by a therapist, a support group, or someone you trust. Afterward, you can ask your witness to be present when you burn the letter. For many, burning the letter is an act of turning hurt, anger, and pain over to a Higher Power; for others, the smoke represents a release of all that has prevented them from moving on.

Steps to Forgiveness

Forgiveness is not an act; it is a process with many steps. They include:

1. Accepting the history—the reality—of what has taken place.

2. Working through your feelings about what has been done to you: anger, sadness, resentment, guilt, shame, fear, and other emotions.

3. Acknowledging your own power and courage in healing. Letting go and forgiving does not compromise the self, but empowers the self. It means moving from victim, to survivor, to human being.

4. Accepting the true nature of the hurt you have experienced. The person who hurt you is still responsible for his or her actions. Forgiveness does not erase responsibility.

5. Accepting the reality of the person you are forgiving and understanding what they are and are not capable of. Set limits on unhealthy behavior if you chose to continue or re-establish a relationship with the person. Reconciliation is always a choice.

6. Accepting that while we didn't create the painful experiences in our childhood, we are responsible for how we respond to them as adults, and how we continue to allow them to affect our lives.

7. Choosing how you wish to forgive: privately—forgiveness in your heart but never spoken; in person—with full realization that forgiving does not necessarily mean the person will acknowledge their behavior; or in letter form—having the letter witnessed, then burned.

8. Letting go of the toxic feelings of anger, resentment, or revenge that are chaining you to the past.

As you go through your process of healing there are some questions that might be helpful to ask yourself on an ongoing basis:

• Do I frequently spend time reliving hurtful events in my life? Does the reliving of the past diminish the quality of my life in the present?

• Do I continually revisit past injustices? If I do, does this process cause me to avoid people I might enjoy relationships with or cause me to carry negativity with me to keep myself safe?

• Am I displacing my anger and resentment toward someone who hurt me in the past to those I am close to in the present?

• Do I feel powerless regarding my past and my family? Does this sense of powerlessness stem from allowing others to continue to define me and the past?

People who are still enraged and resentful about their past have difficulty moving on, fully experiencing the present, or entering new relationships without the presence of past ghosts. Their continued blaming and resentment hold them captive to the past. We do not create the painful experiences of growing up in an alcoholic family, but we are responsible for how we continue to respond to the hurts inside us. We can hold on to bitterness, resentment, or guilt, or we can let them go. With forgiveness comes empowerment and the freedom to move on to all that is in front of us.

18

Finding the Sacred in the Ordinary:
Opening a Window to Spirituality for
Adult Children of Alcoholics

Religion is for those who don't want to go to hell.
Spirituality is for those of us
who have already been through it.

—Anonymous

E VEN DURING EXTREMELY DIFFICULT TIMES in their lives,
hundreds of Adult Children of Alcoholics (ACOAs) have
described feeling "something" next to them. Some call it a "spirit
guide," some call it "God." Others use names like Creator, Jesus,
Goddess, Allah, Buddha, or Nature. Some have no name for it at all:
it just is.

Christina Grof, a pioneer in the transpersonal psychology movement, wrote about her search for this state of being in her book
Thirst for Wholeness: Attachment, Addiction, and the Spiritual Path.

As far back into my childhood as I can remember, I was searching
for something I could not name. Whatever I was looking for would help

me feel all right, at home, as though I belonged. If I could find it, I would no longer be lonely. I would know what it is like to be loved and accepted, and I would be able to love in return. I would be happy, fulfilled, and at peace with myself, my life, and the world. I would feel free, unfettered, expansive, and joyful. (9)

As young children, ACOAs often found peace and strength in the spirituality of ordinary things. A renowned pediatric surgeon and author, Fred Epstein, M.D., spoke about his experience with the healing power of faith for children in his care: "It doesn't matter if you're secular or religious, Jewish or Christian, Hindu or Muslim . . . I've seen kids sustained through terrible ordeals by their belief in Tinker Bell—as long as you believe in something . . . If you don't believe in anything, you're sunk" (102).

In Chapter 5 we met Taylor, whose story helped to illustrate the emotional resiliency of ACOAs. In one of her sessions, Taylor's therapist asked her to draw pictures of her childhood. As they discussed the meaning of each drawing, Taylor described many of the traumas she had experienced. The final two frames fascinated her therapist. One was of a little girl who was crying and walking down a path with a German shepherd trotting along behind her. Although she was crying, her walk seemed brisk and determined. The moon and the stars seemed to light her way; even the fireflies in the picture around the little girl seemed to come to life. The therapist could almost imagine their lights blinking on and off, and the way Taylor had drawn them made them appear as bright miniature angels surrounding the child. In a speech bubble from the little girl's mouth was a song about holding your head up high as you walk through a storm. In the final frame, the little girl sat on a boulder by a stream with a beatific smile and a serene look on her face, the angelic fireflies still surrounding her. She was staring up at the sky and the same song she often heard on the radio surrounded her even though her mouth was closed,

Taylor's therapist was mesmerized by the last two frames of Taylor's story. "You are quite an artist," she commented. "I am really interested in the last two frames. Please tell me about them."

> That spot next to the stream was my safe place. It was where I went after a drunken party or abuse. My dog, Berta, was always with me and I felt surrounded with a love that I can't explain. As it says, I never felt alone. I know my life was a nightmare, it really was, but I always felt something surrounding me that felt like love. I always felt close to God. I never went to Sunday school or church; my family wasn't spiritual or religious. I don't know how I knew but I just knew I wasn't alone and if I could just keep having faith and hope, I would be all right. I would get through it, and I did. Even in the hardest times, I could go to that place in my mind, that boulder by the river with Berta sitting beside me. That was my home, my place of unconditional love. Today, I live by a stream and I still have a German shepherd. As hard as things were then, I just knew I would be all right.

Over the years we have heard hundreds of stories like Taylor's from other ACOAs. Richard, whom we first met in Chapter 3, shared his story with us:

> I think I always felt a spiritual longing. I just didn't know what it was. I think I tried to escape my pain and loneliness through booze, pills, and sex. Then I hit bottom. I felt that I had gone down so far that I would never get up. I had lost my family, my job, everything. It was then I decided to turn my life over to God as I understood him. That surrender brought me home. I will never forget the first time I said the Serenity Prayer: *God grant me the serenity to accept the things I cannot change, the courage to change the things I can, and the*

wisdom to know the difference. Wow, that spoke to me as an alcoholic, but also as an ACOA. I remember thinking, "I'm really not responsible for everything? What a relief."

Christina Grof explored this idea of spirituality in *Thirst for Wholeness*:

> Through surrender of our ego control, we begin to develop a relationship with a deeper Self that brings us increased inspiration, health, and wholeness. A joke around recovery groups is, "Religion is for those who do not want to go to hell. Spirituality is for those who have been to hell and don't want to go back." In order to stay free of the hell of our addictions, we progress towards a direct experience of the divine and its influence on our daily lives . . . As we touch our deeper Self, our experience of alienation slowly disappears. More and more we feel we belong, often for the first times in our lives. (170)

Many ACOAs find connection to a Higher Power through Alcoholics Anonymous. Others find connection to a power greater than themselves in ACOA, Al-Anon, or growth groups. Many, like Taylor, felt a spiritual presence early in life that allowed them to feel belonging, protection, unconditional love, and a sense of hope for the future. Some searched to disconnect from the pain inside them and quench their spiritual longing with alcohol, drugs, religious fanaticism, money, sex, or power, only to genuinely connect with a Higher Power in their recovery. Others never turned to addictions but felt a strong spiritual connection to something beyond themselves at the end of their grief-work process. Some feel connected to a Higher Power as Taylor did, through time spent walking in the woods, on a beach, while gardening, or through creativity—sculpting with clay, painting, or writing music. Paul for instance, was drawn to clay.

There was something about centering the clay. Early on as I worked at the wheel, I felt connected to something in the center of my being and in the center of the universe. All my life I had cursed God for my fate, and then all at once I understood God's creation and love in a way I never had. All of a sudden that place filled with bitterness and pain cleared out and was filled instead with a sense of wonder, belonging, and peace that I had never before experienced.

Last night I was watching *The Wizard of Oz,* a movie that I had seen when I was a kid. I realized the spiritual feeling that had filled the empty place inside me was like the feeling of coming home. It was like when Dorothy was told that she always had the power to return home all along. She just had to learn it for herself. For me it was more like clearing a space for a part of me that was there from the beginning of time.

Some ACOAs find their connection to a Higher Power in prayer, meditation, temple, or church. Here is Joan's experience:

I had just left my therapist's office and was walking home. It was a week before Christmas and I was feeling a sense of serenity, yet I also had a sense that something was missing in my life. I heard music coming from a church that I had passed literally hundreds of times before but never paid much attention to. That day, the sound of the strong voices singing the "Hallelujah Chorus" made me feel like I was soaring, taking flight from some place deep within my spirit. It was like the voices were calling me, asking me to join them. I wasn't dressed for church but it felt like something was pulling me. As soon as I entered the church, I saw the choir—twenty or thirty people of all ages, from different cultures and seemingly all walks of life. I was taken by the joyful expressions on their faces. I just stood, entranced, feeling connected to God in a way I had never felt before. A woman sitting in the back row turned and saw me and she beckoned me to come forward. She made a place for me, whispering, "Welcome. I'm so glad you could join us." She took my hand and introduced herself and her family. I realized that I had gone to church my whole childhood but never truly felt "welcomed in" before. I felt an overwhelming sense of belonging and an odd sense that I had come home.

I still go to that church today. I've found family there and a sense of community. I've also found a connection to God. I didn't even know what denomination the church was. No one asked me my faith or questioned whether I belonged. They just welcomed me.

When I was a kid, the church I had been forced to attend had been a lot like my alcoholic family. I often felt shamed and judged. I was taught that there was only one way to pray, one belief, and I'd better behave and just do what I was told. I couldn't ask questions and was supposed to be loyal. I went every Sunday. I was supposed to believe that I would never get to heaven if I didn't believe what everyone there believed. I never could understand how a loving God who would give some of his children everything and his other kids nothing. I still can't.

Spirituality: Finding the Sacred in the Ordinary

True spirituality is developing faith, connecting to a power greater than ourselves, and finding the sacred in ordinary things. Spirituality is the awareness of the inner connectedness of all of creation. It is having faith in a Higher Power, in ourselves, in others, and in life itself. Spirituality is our candle in the darkness.

Having faith is not a spectator sport. We are not powerless spectators in life. Through faith we can become what we believe ourselves to be and have the strength to get through the darkest of times, joyously celebrate, and feel gratitude for life's gifts. Faith is not a fortress against all danger or hurts of life nor does it prevent suffering. As Thomas Moore wrote, "Faith is a gift of the spirit that allows the soul to remain attached to its unfolding."

Many ACOAs felt a lack of belonging in church early in their lives.

Some were physically, emotionally, and sexually abused as children by religious leaders. Harold Belmont, a wise Native American elder, once told me that one should never confuse "Christianity" with "churchianity." This simple statement illustrates that many people of all faiths confuse dogma, judgment, and righteousness with spirituality. As Joan found, there are many religious people who aren't spiritual. There are also many deeply spiritual people like Taylor and Paul who are not religious. Yet Taylor, Paul, Richard, and Joan all found a connection to a Higher Power in different stages of their lives and through different faiths and beliefs. They found serenity, strength, belief, trust, and dignity. Rollo May defines this idea of connection and spirituality in his book *Existential Psychology*:

> Spiritual growth is movement toward increasing fulfillment of the two great commandments—deepening love for God, others, and self. Dignity is the way God begins the process of spiritual growth in us. Dignity always says we are worth far more than we can ever give ourselves credit for, that we are meant for greater things than those we ever could aspire to, and that we are more loved and more in need of love than we can ever know. (169–170)

It is much the same with families. Some are loving and consistent with deeply held values, and offer compassionate discipline. Their children feel valued, cherished, and safe. There are also hurtful families where children are shamed, harshly punished, fearful, and unsafe. A truly spiritual environment is a welcoming, nonjudgmental, inclusive, and loving place where those who enter feel strength, serenity, empowerment, connection, and trust. That place may be a building where people congregate to celebrate a common spirituality, or it may be something more personal and intimate, where perhaps you are the lone worshiper.

However we choose to honor our Higher Power in our healing journey, there is a time when we finally realize we are not in control of the universe. We are not in control of whether our family members drink or make the choice to become sober. We are not responsible for the behavior and actions of those around us. We begin to be open to the present and open ourselves up to a connection to a Higher Power. It is at that place in our healing journey when we joyfully surrender to a power greater than ourselves as we understand it.

Joan was forced to go to church when she was young and she did what she was told to do. She surrendered to a power greater than herself when she entered that other church as an adult, "The spirituality I felt in the church I entered that night made me feel empowered, not powerless," Joan said thoughtfully. "I felt a sense of belonging rather than exclusion. Religion is often interpreted in a way that makes one feel powerless, not worthy, and excluded. In my healing, I trust my intuition to know the difference." Maxine Schnall discussed this concept of empowerment through surrender in her book *What Doesn't Kill You Makes You Stronger:*

> Surrender is not to be confused with resignation, a feeling of powerlessness that leads to depression and paralysis. Resignation is giving away your power; surrender is getting power back. When you resign yourself to something, you believe there is nothing you can do. When you surrender, you have faith that with the universe on your side, anything is possible . . . Your pain, fear, and anger don't go away when you surrender them, but you gain the strength to take all your outrage and sorrow and turn them into a resolve to make something positive come out of your experience. Loving more, deepening your compassion for those who suffer as you have suffered, is a way to ensure that the goodness of the human spirit will always triumph over tragedy and evil. (59)

Ceremony and Ritual

Involvement in ceremony and ritual is an important way many ACOAs have embraced inclusion and spirituality. Ceremony and ritual allow for the expression of strong emotions, such as grief, joy, sorrow, and gratitude. Rituals help us feel less alone in times of difficulty by strengthening our sense of community, acknowledging life transitions and rites of passage, and providing a sense of belonging.

We can create our own rituals and ceremonies in our lives. We can begin rites of passage for our young men and young women. We can write letters to those who have hurt us. We can send them, or we can have them witnessed and then burn them. We can spread the ashes on the earth and plant seeds that represent the positive things we would like to have grow in us. We can celebrate our successes and those of our children, grandchildren, nieces, or nephews. We can plant trees in honor of our loved ones who have passed on as a symbol of remembrance.

Twenty-three women followed Gloria to the beach at 4:30 AM. They stood in a circle and prayed, and sang songs of thanksgiving as the sun began to rise over the horizon. There were tears in Gloria's eyes as well as in the eyes of the women who had joined her. "I am the first woman in three generations in my family to witness the sunrise at 5:05 AM at the age of fifty-seven on this date. I feel sad for my mother and grandmother, " Gloria said, "But so grateful for all of you."

Gloria had been raised in a alcoholic family filled with pain. Her father had entered the military as a boy of sixteen and had fought in two wars. He had been alcoholic and violent all of Gloria's young life. Her mother (also an alcoholic) had ended her own life before

Gloria was twenty-one years old. She was the second woman on the maternal side of the family to die at the same age on the same date and time of day. (Gloria's grandmother was the first.) Both women had died at age fifty-seven on May 3 at 5:00 AM. Gloria had worked hard not to repeat the legacy in her family and had decided to mark the end of the generational pain by having a ceremony on the beach at the exact time her mother and grandmother had died. The women who joined her also celebrated with her; in one way or another, they all had symbolically broken the legacies of pain in their own families.

Later that afternoon Gloria held a celebration of life ceremony and feast that was attended by three generations of participants' families. Little children were put in a circle and their mothers surrounded them. There was a circle of grandmothers around the mothers, and the grandfathers and fathers surrounded the circle of grandmothers. The circle symbolically represented life today. The children were protected in the center circle by their community of adults; mothers, the life givers, were held up by the grandmothers, who were the wisdom givers, and the men were the protectors of the circle. The children played as the next generation thanked and celebrated their mothers and fathers for breaking the cycle of addiction in the family. After the ceremony ended, everyone joined together to eat, play, and celebrate.

Early the next morning as Gloria was going toward the beach to walk, one of her adult sons called out to her, "Hey Mom! What does it feel like to be the first woman in three generations to see the sunrise on this day? You must feel really proud today. I just wanted to say thank you."

As you connect to the deepest part of yourself in the healing process, the need for chaos lessens and you begin to feel a need for a quiet place where you can feel connected to a Higher Power. You begin to feel the energy that surrounds and touches every living thing, and you begin to acquire a new and special sight that allows you to find the sacred in ordinary things—things that perhaps you had never noticed before.

We invite you to take time every day away from the television, computer, or your hectic pace, and spend time in solitude. Go for a walk along a beach or in a forest, sit by a stream, fish, or just relax. Watch the children playing in your neighborhood. Attune yourself to the energy around you—the strength of the waves lapping on the beach, the amazing beauty and strength of a spiderweb. Pay attention to textures, smells, and sounds. Feel the energy around you and the presence of the sacredness in ordinary things—things you often never allow yourself the time to experience. Make this journey a priority in your life. Celebrate yourself and feel gratitude for the child you were and the adult you have become, after the tears.

Conclusion

IT HAS BEEN MANY YEARS since we first began speaking from our hearts to you, the Adult Children of Alcoholics (ACOAs). We believed then, as we still believe today, that as children raised in alcoholic families you are not crazy or permanently wounded, as many of you secretly think you are. Instead, you are open systems that are affected by, but not determined by, a painful past. The difficulties in your adult lives are not personal shortcomings, but are a result of the normal survival adaptations you developed in response to unhealthy and painful childhoods.

We are humbled to be a small part of a movement that has already transformed millions of lives. Adult children from many other types of dysfunctional families have also benefited from the knowledge that we and our contemporaries in the field have compiled over the years.

When we wrote the original version of our book, *After the Tears: Reclaiming the Personal Losses of Childhood,* we hoped it would serve as a beacon in the healing journey for Adult Children of Alcoholics. We hope this new edition will help to weave the foundation of understanding from the past with the new clinical knowledge of the present, serving as a cornerstone for the hope and healing in children of alcoholics who are reaching adulthood today. We also want to continue to communicate hope to those ACOAs who are familiar with our work and assure you that support is available; you no longer need to keep the secrets that have caused you to suffer in silence for far too long.

Millions of children are still suffering the painful effects of growing up with parents who were addicted, and many of them are now reaching adulthood. Unfortunately, there are fewer ACOA meetings today than in the past. As one writer attests to on acoa-blog. blogspot.com, "Once upon a time there were thousands of ACA, ACOA, and Al-Anon-ACOA meetings. In the Seattle area alone there were once over a hundred . . . Now there are two, and the nearest one to me is forty miles away."

Alcoholism and addiction did not go away just because there was more awareness and discussion about them. Again, we hope that this new edition of *After the Tears* will provide validation and a beacon of hope for Adult Children of alcoholic and addicted families. Over the years, many ACOAs have benefited from the support groups they attended. They cried, laughed, played together, and learned from each other. They were "honest mirrors" who listened and validated each other's painful realities. Today, in many parts of the country, an ACOA has to drive many miles to find a support group. We hope this new edition will also provide an impetus for those on their healing journey to create new support groups and support programs in their local areas through NACOA (National Association for Children of Alcoholics).

It is true that alcoholism is the gift that keeps on giving. It is equally true that the strength and resiliency developed by millions of

Adult Children of Alcoholics, despite—and even because of—their pain, can also be the gifts that keep on giving. Millions of ACOAs like you have dealt with the pain and anger in your lives and moved past them. The energy you used to focus toward your anger is now used to create change in your small corner of the world and in the greater world around you. Collectively, you have used your anger energy and determination to fight for the rights of children, to become supportive relationship partners and supportive adults to your elderly parents, to develop balanced lives, and to become committed role models determined to rebuild a world of health for the generations that follow. Like the phoenix rising from the ashes, Adult Children can heal and can transform the legacy of a painful past into gifts and strengths of the present—after the tears.

Juggler in a Mirror

From that place inside of me
That learning, yearning writer in me
I saw by touch, not from sight
A woman who passed my way in life
Who shared a person I recognized
Surviving like myself.

I watched her juggle as she stood
Words and feelings made of wood
Sticks that talked of *competence*
Of *strength* and *will* and *confidence*
And four or five marked *child* and *home*
And one marked *guilt* that cracked and hit
The others as they flew.

She tossed up two marked *love* and *care*
That hung above her in the air
And one marked *trust* beneath the two
That stopped the lower stick marked *you*
From soaring in the sky.

So skillfully she juggled life
That I would not have recognized
The perspiration on her face
That drew me to her side
If not for one large purple stick
That dropped behind her with a click
And called its name out loud and clear
The one she could not juggle, *fear.*

I could not watch, it hurt too much
And, I thought between the two of us
That we could learn to balance all some way
Beyond the price survivors pay
Who stand alone in streets and crowds
Destined to juggle life.

Perhaps we both could recognize
That none that we had met in life
Had taught us how to juggle sticks.
They had passed them on to us with doubt
With tears that had never made it from the inside out
They had dropped them all, save two or three
The sticks marked *child* and *family.*

by Jane Middelton (Moz) from
Juggler in a Mirror (1980)

Glossary

affect dysregulation. The end product of faulty early attachment experiences between the infant and the primary caregiver; the child fails to learn how to modulate internal emotional states, leading to an inability to self-soothe.

affect tolerance. The experience of affect or emotion entering into consciousness; the ability to feel and tolerate the full range of emotions, including strong feelings such as terror, fear, rage, anger, sadness, joy, and so on.

age of emancipation. The age at which children, who have been provided roots by their parents, are now expected to leave home and begin their own lives—usually between the ages of eighteen and twenty-four.

bondage of past generations. That which is unhealed in prior generations, such as carried feelings, grief around unresolved losses, roles, rules, and family structure, and which is transmitted transgenerationally and becomes the legacy of the next generation.

bond permanence. An individual's pathological fantasy illusion of connection to another in order to defend against the terror and dread of aloneness and separateness, whereby one trades off aloneness for the illusion of security. Also delineates the state of psychological bondage and loss of freedom a child experiences when ensnared by a parent in a fantasy bond.

codependency. Abuse or neglect of self in favor of someone or something else. The "mirror" illness that develops in response to living with an addicted individual. It is considered primary if the addiction was present in the childhood environment, and secondary if in the adult environment. Many ACOAs experience both primary and secondary codependency.

cognitive life raft. A significant component of the grief-work process, which requires both cognitive and emotional mastery for resolution. A cognitive life raft provides a safe holding environment for feelings and a map to the intellectual and emotional terrain of grief work; for instance, the intellectual understanding of the characteristics of Adult Children or the steps necessary for healing.

competent imposter. A role assumed by some adult children of alcoholic and addicted families in their professional and personal lives. When what is mirrored back to children is negative, this negativity is internalized by children—later making it difficult for them recognize and own their talents and abilities. Such adult children have difficulty owning their success, believing they have just duped others who don't know who they "really" are.

continuum-of-life drawings. These are drawings made by individuals of their own life trajectories; a graphic depiction of how each person feels his or her life has been, how it currently is, and how it may be in the future. The drawings are in five- or ten-year segments, representing the artist's feelings at ages five, ten, fifteen, twenty, and so on to the present, as well as depictions of how life may be in the future.

cumulative trauma. Cumulative trauma can comprise a series of events, none of which appears to be major, but when taken together constitute a pileup of wounding life events. The meaning of the term "trauma" can be traced to the Greek word for "wound."

defenses. *See* **denial; suppression; repression.**

defensively self-reliant. The way in which ACOAs learn to not rely on others but only on themselves. This term was developed by Jane Middelton-Moz and Lorie Dwinell in their Adults Kids Workshops in the late 1970s and early 1980s.

delayed grief. Grief work put on a psychic backburner until a safer time. Grief work requires the individual to fully feel his or her feelings in a safe environment that does not impede the emotional work of acknowledging losses and working through them. An individual in a grief-suppressing

environment with a pileup of losses and cumulative trauma will unconsciously put the process of working through losses on a "backburner"
until a later time when circumstances can both tolerate and facilitate the
grief.

delayed stress. When stressors pile up and become cumulative without the
individual being aware of the degree to which he or she is compromised
and stressed.

delirium tremens. A potentially fatal alcohol withdrawal syndrome that
may include hallucinations, seizures, and elevated temperature.

denial. An ego defense by an individual who unconsciously attempts to allay
anxiety and lessen conflict between competing aspects of a situation or
circumstance. This is accomplished by banishing some or all of the anxi-
ety-provoking material from awareness.

disowned child. All individuals have three "child selves": one, the precious
child they were at birth; two, the loyal child who maintains loyalty to the
parents no matter what parents do; and three, the wounded child whose
trauma is healed through "inner-child" and grief work. When children
internalize punitive parental figures, they may become complicit with
the parents in wounding and disowning their own precious child self.

ego ideal. The way Adult Children unconsciously believe they *should* be,
based on what they believe their parents, family, and culture expect them
to be, rather than how they actually are. If parents need an exemplary
child, Adult Children suppress the feelings and behavior of their real self
and produce what parents need them to be.

emotional net. A safe holding environment within which Adult Children
can fully feel their feelings as part of working through and resolving loss.
An emotional net is a safe person or group of people who can mirror the
Adult Child as he or she is and show empathy for the child he or she was.

enmeshed family. When family members do not separate in a natural way
and instead maintain bonds in a "super-glue" fashion.

fantasy ideal. When an individual denies all negative aspects of an object—by
self-deluding and distorting reality—and establishes an unattainable,
fantasy standard of the perfect mate, perfect family, and/or perfect parents.

fantasy parents. A child's creation of the parents he or she longs for rather
than the reality of who and how they are.

faulty mirroring. When parents unconsciously impose their own unmet expectations on their children. Such parents do not act as healthy and normal "mirrors" for their children. Out of their own wounding, they expect their children to fulfill their unmet childhood needs by becoming a particular kind of child. When parents were not lovingly mirrored and prized for exactly who they were as children, they are incapable of mirroring their own children.

flashbacks. A symptom of post-traumatic stress disorder in which vivid memories or pieces of memory of a traumatic experience are triggered or restimulated. These are experienced by the individual as if they were happening again in present time.

genogram. A diagram detailing the current generation, three preceeding generations, and the history of behavior patterns (divorce, abortion, substance abuse, suicide, and so forth) or medical conditions of a family over those generations. This family map is color-coded for trauma—a colored dot representing each trauma—so the history of trauma can be easily identified.

grief/grief work. A subjective process which follows loss. It is a socially facilitated process in that individuals need to share their feelings around what has been lost with God or one other human being. The pain heals itself when the environment in which it is shared can support the strong feelings that accompany grief.

guilt. A feeling state and a thought process characterized by words such as *blame, should have, fault, responsibility.* It is about what one does rather than about who one is.

hypervigilant. A state of exaggerated, alert watchfulness that is a consequence and a symptom of post-traumatic stress disorder.

ideal child. *See* **ego ideal.**

identification with the aggressor. Unconscious defense mechanism whereby an abused person takes on the role and the behavior of the abuser, treating others as they have been treated.

integrating feelings. Revisiting the losses of the past in an emotionally supportive environment. This affords the opportunity to connect the memories, events, and feelings and work through them. In so doing, it is no longer necessary to suppress or deny the reality of the past. An individual's feelings become available to him or her and are integrated.

intellectualization. A psychological defense in which individuals have the ability to think about an event but suppress the feelings associated with the event. By being "in our head," the feelings about the event are split off and unavailable to us.

internalized abusive parent. Process by which the child identifies with the actual abusive parent, leading to the child's treating himself or herself in the same way he or she was treated by the parent.

looking glass. Parents' views of children are reflected back to the children like a looking glass; children in turn internalize those views and see themselves the way they are seen and responded to by their parents.

loyal child. One of our three child selves (the precious child, the loyal child, and the wounded child); the loyal child is the parental protector who will take their side regardless of how the parents have behaved. Before completing one's grief work, this is the child self who always says, "They did the best they could." In recovery, this child self can say the same words, but the words come from a place of healing, acceptance, and possibly forgiveness.

mirror projection. Projection is an unconscious ego defense that allows one to deny and disown parts of self that are unacceptable and do not fit a picture of the ideal self. These qualities or traits are then seen in another. In a mirror projection, a parent sees his or her own despised traits in the child and attributes these traits as the child's own.

mourning. A psychological process set in motion by loss. Tasks of mourning include: one, making real the loss in one's external world; two, working through the feelings associated with the loss in one's internal world; and three, withdrawing emotional investment in that which has been lost and reinvesting in life.

multigenerational loss. Loss that has not metabolized and resolved in prior generations and is transmitted to subsequent generations.

need-satisfying object of parents. Adults come to parenting with unfinished business when their own psychological needs were not met in childhood by their parents. They look to their children to meet needs that should have been met by their own parents.

normalizing of responses. A state of being in recovery where ACOAs discover their responses are normal responses to abnormal events. Before recovery they tend to live in silence and isolation, believing that their responses are pathological.

post-traumatic stress disorder (PTSD). An anxiety state created by the individual's ego being overwhelmed by an inordinately stressful event or circumstance. Distressing psychological symptoms include flashbacks, nightmares, a recurrent re-experiencing of the event as if it were currently happening, psychic numbing, startle response, problems with concentration and memory, sleeplessness, survival guilt, and a loss of interest in usual activities.

pseudopartners. Children in dysfunctional families are often drafted to meet the needs of the parent. A child can be recruited as a surrogate spouse to one of the parents, which violates the boundary between the generations and denies the child the opportunity to take ownership of his or her own appropriate development.

psychological muscle. Created by the development and use of coping skills for psychological strength; similar to the way development and practice of exercises for physical strength build physical muscle.

psychologically unemployed. The feeling of uselessness experienced by some codependent individuals when healing begins and attention is paid to the self instead of others

repression. An ego defense that is automatic and unconscious. Unwelcome material is warded off and not allowed into consciousness, while the individual continues unaware of the existence of the material.

resilience. An individual's ability to bounce back after stressful life events. Resilience is both part of an individual's biological and psychological endowment as well as the end result of confronting life circumstances with creativity, openness to learning from the experience, hopeful perseverance and hardiness of spirit, a willingness to ask for and accept help while maintaining autonomy and boundaries, an ability to tolerate pain, and a commitment to eventually wresting meaning from what has happened.

shame. A thought process and a feeling state characterized by words like *humiliation, embarrassment, disgrace, ridiculousness,* and *flawed.* It is the belief and feeling that one is defective.

startle reaction. One of the manifestations of post-traumatic stress disorder. The traumatized individual maintains high levels of cortisol and startles at any stimulus that the amygdala (one of the limbic centers of the brain) interprets as possible danger.

suppression. An ego defense in which the individual consciously banishes from awareness material that is distressing and therefore is not welcome in conscious awareness.

trauma. A psychic wound caused by an event of such magnitude that the individual's normal coping capacity is overwhelmed to the point of not being able to metabolize, master, and work through what has happened.

trigger. Any stimulus that can evoke the emergence into conscious awareness of memories, thoughts, feelings, or body sensations that have been suppressed or repressed as a defense on the part of the ego because they threaten the psychological integrity of the individual. Triggering events often include anniversary dates, seasons of the year, sights, smells, places, gestures, words, ages children turn—anything potentially reminiscent of the disavowed event.

Resources

Adult Children of Alcoholics (ACA)
website: www.adultchildren.org • email: info@adultchildren.org
A twelve-step program for individuals who grew up in addicted or
dysfunctional families.

Al-Anon/Alateen
888-4AL-ANON for meeting schedules
757-563-1600 for Al-Anon Family Group Headquarters
website: www.al-anon.alateen.org • email: wso@al-anon.org
A twelve-step program for family members and other individuals
affected by another's alcohol addiction.

Alcoholics Anonymous (AA)
212-870-3400
website: www.aa.org
A twelve-step program for alcoholics and alcohol abusers.

Caregiver Wellness
website: www.caregiverwellness.ca • e-mail: caregiverwellness@shaw.ca
A resource for caregivers looking for support for compassion
fatigue or chronic sorrow.

Codependents Anonymous (CoDA)
602-277-7991
website: www.coda.org • email: outreach@coda.org
A twelve-step program for codependency recovery.

Codependents of Sex and Love Addicts Anonymous (COSLAA)
860-456-0032 • website: www.coslaa.org
A twelve-step program for family members and intimate others
who have been affected by relationship with a sex and love addict.

COSA
763-537-6904
website: www.cosa-recovery.org • email: info@cosa-recovery.org
A twelve-step program for those affected by individuals with
compulsive sexual behavior.

National Alliance for Care Giving (NAC)
website: www.caregiving.org
A resource for those providing care for sick or elderly parents.

Parenting—Sponsored by Boys Town
Hotline for parents: 1-800-448-3000 • website: www.parenting.org
A website for parenting help, commonsense parenting, and
parenting tips sponsored by Boys Town.

S-Anon
800-210-8141 • website: www.sanon.org
A twelve-step group for friends or family members of individuals
with sexual addiction.

Sex and Love Addicts Anonymous (SLAA)
210-828-7900
website: www.slaafws.org • email: generalinfo@slaafws.org
A twelve-step program for individuals who feel they are acting out sex
addiction and love addiction.

Today's Caregiver: For, About, and By Caregivers
website: www.caregiver.com
A resource for those providing care for sick and elderly parents.

Selected References

Ackerman, Robert J. *Same House, Different Home: Why Adult Children of Alcoholics Are Not the Same.* Pompano Beach, FL: Health Communications, Inc., 1987.

Anderson, Susan. *The Journey from Abandonment to Healing.* New York: Berkley Books, 2000.

Anthony, E. James, and Bertram J. Cohler. *The Invulnerable Child.* New York: Guilford Press, 1987.

Bank, Stephen P., and Michael D. Kahn. *The Sibling Bond.* New York: Basic Books, 1982.

Baures, Mary. *Undaunted Spirits: Portraits of Recovery from Trauma.* Philadelphia: Charles Press, 1994.

Bettelheim, Bruno. "Trauma and Reintegration" in *Surviving and Other Essays.* New York: Knopf, 1979.

Brenner, Avis. *Helping Children Cope with Stress.* Lexington, MA: Lexington Books, 1984.

Brown, H. Jackson, Jr. *Life's Little Instruction Book.* Nashville, TN: Thomas Nelson, 1991.

Burgan, Jean, ACSW. Unpublished Works. Tacoma, WA, 1974.

Cermak, Timmen. "Children of Alcoholics: The Power of Reality and the Reality of Power." Paper presented at the Children of Alcoholics Conference. Seattle, Washington, 1984.

————. *A Time to Heal: The Road to Recovery for Adult Children of Alcoholics.* Los Angeles: Jeremy P. Tarcher, 1988.

Dayton, Tian. *Daily Affirmations for Forgiving and Moving On.* Deerfield Beach, FL: Health Communications, 1992.

————. *Emotional Sobriety: From Relationship Trauma to Resilience and Balance.* Deerfield Beach, FL: Health Communications, 2007.

DesJardins, Carole. *Schenectady Gazette.*

Flach, Frederic F. *The Secret Strength of Depression.* Philadelphia: Lippincott, 1974.

Follette, Victoria M., and Jacqueline Pistorello. *Finding Life Beyond Trauma.* Oakland, CA: New Harbinger Publications, 2007.

Fromm, Erich. *The Art of Loving.* New York: Harper & Row, 1956.

Freud, Anna. "Comments on Trauma" *Psychic Trauma,* Sidney Furst, Ed. New York: Basic Books, 1967.

Gabor, Mate. Lecture January 26, 2010. *American Podium Series: Addiction.* Presented by Town Hall Seattle, seattlechannel.org.

Goleman, Daniel. "The Healing Power of Relationships—Health & Science—*International Herald Tribune.*" *New York Times,* October 11, 2006

Grof, Christina. *The Thirst for Wholeness: Attachment, Addiction, and the Spiritual Path.* San Francisco: HarperCollins, 1993.

Kahn, Michael D., and Karen Lewis. *Siblings in Therapy: Lifespan and Clinical Issues.* New York: W. W. Norton, 1988.

Lerner, Harriet Goldhor. *The Dance of Intimacy: A Woman's Guide to Courageous Acts of Change in Key Relationships.* New York: Harper & Row, 1989.

Levine, Peter A., and Maggie Kline. *Trauma Through A Child's Eyes: Awakening the Ordinary Miracle of Healing.* Berkeley, CA: North Atlantic Books, 2006.

Levine, Stephen. *Unattended Sorrow: Recovering from Loss and Reviving the Heart.* Emmaus, PA: Rodale Books, 2005.

Mahler, Margaret S. *On Human Symbiosis and Vicissitudes of Individuation.* New York: International Press, 1968

May, Rollo. *Existential Psychology.* New York: Random House, 1988.

Middelton-Moz, Jane. *Shame and Guilt: The Masters of Disguise.* Deerfield Beach, FL: Health Communications, 1990.

————. *Values from the Front Porch: Remembering the Wisdom of Our Grandmothers.* Deerfield Beach, FL: Health Communications, 2005.

Middelton, Jane, and Susan Harris. *Juggler in a Mirror.* Kirkland, WA: Arthur-Ward, 1980.

Middelton-Moz, Jane, Lisa Tener, and Peaco Todd. *The Ultimate Guide to Transforming Anger.* Deerfield Beach, FL: Health Communications, 2004.

Moe, Jerry. *Understanding Addiction and Recovery Through a Child's Eyes.* Deerfield Beach, FL: Health Communications, 2007.

Moore, Thomas. *Care of the Soul.* New York, NY: HarperCollins, 1992.

Reid, Jack. From "Adolescent Families: Loosening the Superglue," lecture given at First Annual Western Conference on Alcoholism in the Family, Anaheim, CA, June 9–13, 1985

Sandler, Joseph. "Trauma, Strain, and Development" in *Psychic Trauma.* Sidney Furst, Ed. New York: Basic Books, 1967.

Satow, Roberta. *Doing the Right Thing: Taking Care of Your Elderly Parents Even if They Didn't Take Care of You.* New York: Jeremy P. Tarcher/ Penguin, 2005.

Schnall, Maxine. *What Doesn't Kill You Makes You Stronger: Turning Bad Breaks into Blessings.* Cambridge, MA: Perseus Publishing, 2002.

Siegel, Daniel J. *The Developing Mind: How Relationships and the Brain Interact to Share Who We Are.* New York: Guilford Press, 1999.

————. *Mindsight: The New Science of Personal Transformation.* New York: Bantam Books, 2010.

————. "An Interpersonal Neurobiology of Psychotherapy: The Developing Mind and the Resolution of Trauma," in *Healing Trauma: Attachment, Mind, Body and Brain.* M. F. Solomon and D. J. Siegel Eds. New York: W. W. Norton, 2003.

Sirota, Marcia, "Sibling Betrayal and Estrangement in Dysfunctional Families," http://ezinearticles.com, 2010.

Spring, Janis A. *How Can I Forgive You? The Courage to Forgive and the Freedom Not To.* New York: HarperCollins, 2004.

Steinglass, Peter. *The Alcoholic Family.* New York: Basic Books, 1987.

Van der Kolk, Bessel A. "Post Traumatic Stress Disorder and the Nature of Trauma," in *Healing Trauma: Attachment, Mind, Body, and Brain.* M. E. Solomon and D. J. Siegel, Eds. New York: W. W. Norton, 2003.

Van der Kolk, Bessel A., Alexander C. McFarlane, and Lars Weisaeth, Eds. "The Black Hole of Trauma." In *Traumatic Stress: The Effects of Overwhelming Experience on Mind, Body, and Society.* New York: The Guilford Press. 1996.

Waelder, R. *The Basic Theory of Psychoanalysis.* New York: International Universities Press, 1960.

Wegscheider-Cruse, Sharon. *Another Chance.* Palo Alto, CA: Science and Behavior Books, 1981.

Williams, Mary Beth, and Soili Poiujula. *The PTSD Workbook: Simple, Effective Techniques for Overcoming Traumatic Stress Syndrome.* Oakland, CA: New Harbinger, 2002.

Woititz, Janet Geringer. *Home Away From Home: The Art of Self-Sabotage.* Pompano Beach, FL: Health Communications, 1987.

Wolin, Steven J., and Sybil Wolin. *The Resilient Self: How Survivors of Troubled Families Rise Above Adversity.* New York: Villard Books, 1993.

Worden, William J. *Grief Counseling and Grief Therapy: A Handbook for the Mental Health Practitioner* (Second Ed.). New York: Springer, 1991.

Index

About the Authors

Jane Middelton-Moz, M.S., is an internationally known speaker and author with more than forty years experience in consultation, training, and community intervention. She is the director of the Middelton-Moz Institute, has served on the Board of NACOA (National Association of Children of Alcoholics), and the Advisory Board of NANACOA (National Association of Native American Children of Alcoholics). Skilled at meeting the particular needs of an organization, Ms. Middelton-Moz is a dynamic keynote presenter and is known for her highly successful "hands on, participant driven" workshops. She is recognized for her work in the areas of Adult Children of Alcoholics; multigenerational grief and trauma in individuals, families, and communities; ethnic and cultural awareness; anger, shame, and guilt; differential diagnosis; sexual abuse and sexual assault; values in the workplace and in families; and community intervention and empowerment.

Ms. Middelton-Moz has appeared on national television shows including *Oprah, Maury Povich,* and *Montel Williams,* and on the Discovery Channel, and has had her own PBS special, *Boiling Point.*

She is the author of *Children of Trauma, Shame and Guilt, Boiling Point, Welcoming Our Children to a New Millennium,* and *Values from the Front Porch,* and coauthor of *Bullies, Good and Mad,* and *The Ultimate Guide to Transforming Anger.* Learn more at http://www. middeltonmozinstitute.org.

Lorie Dwinell, M.S.W., has almost forty years of experience in the field of addiction and recovery, and was a pioneer in the recognition of the special needs of addicted women as well as in the use of innovative approaches to their treatment. She was also a pioneer in helping parents in recovery learn to deal with their remorse and shame concerning the effect their life problems had on their adult children. Her groundbreaking work in applying grief-work concepts to the recovery efforts of recovering addicts, alcoholics, and ACOAs led to the writing and publication of the original version of *After the Tears* in 1986.

A well-known therapist in the United States and Canada since the 1970s, Ms. Dwinell taught for nine years in the Seattle University Alcohol Studies Program and was the addiction specialist at the University of Washington's School of Social Work in the 1970s. On behalf of the Washington State Office of Alcoholism, she taught the first state-wide training seminars on the treatment of addicted women. Ms. Dwinell had the pleasure of training many of the leaders in the chemical-dependency field who went on to esteemed careers in Washington State and throughout the United States, and has also appeared on *Oprah* as a guest therapist. She has been full-time private practice in Seattle since 1977, and specializes in all aspects of addictive disorders, grief, depression, stressful life events, and transitions.